New Approaches to
Teaching Folk and Fairy Tales

New Approaches to Teaching Folk and Fairy Tales

Edited by
Christa C. Jones
Claudia Schwabe

Utah State University Press
Logan

Published by Utah State University Press
An imprint of University Press of Colorado
5589 Arapahoe Avenue, Suite 206C
Boulder, Colorado 80303

 The University Press of Colorado is a proud member of
The Association of American University Presses.

The University Press of Colorado is a cooperative publishing enterprise supported, in part, by Adams State University, Colorado State University, Fort Lewis College, Metropolitan State University of Denver, Regis University, University of Colorado, University of Northern Colorado, Utah State University, and Western State Colorado University.

∞ This paper meets the requirements of the ANSI/NISO Z39.48-1992 (Permanence of Paper).

ISBN: 978-1-60732-480-5 (paperback)
ISBN: 978-1-60732-481-2 (ebook)

Library of Congress Cataloging-in-Publication Data
Names: Jones, Christa, editor. | Schwabe, Claudia (Claudia Mareike Katrin), editor.
Title: New approaches to teaching folk and fairy tales / edited by Christa C. Jones, Claudia Schwabe.
Description: Logan : Utah State University Press, 2016.
Identifiers: LCCN 2015039582| ISBN 9781607324805 (pbk.) | ISBN 9781607324812 (ebook)
Subjects: LCSH: Fairy tales—Study and teaching. | Tales—Study and teaching. | Fairy tales in motion pictures—Study and teaching. | Tales—Film adaptations—Study and teaching.
Classification: LCC GR45 .N49 2016 | DDC 398.207—dc23
LC record available at http://lccn.loc.gov/2015039582

Cover images. Top row, left to right: © veron_ice/Shutterstock; caravan of pilgrims in Ramleh by Yahyâ ibn Mahmûd al-Wâsitî, public domain image; "The Little Mermaid," Edmund Dulac. Middle row, left to right: © Elena Schweitzer/Shutterstock; © Fotokostic/Shutterstock; © Elena Schweitzer/Shutterstock. Bottom row, left to right: © Falcona/Shutterstock; © Kotin/Shutterstock; © Lightspring/Shutterstock.

Contents

Foreword

Donald Haase

Iт's about time. Time, that is, for a collection of essays like this. Time for scholars of folktales and fairy tales to acknowledge the role that teaching plays in their work. The study of folktales and fairy tales has a long history that took a radical turn in the 1970s and '80s, a turn that reinvented, revitalized, and expanded the field across disciplines. That burgeoning interest generated new university courses on fairy tales that over the last thirty years have introduced countless students to a new, critical understanding of the fairy tale and to a host of new tales, traditions, and adaptations in every conceivable medium. In tandem with scholarly research, these courses have challenged the fairy-tale canon—especially as represented by the Brothers Grimm, Charles Perrault, Hans Christian Andersen, and Walt Disney—and revealed a much more diverse fairy-tale landscape. Although fairy-tale courses continue to thrive and develop along with research in fairy-tale studies, the scholars who teach them have had little to say about their teaching or how their teaching relates to their research. A mixed bag of course websites, syllabi, and resources has been available on the Internet; and brief exchanges and questions about teaching have occasionally occurred on fairy-tale blogs and discussion boards such as surlalunefairytales.com. Beyond this, however, and outside of personal conversations at conferences, email exchanges among themselves, and shared syllabi, college and university teachers have said relatively little publicly, in print or otherwise, about teaching folktales and fairy tales.

Teaching, of course, reflects local contingencies—institutional specs for courses, the students for whom the course is intended, the availability of resources, and the instructor's personal choices and familiarity (or lack of familiarity) with research. Everyone who has taught fairy tales, at whatever level and in whatever kind of educational setting, will have his or her own story to tell about the path that led to the fairy-tale classroom. Mine begins in 1982–83, the very time when what we have come to view as "fairy-tale studies" was taking shape. Motivated by my department's pragmatic interest in offering a new general education course with the potential to draw undergraduate students otherwise oblivious to German literature, I wondered whether a course on the fairy tale might not fit the bill. As a specialist in German Romanticism, I thought—perhaps naively—that the literary tales of writers such as Ludwig Tieck and E. T. A. Hoffmann would have some appeal, especially if students could be lured into the course with a clever title, provocative description, and a selection of Jacob and Wilhelm Grimms' popular folktales. Bruno Bettelheim's bestselling book, *The Uses of Enchantment,* which had been published to great acclaim only six years earlier in 1976, was also on my mind. Certainly Bettelheim's psychoanalytic interpretations and his views on the "meaning and importance" of fairy tales would provoke students and generate a helpful buzz. I had also learned that there was some new, especially interesting scholarship on folktales and fairy tales, including Grimms' *Kinder- und Hausmärchen* (Grimm and Grimm 1974), which I imagined would be useful in designing and teaching the course. So, as I developed the new course proposal, I assembled a selection of primary texts, tracked down recent scholarship, and began reading. That's when everything changed—my ideas about the course, my understanding of fairy tales, the focus of my research, and the course of my career (in both senses).

What I encountered was a rich field of research that was teeming with questions and controversy. Conventional wisdom—both popular and scholarly—about folktales and fairy tales was being challenged on multiple fronts. The feminist critique of the fairy tale's powerful gender bias, which began playing out in the public sphere in the early 1970s, gained momentum later in the 1970s and early '80s thanks to work such as Kay Stone's (2008) influential article "What Walt Disney Never Told Us" (1975), and Madonna Kolbenschlag's trade book *Kiss Sleeping Beauty Good-Bye: Breaking the Spell of Feminine Myths and Magic,* which had appeared in 1979, just a few years before I started reading to prepare my course (Kolbenschlag 1979). I also encountered another book from 1979, Jack Zipes's *Breaking the Magic Spell: Radical Theories of Folk and Fairy Tales* (Zipes 1979). Like Kolbenschlag's, Zipes's title announced a disenchantment, a critical turn that could liberate us and the tales from repressive ideology. Zipes offered a new way of understanding the sociocultural power of fairy tales and essentially issued a call to radical action in literary and folklore studies that was, in the final analysis, also a call to sociopolitical action. Drawing on German critical theory and calling for a critical reexamination of the fairy tale in its social, cultural, and historical contexts, Zipes's "radical theories of folk and fairy tales" were attractive to a generation of scholars educated in the 1960s, including me. And it didn't hurt that feminist and sociopolitical readings of the fairy tale also promised just the sort of fresh, provocative content I wanted to drive the course.

While preparing my course, I also encountered Heinz Rölleke's recent scholarship on Grimms' *Kinder- und Hausmärchen* (Grimm and Grimm 1980), especially his editions of the now-famous Ölenberg manuscript of 1810 and the Grimms' seventh edition, of 1857 (Rölleke 1975, 1993, 2000). Rölleke's textual-philological work showed without a doubt that widely held beliefs about the extent of Grimms' editing, the tales' oral authenticity, and their folk origins were at best oversimplified and at worst simply wrong. Rölleke's work was readily adopted by Zipes and other sociohistorical crit-ics who built on it to demonstrate how the fairy tale had been appropri-ated for the sociopolitical interests of patriarchy and the bourgeoisie. In another book from that period, *One Fairy Story Too Many* (1983), British-born scholar John M. Ellis relied on Rölleke's work to accuse the iconic Brothers Grimm of having intentionally perpetrated a folklore fraud in order to promote German nationalism (Ellis 1983). Rölleke's findings were astonishing in their own right, but enlisted in the culture wars—domestic or international—they became sensational and controversial (and still are).

The contemporary scholarship I encountered in designing the course fundamentally changed my own critical approach and my pedagogical goals. What began as a pragmatic tactic to bolster my department's student enroll-ments became a project to participate in the reassessment of the fairy tale. Informed by the latest research, the course would engage students in that critical undertaking and its controversies and lead to an understanding of what was at stake socially, culturally, and politically in the production, recep-tion, and study of folktales and fairy tales. To signal to students (and, to be completely candid, to colleagues) that the class would be no lighthearted romp through fairyland, a sexy course title gave way to "Understanding the Fairy Tale," which was (and still is) a sober but accurate description.

Contemporary fairy-tale research invigorated and motivated my teach-ing by giving it a contemporary significance and relevance that I had not experienced before. My great fortune as a university professor was falling into fairy-tale studies and doing work that clearly resonated beyond the university. From the start, fairy-tale research and teaching were interrelated and part of a project to reach and teach beyond academe.

This may sound like an ambitious project—I might even say mission—but the 1980s were a heady time for fairy-tale research and teaching. In addi-tion to the game-changing scholarship of Rölleke and Zipes—which was complemented by a steady stream of influential work by Alan Dundes, Ruth B. Bottigheimer, Wolfgang Mieder, James McGlathery, Kay Stone, Maria

Tatar, and others—celebration was in the air. The bicentennial of the births of Jacob and Wilhelm Grimm in 1985 and 1986 occurred in the very midst of the surge of new fairy-tale scholarship, and the numerous exhibits, conferences, and symposia around the world fueled wide interest in the fairy tale. Celebrations, controversies, and radical research generated an excitement that made it both natural and easy to reach out and extend the teaching mission to a much broader audience. So, in keeping with my project, in 1985 and 1987, and again later in 1994, I conducted Summer Seminars for School Teachers funded by the National Endowment for the Humanities (NEH), which gave me the opportunity to disseminate the new scholarship on Grimms' tales to school teachers. Since then, other fairy-tale scholars have also reached out to teachers through NEH Summer Seminars and to the public through workshops, exhibits, storytelling events, and lectures. The work we do in our research and in our classrooms lends itself perfectly to public engagement and outreach, allowing us to conceive of our teaching in a much broader context.

Since the emergence of contemporary fairy-tale studies in those early years, the excitement has barely waned, the research has not ebbed, the fairy tale has remained a popular topic of courses on college and university campuses, and fairy-tale scholars have continued to educate audiences beyond the university. The interplay of teaching and research has been facilitated by the endless production of new editions, anthologies, translations, and textbooks. New technologies and access to seemingly endless digital resources make it easier than ever to incorporate illustrations, artwork, photographs, film, video, music, rare texts, and a host of other artifacts and experiences into the fairy-tale classroom. The infrastructure and resources are in place for courses we could not have envisioned thirty years ago.

The new possibilities for teaching the fairy-tale remind us that it is time to take stock of the present state of our teaching. Having evolved from cultural events and the radically new scholarship of the 1970s and '80s, fairy-tale pedagogy should similarly keep pace with the developments that have occurred over the last decades. Teaching the fairy-tale in the twenty-first century should not rely on the models of the twentieth. New generations of fairy-tale scholars necessarily give rise to new directions in both research and teaching. It is no wonder these scholars have been the ones to initiate a discussion about the teaching of fairy tales. In 2009, Nancy Canepa invited a small but diverse group of scholars to Dartmouth University to participate in a colloquium on New Critical and Pedagogical Perspectives on the Fairy Tale. For the 2013 Annual Meeting of the American Folklore Society, four young scholars—Linda J. Lee, Robin Gray Nicks, K. Elizabeth

Spillman, and Adam Zolkover—organized a panel on Little Red Riding Hood's Pedagogical Possibilities in the General Education Classroom. Another telling example from 2013 is Christine A. Jones and Jennifer Schacker's new textbook, *Marvelous Transformations: An Anthology of Fairy Tales and Contemporary Critical Perspectives* (Jones and Schacker 2012). It is clear from the book's innovative concept and composition, and explicit in its introduction, that Jones and Schacker are critically rethinking the way fairy tales have been taught over the last three decades. Directly challenging the common pedagogical strategy of organizing textbooks and courses according to motifs and national traditions, Jones and Schacker seek to foreground the diversity and differences in fairy-tale studies and put those ideas into productive dialog. Refreshingly self-reflective about their research and teaching, Jones and Schacker have produced a book designed to encourage new ways of thinking—and teaching—among future generations of fairy-tale scholars.

These recent acts of pedagogical self-reflection signal the continuing vitality of fairy-tale studies. In fact, the sustainability of meaningful fairy-tale research and teaching depends on critical self-reflection and the conversation that it promotes. With this collection of essays, Christa C. Jones and Claudia Schwabe recognize that the time has come to give serious attention to teaching as an important part of the work we do in fairy-tale studies. The diverse voices and approaches that they have mobilized here not only remind us how far we have come as scholars and teachers since the first clarion call to "break the magic spell." They also encourage us to imagine what possibilities for research and teaching lie still ahead.

New Approaches to Teaching Folk and Fairy Tales

Introduction

Cross-Disciplinary Perspectives on Teaching Folklore and
Fairy Tales in Higher Education

Christa C. Jones and Claudia Schwabe

> *Imagination is more important than knowledge. For knowledge is limited, whereas imagination*
> *embraces the entire world, stimulating progress, giving birth to evolution. It is, strictly speaking, a*
> *real factor in scientific research.*

—Albert Einstein (1931), *Cosmic Religion,* 97

FROM THE EARLIEST STAGE OF STORYTELLING, ORAL TALES and their manifold retellings have served not only to mesmerize, entertain, and captivate
listeners, but also to educate audiences about valuable life lessons and universal truths. Early tales contained examples of human conduct and provided guidelines on how to overcome serious challenges, survival struggles,
or master problematic interpersonal relations. As Jack Zipes (2012) states
in his recent study *The Irresistible Fairy Tale,* "For once a plethora of stories began to circulate in societies throughout the world, they contained
the seeds of fairy tales, ironically tales at first without fairies formed by
metaphor and metamorphosis and by a human disposition to communicate
relevant experiences" (Zipes 2012, 4). These primary tales, as Zipes calls
the early form of fairy tales, "enabled humans to invent and reinvent their
lives" (4). In other words, primary tales invited human beings to propel
themselves into a fantastic world filled with supernatural creatures, demons,
and deities. Stories allowed listeners to mentally engage with these dangerous powers and forces of nature in the contained framework of the story
and the safe space of their imagination, without putting their lives in jeop-
ardy. Interestingly, fairies were not yet an integral part of these early tales or
traditional storytelling, at least up until the sixteenth and seventeenth centuries, which saw the rise of the French *contes de fées* (fairy tales) written by the
likes of Madame D'Aulnoy, Charles Perrault, Mademoiselle Marie-Jeanne
L'Héritier, Mademoiselle de La Force, Jeanne-Marie Leprince de Beaumont,

DOI: 10.7330/9781607324812.c000

3

and, earlier on, Italian folklorists such as Francesco Straparola, Giambattista Basile, and Giovanni Boccaccio.

In the French fairy-tale tradition the literary fairy tale (in contrast to the *contes populaires*, or popular tales) emerged as an institutionalized phenomenon that addressed a dual audience made up of foremost women of the aristocracy and bourgeoisie on the one hand, and their children on the other. These literary tales, which were meant to reinforce the rules of courtly behavior and social mores, contained strong moral messages (*morales*, also referred to as *moralités*). They reflected primarily the tastes, values, and concerns of the French court society such as civility and propriety. The tales further highlighted the importance of reinforcing power alliances through advantageous marriages, for instance in Perrault's "Peau d'âne" (Donkey Skin) and "Riquet à la houppe" (Riquet with the Tuft), or prepared young court ladies for wedlock as in De Beaumont's "La Belle et la Bête" (Beauty and the Beast) (Perrault 1697). Perrault's "Le petit chaperon rouge" (Little Red Riding Hood), a classic cautionary tale, inspired the twentieth-century writers James Thurber, Roald Dahl, Angela Carter, and Anne Sexton, and continues to influence contemporary authors and filmmakers, including Karen Duve, Tahar Ben Jelloun, Catherine Hardwicke, Cory Edwards, and many others.

Though less didactic in nature than Perrault's moralistic tales, the Grimms' *Kinder- und Hausmärchen* (*Children's and Household Tales*) encapsulate fundamental educational and social values for adults and children alike (Grimm and Grimm 1974). Initially composed with an adult readership in mind, the Grimms later on embellished, sanitized, and reworked their tales to tailor them to what they perceived to be of educational benefit to children. They eliminated profanity and sexual references, added Christian prayers and values, expanded on narrative, and added illustrations. The most common didactic guidelines and mores that they incorporated into their stories include modesty, honesty, diligence, obedience, patience, courage, perseverance, and shrewdness. Although the *Märchen* reflect the social norms and cultural codes of nineteenth-century Germany, many of those values are still considered paramount in Western civilization, attesting to the universality of the Grimms' oeuvre.

In the Anglophone world, the connections between fairy tales, cautionary tales, and children as intended audience have been made through publications in nineteenth-century children's literature such as Joseph Cundall's (1850) *Treasury of Pleasure Books for Young Children*—which included Robert Southey's (1837) *The Story of the Three Bears*—and James Orchard Halliwell-Phillipps's (1886) *The Nursery Rhymes of England*, which contained the fairy tale "The Three Little Pigs." This link was also emphasized by Heinrich Hoffmann's (1845) *Der Struwwelpeter* (translated as *Shockheaded Peter*, first published in Frankfurt am Main in 1845, so interestingly during the lifetime of the Brothers Grimm), and by critics, most famously Austrian Holocaust survivor and child psychoanalyst Bruno Bettelheim (1976) in his seminal study *The Uses of Enchantments: The Meaning and Importance of Fairy Tales*. Today's entertainment industry, be it Walt Disney or Pixar Studios, continues to massively capitalize on classic fairy tales, putting out innumerable film productions which, as Jessica Tiffin (2009) points out in her study *Marvelous Geometry: Narrative and Metafiction in Modern Fairy Tale*, is "reassuring to children as well as to their parents, who can send children to see Disney films secure in the knowledge that sex and realistic violence will not be on the menu" (211–12).

In this collection, we dare to de-compartmentalize traditional fairy-tale research-based, analytical scholarship by shifting and expanding our focus of analysis to include international research on pedagogy in a higher-education setting. As we have come to realize while teaching fairy tales at Utah State University, pedagogy remains a much overlooked aspect of fairy-tale studies. Acknowledging the recent rise in important fairy-tale scholarship—such as Christine A. Jones's and Jennifer Schacker's (2012) *Marvelous Transformations*, Cristina Bacchilega's (2013) *Fairy Tales Transformed?*, and Jack Zipes's (2012) *The Irresistible Fairy Tale*—we have decided that the time has come to turn our attention to the neglected field of fairy-tale pedagogy and teaching methods. While there is a plethora of academic studies on folk and fairy tales, there is to date no comprehensive study on teaching fairy tales in English or foreign-language undergraduate and graduate student classrooms. Our edited collection fills this gap in contemporary folk and fairy-tale studies and is especially relevant, given that language teachers routinely use fairy tales in beginning, intermediate, and advanced foreign-language and -culture classrooms to improve students' linguistic proficiency, and their cultural and intercultural competency. With this in mind, our edited collection focuses on the implementation of teaching strategies and methodologies in folklore, storytelling, and fairy-tale classrooms, and in other academic disciplines that use the age-old device of storytelling, including anthropology, cultural studies, history, linguistics, literature, philosophy, political studies, psychology, theology, women and gender studies, and beyond. To this end, we decided to bring together a number of international and cross-disciplinary approaches to provide materials and inspiration to first-time as well as experienced instructors teaching folk and fairy tales in the graduate and undergraduate classrooms. In this volume, we thus recognize the universal appeal and teaching potential of fairy tales and their adaptability to different instructional classroom settings, both traditional and online. We wish to emphasize the educational opportunities offered by fairy tales, which can fill a broad range of curricular needs: instructors in a variety of academic fields can draw on fairy tales to help students improve critical-thinking abilities, strengthen writing skills, and explore cultural values.

As instructors of foreign language, culture, literature, and fairy-tale classes at Utah State University, a doctoral land-grant institution with high research activity, we have experienced firsthand a significant lack of hands-on resources and pedagogical tools for teaching fairy tales. While conversing about our experiences teaching fairy tales, we identified the need for a teaching volume that addresses this issue, and reflects the vitality and diversity of the field of folk and fairy-tale studies. With this in mind, we set out to give voice to an international group of experts in the fairy-tale and folklore fields with close ties to Algeria, Canada, Germany, France, Italy, Portugal, Switzerland, the United Kingdom, and the United States. Their rich scholarship and diverse teaching methodologies all highlight the use of fairy tales in courses where they might not initially be seen as relevant, such as in courses focusing on second language acquisition. Rather than restricting fairy tales to the fields that traditionally subsume the fairy tale within their purview, the chapters in this collection introduce fresh scholarly perspectives that expand the scope of courses beyond strict disciplinary boundaries. Building on an ever-growing body of fairy-tale research, which encompasses varied intermedial and intertextual approaches and academic disciplines—such as anthropology, creative writing, children's literature, film studies, women and gender studies, cultural studies, sociocultural and sociohistorical approaches, translation studies and linguistics, developmental psychology, and the fantastic in the arts—we hope to provide instructors with fresh ideas, teaching materials, and out-of-the-box teaching strategies they can draw on or implement in their own classrooms. We aim to offer new and adaptable pedagogical models that can easily be applied to fairy-tale texts and films and that invite students to engage with class materials in intellectually stimulating ways. This collection is intended first and foremost as a resource for specialized and nonspecialized higher-education instructors, fairy-tale and folklore scholars, or fairy-tale aficionados and aficionadas. We also hope to inspire instructors in other fields to take on the challenge of teaching fairy tales in their respective areas, for example second language (L2), cultural studies, translation or gender studies, and elsewhere, and thus contribute to the already existing cross-disciplinary dialog and scholarship. The teaching suggestions presented in the following chapters are meant as platforms for lively and controversial class discussions, group projects, and independent research. While devising their own courses, instructors can adapt specific methodological approaches to their own needs.

We envision that our volume will help debunk the deeply ingrained misconception that the pedagogical use of fairy tales limits itself to kindergarten and elementary school settings, or children's literature departments. Likewise, our contributors unanimously stress the universal value and importance of fairy tales. By focusing specifically on pedagogy and student-centered research activities, our study aims to fulfill a pioneering role. Further, as editors, we are confident that this work will open the door to a new understanding and appreciation of the value of fairy-tale studies in higher-education teaching, and hence pave the way to further research in this area.

The four parts of this fourteen-essay-strong collection address diverse cross-disciplinary and fundamental, critical, and methodological approaches to teaching folk and fairy tales. Instead of organizing the essays by fairy-tale authors, their countries of origin, and time periods—a common thread found in many annotated anthologies—we organized the volume with a view to facilitating easy access for instructors' respective teaching agendas. The first part firmly grounds the teaching of fairy tales in the academic discipline of folkloristics, exploring key terminology, including fairy tale, myth, fantasy, folktale, folklore, and the Otherworld. The second part delves into sociopolitical, historical, ideological, and intercultural topoi underlying the canonical fairy tales and fairy-tale retellings of the Grimms, Charles Perrault, and the *Arabian Nights*. Translation issues, linguistics, and semantics are the focal points of the third part, which ties together European fairy tales from Germany, Italy, France, Denmark, and Britain. The final part introduces iconoclastic teaching ideas pertaining to canonical fairy tales and the interpretation thereof, by offering interpretations of classic fairy tales in light of new research in the areas of lesbian, gay, bisexual, transgender (LGBT), gender, and women's studies, thus reinvigorating the discipline. It also features a chapter (see chapter 13, Greenhill and Orme) providing hands-on advice and directions for teaching a class online using fairy-tale films and folklore.

PART I. FANTASTIC ENVIRONMENTS: MAPPING FAIRY TALES, FOLKLORE, AND THE OTHERWORLD

In their essay "Fairy Tales, Myth, and Fantasy," Christina Phillips Mattson and Maria Tatar, both from Harvard University, outline a class that invites students to explore the porosity of generic borders that characterize malleable, fictional or, as they put it, "Wonder Worlds." Works studied include classics, such as "Hansel and Gretel," "Little Red Riding Hood," "Beauty and the Beast," *Alice in Wonderland*, and *Peter Pan* but also modern works, such as *Harry Potter* and *The Hunger Games*. The authors move along the spectrum between fairy tales, fantasy literature, myth, and history, by analyzing fairy-tale hypertexts, mythical subtexts, allusions, tropes, and parallels in a variety of works. In this decidedly student-centered class or, as Ernest Hemingway famously said, "moveable feast" that links (Roland) Barthian reading pleasure, his *plaisir du texte*, to cognitive gain, students learn to apply the tools of close reading, discourse analysis, intertextuality, and poetics. They delve into the works of cultural critics, structural anthropologists, postmodernists, reader response theorists, philosophers, novelists, and linguists working in the field of folklore and fairy-tale studies.

Fairy-tale scholars Pauline Greenhill and Sidney Eve Matrix (2010) have defined fairy tales as "fictional narratives that combine human and nonhuman protagonists with elements of wonder and the supernatural. They come in traditional (usually collected from oral tellers) or literary (formally composed and written) forms" (1). This definition reflects our own understanding of the genre which, for the purpose of this edited collection, needs to be clearly demarcated from related concepts such as myth, fantasy, folklore, folktale, and the Otherworld. In the *Greenwood Encyclopedia of Folktales and Fairy Tales*, Estonian folklorist Ülo Valk provides an in-depth definition of myth: "Folklorists see myths as stories about grand events in ancient times . . . , held to be true in the culture where they belong. As sacred narratives, they are included in religious canons and acted out in rituals; as a prominent genre of folklore, they have spread worldwide at different time periods from the Stone Age to the present day" (Haase 2008, 652). Out of fairy tales and myths grew the genre that is now referred to as fantasy, which, as children's literature scholar Maria Nikolajeva pertinently writes, "stands close to the literary fairy tale, as it is created by a specific author, even though it may be based on a traditional narrative. Similar to literary fairy tales, fantasy is less rigid in plot structure and character types" (Haase 2008, 329). It is, she writes, a "modern genre, tightly connected with the development of Modern Age philosophy, psychology, natural sciences, and general worldview" (329). Many of the tropes, motifs, and fantastic elements of fantasy are rooted in traditional folklore.

Folklorist Lisa Gabbert in her class "Introduction to Folklore" at Utah State University, raises students' awareness of the manifold possibilities of storytelling, as she relates in her chapter "Teaching Fairy Tales in Folklore

Classes." Her class familiarizes students with basic disciplinary terminology, such as tale type, variation, and fundamental principles in the discipline of folklore. Students are invited to discover the metaphorical dimensions of folktales and their relationship with reality in well-known German, French, and Russian fairy tales. Furthermore, they are confronted with materials that do not fit their assumptions of what constitutes folklore, such as email scams, practical jokes, and graffiti. Materials cover staple fairy tales, such as Alexandr Afanas'ev's (1945) *Russian Fairy Tales*, Grimms' *Kinder- und Hausmärchen*, and Native American tales and other twentieth-century texts, such as Zora Neale Hurston's (2008) *Mules and Men*, and Kirin Narayan's (1997) *Mondays on the Dark Night of the Moon*, which are discussed against cultural and comparative contexts and theories outlined by Max Lüthi, Elliott Oring, Alan Dundes, and others. Gabbert also includes a teaching unit centered on issues of transcription, translation, and orthography, as well as a unit on collectors, tellers and settings, the latter emphasizing the performative nature and social context of tales. As folklorist and story-teller Kay Stone (2008) points out in her collection of essays *Some Day Your Witch Will Come*, *Märchen* most often mean "printed texts in books, for some scholars and most general readers," while folklorists "are aware that behind each printed text are countless unrecorded tales by innumerable traditional oral artists, with no single telling capturing the full potential of any given story" (78). For their final project, students complete a hands-on assignment by doing fieldwork: they collect examples of folklore and thus obtain the experience of collecting, documenting, classifying, and interpreting folklore materials. Students learn that folk and fairy tales are not merely entertainment for children but carry deeper meanings.

The term *folktale*, a direct translation from the German *Volksmärchen*, is often used interchangeably with the term *fairy tale* (*Märchen*), which in fact comprises both oral (*Volksmärchen*) and literary fairy tales (*Kunstmärchen*). As folklorist JoAnn Conrad clarifies, the term *folklore* itself was an appropriation of the concept of *Volkskunde*, the lore of the people, into the English language (Haase 2008, 364). According to Swedish ethnologist Barbro Klein (2001), folklore has four basic meanings: "First, it denotes oral narration, rituals, crafts, and other forms of vernacular expressive culture. Second, folklore, or 'folkloristics,' names an academic discipline devoted to the study of such phenomena. Third, in everyday usage, folklore sometimes describes colorful 'folkloric' phenomena linked to the music, tourist, and fashion industries. Fourth, like myth, folklore can mean falsehood" (5711).

The Irish folklore of the Otherworld—rich in its manifestations, super-natural creatures, and environments—is at the center of Juliette Wood's course (and chapter 3), "At the Bottom of a Well: Teaching the Otherworld as a Folktale Environment." The course caters to students seeking degrees in folklore and cultural studies, English literature, and European languages at Cardiff University in Wales. The Otherworld can be broadly defined as "a realm beyond the senses, usually a delightful place, not knowable to ordinary mortals without an invitation from a denizen" (MacKillop 2004, 359). According to folklorist Hilda Roderick Ellis Davidson, "The Otherworld may be reached through the air, perhaps on a magic horse or an eagle's back, or by descending into the earth, and the general impression is of a land of richness and beauty, where enormous distances may separate one kingdom or supernatural being from another" (Davidson and Chaudhri 2003, 119). Wood's class examines various ways in which the Otherworld can be presented in the context of teaching folktales. Using examples from different cultures and existing folktale collections, she surveys the Otherworld topos exemplifying the diverse ways in which it was adapted to "folktale" environments across cultures and through time. Some of the selected Otherworld tales and variants under consideration are "The Star Husband," "Jack and the Beanstalk," "Frau Holle," "The Search for the Water of Life," and "East of the Sun and West of the Moon," with a special focus on the Celtic Otherworld and Welsh tales. While the course draws attention to the approaches and tools used by scholars to address fundamental questions about the meaning and origin of the Otherworld trope, students-centered approaches are at the heart of this class: students engage in creative-writing projects, conceptualize their own Otherworlds and folktales, and learn about the basic concept of spatial otherness through explorations of medieval maps illustrating fantastic worlds. The class aims to teach students how the Otherworld topos, with its narrated journey to an alternative environment, functions within specific tales as a way to express fundamental human needs, desires, and anxieties. Together with her students, Wood also pursues the question of archetype as a way of understanding and explaining the notion of the Otherworld, and the discourses surrounding interpretations of the Otherworld in folk narrative.

PART II. SOCIOPOLITICAL AND CULTURAL APPROACHES TO TEACHING CANONICAL FAIRY TALES

In "The Fairy-Tale Forest as Memory Site: Romantic Imagination, Cultural Construction, and a Hybrid Approach to Teaching the Grimms' Fairy Tales and the Environment," German professor Doris McGonagill ties the study of fairy tales to ecocriticism, that is, the focus on nature and questions about the interaction between humans and the environment. In her upper-division, undergraduate-level class taught at Utah State University, McGonagill invites students to follow "the trail into the woods" as a path to social memory and to examine trees and forests in the Grimms' tales as constructions, expressions, and repositories of the cultural imagination. By pairing fairy-tale studies with an interest in the physical environment as a lens to examine cultural memory, McGonagill's hybrid teaching approach suggests several distinct lines of synchronic and diachronic investigation that both focus and enrich the textual and contextual analysis of fairy tales. A catalog of questions concerning fundamental concepts—such as nature and the environment, narrative, fairy tales and folklore, and collective memory—serves as a valuable assessment tool to determining students' level of knowledge before and after the teaching unit. This innovative class is designed to make students' learning a truly transformative experience by drawing on multiple disciplines and promoting a deeper appreciation of the tales' historical specificity. McGonagill offers students profound insights into the Grimms' romantic project and their attempt to compensate experiences of longing and loss with the nostalgia of literary imagination. At the same time, students in this class benefit from close readings of individual tales, topical contextualizations, and informed discussions on German mystification of the forest.

Claudia Schwabe's chapter "Grimms' Fairy Tales in a Political Context: Teaching East German Fairy-Tale Films" brings Deutsche Film-Aktiengesellschaft (DEFA) fairy-tale productions and their subliminal socialist messages and anticapitalist tropes into keen focus. In her upper-division, undergraduate-level course at Utah State University, German professor Schwabe and her students investigate relevant links and political connections between the Grimms' fairy tales and the former German Democratic Republic. Through sociohistorically sensitive discussions about state propaganda, students are encouraged to critically engage with the East German past, examine the functions of socialist realism and ideology in the Workers' and Peasants' State (*Arbeiter- und Bauernstaat*), and relate their findings to DEFA's fairy-tale adaptations. Drawing on an intermedial teaching approach that incorporates literary texts, films, songs, posters, paintings, and online resources, Schwabe's constructive class provides students with fresh insights into how fairy tales and their innumerable retellings serve as cultural signifiers by reflecting a society's cultural traditions, moral sensibilities, values and virtues, accepted gender norms and roles, and attitudes toward life. Students not only conduct in-depth film analyses, but also explore the fundamental concepts of gender equality, social classes,

political propaganda, and punishment and reward systems in DEFA productions, such as *Rumpelstiltskin* (1960), *Snow White* (1961), *Little Red Riding
Hood* (1962), *Mother Holle* (1963), *The Golden Goose* (1964), *Sleeping Beauty*
(1970), and *Three Wishes for Cinderella* (1973).

Christa C. Jones, in her communication- and writing-intensive under-
graduate course at Utah State University "Teaching Charles Perrault's
Histoires ou contes du temps passé in the Literary and Historical Context of the
Sun King's Reign," offers close readings of Charles Perrault's *Contes* and
surveys works by other key seventeenth-century writers, such as Jean de
La Fontaine, François de La Rochefoucauld, Jean de La Bruyère, Marie-
Catherine D'Aulnoy, Madame de Lafayette, La Comtesse de Ségur, and
Jeanne-Marie Leprince de Beaumont. Students learn about French absolutism and about historical and literary concepts, such as classicism, *honnête
homme*, propriety, salon culture, and intertextuality. Throughout the semester, they investigate the magnetism and longevity of Perrault's tales and try
to answer why, as Jack Zipes puts it, these tales "stick." Reading Perrault's
source tales against contemporary rewritings and cinematic adaptations, students examine how heteronormative stereotypes are either perpetuated or
undermined today, for example, in Jean Bacqué's *Cendrillon* (1966), Jacques
Demy's musical comedy *Donkey Skin* (1970), in Olivier Dahan's television
film *Le Petit Poucet* (2001, "Hop-o'-My-Thumb"), or in Catherine Breillat's
television production *The Sleeping Beauty* (2010). By studying Perrault's tales
in their sociohistorical context and against contemporary remakes, students
develop their literary and historical knowledge and gain a better understanding of both seventeenth-century and modern-day France.

Anissa Talahite-Moodley's discussion-centered gender studies course
"Lessons from Shahrazad: Teaching about Cultural Dialogism" at the
University of Toronto is focused on feminist and postcolonial readings
of *The Arabian Nights*, examining how its framing narrative, Shahrazad's
story, has been reinterpreted and rewritten through a variety of media in
the past and in the present. Students apply key concepts of literary theory and cultural and historical studies to this hybrid text as they analyze
East/West relations and the concept of the exoticized cultural, or gendered
"Other." Centering on cultural dialogism and drawing on key theorists such
as Julia Kristeva, Fatema Mernissi, Roland Barthes, Mikhail Bakhtin, Gérard
Genette, and Edward Said, they analyze Orientalism and issues of gender,
and they revisit mediatized, stereotypical concepts of "Arab culture," or the
"Muslim world." During the course of the semester, students engage with
questions such as "Can the story of Shahrazad be read as a reflection of
the society and culture within which it is set? And, if so, to what extent? To

what extent can we consider a work of fantasy as the 'true' reflection of a culture? What are the processes at work in such imaginings of the Middle East and Muslim/Arab culture in particular?" The manifold translations and retellings of the *Nights* underline the porosity of the border between historical objectivity and the collective imaginings of community, nation, and culture.

PART III. DECODING FAIRY-TALE SEMANTICS: ANALYSES OF TRANSLATION ISSUES, LINGUISTICS, AND SYMBOLISMS

Christine A. Jones's class, "The Significance of Translation," teaches students at the University of Utah that translations constitute creative writings in and of themselves, since they are based on interpretation and adaptation. Her three-pronged class unit focuses on first, translation and second-language (L2) pedagogy, taking "Cinderella" as an example; second, comparison and idiosyncrasy, taking "Little Red Riding Hood" into the English-language classroom to reveal the female figure's unstable character; and third, translations over time, using the figure of Sleeping Beauty to uncover the impact her English personae had on her reception in France. Students compare a number of English-language translations of Perrault's *Contes* with various English-language translations from different periods of the texts' print history, such as Robert Samber's 1729 adaptation of "Cinderella" or American A. E. Johnson's 1962 rendition of "Little Red Riding Hood." Delving into the cultural palimpsest of fairy-tale reception and transmission, students learn that translations are more than a tool to transmit foreign-language stories. They thus come to credit translators for their creativity and immense influence on the fairy-tale history.

"Giambattista Basile's *The Tale of Tales* in the Hands of the Brothers Grimm" is the title of Armando Maggi's valuable contribution to this collection. As Italian professor at the University of Chicago, Maggi teaches an undergraduate, ten-week course "Baroque Fairy Tales and Their Modern Rewritings." Maggi's illuminating piece centers on the rewriting of classic fairy tales, and in particular on Basile's *Lo cunto de li cunti* (published posthumously in 1634–36) and the subsequent appropriations of his texts. The main goal of the class is to teach students how to critically engage with folktales and fairy tales, to treat the tales with the same respect as they grant other literary genres, and to appreciate them as artistic artifacts. As an integral part of his effective teaching strategy, Maggi foregrounds the complex interaction between oral and written texts through close readings of selected fairy tales. At the same time, Maggi integrates creative and unconventional, fun teaching activities into his curriculum, such as the use of fairy-tale tarot cards when discussing the crucial concept of "motif." The students in this course examine how skillfully the Brothers Grimm reshaped and manipulated several of Basile's fifty Italian tales in order to bring the tales closer to their poetics. By dissecting the Grimms' literary style, the students learn that the German tales do not result from a faithful transcription of an oral performance, but rather from a meticulous stylistic procedure.

Cyrille François, senior lecturer at Université de Lausanne (Switzerland) presents in his chapter "Teaching Hans Christian Andersen's Tales: A Linguistic Approach" a new modality for studying Andersen's tales through a linguistics-oriented analysis. François's well-conceived teaching approach is based on close readings of tales from a linguistic perspective with an emphasis on translation. Through class discussions, lectures, comparative studies, and linguistic analyses, students learn that fairy tales differ significantly in the way in which they are told and gain deeper insights into the revolutionary impact of Andersen's tales on the Danish language. In order to better understand Andersen's productive fairy-tale output in its European context, François encourages his students to compare the paratexts of collections by Andersen, Perrault, and the Grimms. By drawing on the works of Viggo Hjørnager Pedersen, Diana and Jeffrey Frank, and Sven Hakon Rossel, students better comprehend the challenges associated with translations and how to successfully overcome those challenges when translating Andersen's tales. One crucial objective of the class is for the students to develop a fine sense for Andersen's special language by comparing his tales, for example, "The White Swans," with similar texts by Mathias Winther and the Grimms. Focusing on punctuation, deixis, and reported speech in the classroom, the chapter reveals how students and instructors who do not know Danish can still make useful comparisons between Andersen's tales and their translations.

In his essay "Teaching Symbolism in 'Little Red Riding Hood,'" Francisco Vaz da Silva, professor of folklore and anthropology, focuses on a two-week introduction of his fairy-tale class at Instituto Universitário de Lisboa (Portugal). Students in this course learn that grasping symbolism in fairy tales demands taking into account thematic variations, that is, focusing on intertextual links rather than on any single text. As an integral part of his introduction to symbolic analysis, Vaz da Silva employs an effective hands-on approach: together with his students he explores four variants of the popular tale "Little Red Riding Hood"—the literary texts by Charles Perrault and the Brothers Grimm, and two oral variants (one

French, the other Portuguese)—to reach beyond the commonplace knowledge of the theme. By teaching his students about the common misconceptions that orally transmitted stories are based on a specific fairy-tale urtext or authorial story, Vaz da Silva uses a strategy he calls "a flip of the mind" to help students understand *why* intertextual readings of a given tale are of paramount importance. Students critically engage with seminal works by Frederic Bartlett, Roman Jakobson, and Petr Bogatyrev, and they discuss Alan Dundes's ideas on the symbolic equivalence of *allomotifs* —the different motifs occupying the same narrative slot in different texts. Thanks to Vaz da Silva's scaffolding strategy and a constructive course design, students then learn *how* to undertake intertextual readings and to explore the symbolic codes underlying all the variants of "Little Red Riding Hood."

PART IV. CLASSIC TALES THROUGH THE GENDERED LENS: CINEMATIC ADAPTATIONS IN THE TRADITIONAL CLASSROOM AND ONLINE

Anne E. Duggan's class "Binary Outlaws: Queering the Classical Tale in François Ozon's *Criminal Lovers* and Catherine Breillat's *The Sleeping Beauty*," at Wayne State University, introduces students to queer theory (drawing on theorists Alexander Doty, Steven Angelides, Lauren Berlant, and Michael Warner) and the "queer possibilities" of the fairy-tale genre. Students do comparative readings of classic source tales (Charles Perrault's "Sleeping Beauty," Hans Christian Andersen's "The Snow Queen," and the Grimms' "Hansel and Gretel"), and Breillat's and Ozon's contemporary French fairy-tale films. Both filmic remakes destabilize normative gender roles, calling into question their heteronormative plots and the traditional configuration of gender roles. In this communication-intensive course, students carry out comparative analyses of the films and their source tales in ways that foreground the queering techniques of the films, and the queer possibilities of traditional source tales. By weaving Perrault's "Sleeping Beauty" and Andersen's "Snow Queen" into her film, Breillat subverts gender oppositions that mark Perrault's heteronormative source tale. Students learn that the concept of "binary outlaws" (characters that move between masculine and feminine, heterosexual and homosexual, active and passive) in both films challenges heteronormativity and points to new, queer fairy-tale forms.

In "Teaching 'Gender in Fairy-Tale Film and Cinematic Folklore' Online: Negotiating between Needs and Wants," fairy-tale and gender studies scholars Pauline Greenhill and Jennifer Orme share their longtime experience teaching online (starting 1989 for Greenhill and 2009 for Orme), and here, teaching a third-year undergraduate online women's and gender studies class at the University of Winnipeg, Canada (also see Greenhill and Matrix 2010, which contains materials for their course). Negotiating pedagogical goals, available materials, and analytical approaches to the content are challenging when teaching online. Audio and video lectures, readings, and films made available online include *Little Red Riding Hood* (1997, Kaplan), *The Juniper Tree* (1990, Keene), *The Wolves of Kromer* (1998, Gould), *Donkey Skin* (1970, Demy), *Atanarjuat: The Fast Runner* (2001, Kunuk), and *Capturing the Friedmans* (2003, Jarecki), among others. Challenges tied to time, technical, and quality-feedback issues are outweighed by the benefits of independent and collaborative learning, analytic, peer-reviewed writing, and web discussion assignments. Orme cautions that preparing a course online takes about twice as long as preparing for a traditional course.

Fairy-tale and women's studies scholar Jeana Jorgensen in her stimulating essay "Intertextuality, Creativity, and Sexuality: Group Exercises in the Fairy-Tale/Gender Studies Classroom" puts her students in the driver's seat in an upper-division class taught at Butler University. This chapter is particularly valuable and thought provoking, given that Jorgensen—as do Greenhill and Orme—reflects on why certain approaches worked or failed in her classroom. She details three specific group exercises focused on the depiction of sexuality and the intersections of gender, sexuality, and intertextuality. Students analyze a broad range of classic German, French, and Danish fairy tales and contemporary retellings such as the film *The Company of Wolves*, the television show *Dollhouse*, and Angela Carter's *The Sadeian Woman*. Guided by a catalog of questions, prompts, and specific instructions, her students become creative participants in the production of tales. Assignments include blog posts, presentations, lectures, and three short essays —"Versions and Variations," "Revisiting Disney," and "Scholarly Sources"—in addition to other creative writing exercises and fairy-tale retellings.

The importance of studying fairy tales is clear to scholars in the field, yet needs to be reiterated to a wider public. As Christina Phillips Mattson and Maria Tatar eloquently put it, their teaching goals are tailored to their students' needs and interests, because students acquire skills and insights they can use in their major programs. They further enrich their personal worldviews by learning to call into question long-held convictions: "Our students acquire the critical skills they need to be successful in this course and in their other college courses, as well as in their postcollege lives (e.g., critical thinking, close reading, thorough research, and composing a clear and logical argument)" (personal communication). Another recurrent teaching goal, stressed by contributor Anne E. Duggan, is to recognize the importance of reading fairy tales critically. All too often, they are taken for granted as being "innocent," nonideological texts for children.

As the following chapters show, fairy-tale pedagogy—or as the Germans put it, *Märchenpädagogik*—is highly diverse. Most instructors in this collection use a mixed approach that combines several teacher- and learner-centered strategies. Teacher-centered approaches include lectures, lecture-discussions, demonstrations, and direct instruction, whereas learner-centered approaches include small-group work, fairy-tale retellings, games, reading reports, role-plays, discussion groups (in the classroom or online), creative projects, student presentations, case studies, discovery learning, graphic organizers, journals, blogs, scaffolding, Know—What to Know—Learned (K-W-L), problem-based learning and inquiry, research papers, and simulations. Virtually all teaching methodologies to some extent emphasize comparative close readings of texts or film materials, interpretation and analysis of literary texts or cinematic adaptations, discourse analysis, semantics, and poetics. As instructors, we constantly need to remind ourselves that we are responsible for the quality of the ongoing intellectual dialog in our classrooms and that by making our lessons as interactive as possible, we can considerably enhance the quality of class discussion and the free-flowing exchange of ideas. Finally, it is essential to appropriately frame fairy tales in their respective cultural and historical contexts so that students may develop a deeper understanding of the intricate and complex ways that continue to shape the fairy-tale web (see Bacchilega 2013). May this collection serve as a "compass" to guide your teaching and steer your students safely through the web of stories.

REFERENCES

Afanas'ev, Aleksandr. 1945. *Russian Fairy Tales*. Trans. Norbert Guterman. New York: Pantheon.

Bacchilega, Cristina. 2013. *Fairy Tales Transformed?: Twenty-First Century Adaptations and the Politics of Wonder*. Detroit: Wayne State University.

Bettelheim, Bruno. 1976. *The Uses of Enchantment: The Meaning and Importance of Fairy Tales*. New York: Vintage Books. http://dx.doi.org/10.1037/e309842005-008.

Cundall, Joseph. 1850. *Treasury of Pleasure Books for Young Children: With More than One Hundred Illustrations*. London: Grant and Griffith.

Davidson, Hilda Roderick Ellis, and Anna Chaudhri. 2003. *A Companion to the Fairy Tale*. Cambridge: D.S. Brewer.

Einstein, Albert. 1931. *Cosmic Religion: With Other Opinions and Aphorisms*. New York: Covici-Friede.

Ellis, John M. 1983. *One Fairy Story Too Many: The Brothers Grimm and Their Tales*. Chicago: University of Chicago Press.

Greenhill, Pauline, and Sidney Eve Matrix, eds. 2010. *Fairy Tale Films: Visions of Ambiguity.* Logan: Utah State University Press.

Grimm, Jacob, and Grimm, Wilhelm. [1812] 1974. *Kinder- und Hausmärchen gesammelt durch die Brüder Grimm.* 3 vols. Frankfurt am Main: Insel.

Grimm, Jacob, and Wilm Grimm. 1980. *Kinder- und Hausmärchen: Ausgabe letzter Hand mit den Originalanmerkungen der Brüder Grimm*, ed. Heinz Rölleke. Stuttgart: Philipp Reclam.

Haase, Donald, ed. 2008. *The Greenwood Encyclopedia of Folktales and Fairytales.* 3 vols. Westwood: Greenwood Press.

Halliwell-Phillipps, Orchard. 1886. *The Nursery Rhymes of England.* London: Frederick Warne & Co.

Hoffmann, Heinrich. 1845. *[Der Struwwelpeter] Lustige Geschichten und drollige Bilder mit 15 schön kolorierten Tafeln für Kinder von 3–6 Jahren.* Frankfurt am Main: Zacharias Löwenthal.

Hurston, Zora Neale. 2008 (1935). *Mules and Men.* New York: Harper Perennial.

Jones, Christine A., and Jennifer Schacker, eds. 2012. *Marvelous Transformations: An Anthology of Fairy Tales and Contemporary Critical Perspectives.* Peterborough: Broadview Press.

Klein, Barbro. 2001. "Folklore." In *International Encyclopedia of the Social and Behavioral Sciences*, vol. 8, ed. Neil J. Smelser, 5711–55. New York: Elsevier. http://dx.doi.org/10.1016/B0-08-043076-7/00869-X.

Kolbenschlag, Madonna. 1979. *Kiss Sleeping Beauty Good-Bye: Breaking the Spell of Feminine Myths and Models.* Garden City: Doubleday.

MacKillop, James. 2004. *Dictionary of Celtic Mythology.* Oxford: Oxford University Press.

Narayan, Kirin. 1997. *Mondays on the Dark Night of the Moon.* Oxford: Oxford University Press.

Perrault, Charles. 1697. *Histoires ou Contes du Temps Passé.* Paris: Claude Barbin.

Rölleke, Heinz. 1975. *Die älteste Märchensammlung der Brüder Grimm: Synopse der handschriftlichen Urfassung von 1810 und der Erstdrucke von 1812.* Cologny-Genève: Fondation Martin Bodmer.

Rölleke, Heinz. 1993. *Grimms Märchen wie sie nicht im Buch stehen.* Frankfurt am Main: Insel.

Rölleke, Heinz. 2000. *Die Märchen der Brüder Grimm: Quellen und Studien: Gesammelte Aufsätze.* Trier: WVT, Wissenschaftlicher Verlag.

Southey, Robert. 1837. *The Story of the Three Bears.* London: Porter and Wright.

Stone, Kay. 2008. *Some Day Your Witch Will Come.* Detroit: Wayne State University Press.

Tiffin, Jessica. 2009. *Marvelous Geometry: Narrative and Metafiction in Modern Fairy Tale.* Detroit: Wayne State University Press.

Zipes, Jack. 1979. *Breaking the Magic Spell: Radical Theories of Folk and Fairy Tales.* Austin: University of Texas Press.

Zipes, Jack. 2012. *The Irresistible Fairy Tale: The Cultural and Social History of a Genre.* Princeton: Princeton University Press.

Part I

Fantastic Environments
Mapping Fairy Tales, Folklore, and the Otherworld

1

Fairy Tales, Myth, and Fantasy

Christina Phillips Mattson and Maria Tatar

THE COURSE "FAIRY TALES, MYTH, AND FANTASY LITERATURE" takes up the study of foundational stories from the childhood of culture and also from the culture of childhood. It tracks how narratives are recycled as they migrate into new media and old—how the story of Demeter and Persephone, for example, shows up in J. M. Barrie's play *Peter Pan* or how "Little Red Riding Hood" is refashioned in contemporary films ranging from David Slade's *Hard Candy* (2005) to Joe Wright's *Hanna* (2011). It seeks to dismantle the divide between what we read to children and what we read as adults by constructing networks of storytelling cultures that intersect and overlap. Its focus is on both ethics and aesthetics, showing how counterfactuals and the construction of alluring Other Worlds challenge us to think harder and to connect with others through conversations and debate about what could be, should be, or ought to be.

Tolkien told us long ago that the cauldron of story has "always been boiling, and to it have continually been added bits, dainty and undainty" (Tolkien 1966, 32). For him, story is one thick brew—flavorful, zesty, and aromatic, with a wide range of ingredients, refined and unrefined. Tolkien's statement captures the dainty, or aesthetically pleasing, elements of stories as well as the undainty coarseness, crude grotesqueries, and over-the-top violence in them. We always borrow a phrase from Philip Pullman to warn our students that what they see will "shock and startle" them, and we advise them to fasten their seat belts for a (somewhat) bumpy ride (Pullman 2000, 710). The metaphors we use are chosen with a purpose. The stories we read make direct visceral hits, evoking a somatic response in many cases, but they also animate us, crying out for critical analysis that will enable us to understand exactly what moves us in the words used to tell tales. This

DOI: 10.7330/9781607324812.c001

course promotes bifocal vision as students probe the manifest content of texts and also begin to discover latent meanings.

Our course draws undergraduate students from all levels and many different majors at a liberal arts university. One of the first challenges facing us as teachers was to train our students in the art of analyzing print materials derived from oral traditions as well as in the craft of interpreting literary texts. We use the tools of close reading, discourse analysis, and poetics in both domains, but we also introduce students to Claude Lévi-Strauss's structural analysis of myth as well as to Vladimir Propp's morphology of the folktale, along with the work of other cultural critics, anthropologists, and linguists working in the field of folklore.

Many of our students are familiar with Salman Rushdie's *Haroun and the Sea of Stories* and recall the description in that book of "The Ocean of the Streams of Story," which is also known as the "biggest library in the universe." There they learned about oral traditions held "in fluid form" that retain the ability "to change, to become new versions of themselves, to join up with other stories and so become yet other stories" (72). Rather than a stable text and artifact—a library of books—the ocean of the Streams of Story is magically alive, "a liquid tapestry of breathtaking complexity" (Rushdie 1991, 72). The passages from Rushdie's novel give students a platform for meditating on the various metaphors we use for stories (kaleidoscopes, carpets, yarns, tapestries, soups, and so on) and their component parts (threads, strands, tropes, memes, and motifs).

Students quickly discover that tales from the culture of childhood have a mythical power and are more than "just" nursery stories or old wives' tales. Little Red Riding Hood picks flowers in a meadow, much like Europa and Persephone before their abductions. The mythical Atreus and Thyestes haunt the Grimms' "This Juniper Tree" (Tatar 1998). And the giant in "Tom Thumb," who mistakenly eats his seven daughters, can be seen as a folkloric analogue to Kronos, who devours his own children. As Italo Calvino tells us: "Through the forest of fairy-tale, the vibrancy of myth passes like a shudder of the wind" (Calvino 1986, 18).

"All versions belong to the myth," Lévi-Strauss tells us, and this course tries to show how the multiforms of folklore and mythology enable us to use a wide lens in analyzing cultural stories (Lévi-Strauss 1963, I: 217). If fairy tales miniaturize myth and make it up close and personal, fantasy literature aspires to create new mythologies that rival the old. Fantasy opens up other worlds, secondary worlds, offering what Susan Cooper calls "magnificent bubbles" (Nel and Pau 2011, 83) marked by beauty but invoking also horror and dread. We explore a range of Wonder Worlds: Wonderland,

Neverland, Narnia, Hogwarts, along with Philip Pullman's multiverses. The make-believe operations of these worlds do the work of mythopoesis, making beliefs and using the tropes of prophecy, miracle, revelation, and transformation in their fictional elaborations.

Fairy tales and fantasy literature have often been positioned as escapist. But they are less a way out than a way in, an escape into perils and possibilities. Moving in the optative mode, they tell us how things might be, should be, could be, or ought to be. These stories give us the great "what ifs?" and they introduce students to hypotheticals, giving them worlds that may not be real yet also characters who shape their identities in much the same way as people do in real life. They have what Paul Ricœur refers to as ontological vehemence, and what Dumbledore affirms in a head-spinning, self-reflexive moment in the Harry Potter series, as having the same status as reality (Ricœur 1981, 76). "Of course it is happening inside your head," he tells Harry. "But why on earth should that mean that it is not real?" (Rowling 2007, 723). We are after all still "on earth" as we read, witness, wonder, navigate, and explore with Harry and his companions.

In this course, we aim to promote what Tim Wynne-Jones calls the "deep-read," an immersive experience ("you get gut-hooked and dragged overboard down and down through the maze of print") that begins by seizing hold of us and then letting us go, enabling us to read and think between the lines, "where you are fleetingly aware of your own mind at work" (Wynne-Jones 1998, 165–66). We take up the aesthetic pleasure of reading and explore cognitive gains (nothing challenges us more than making sense of Lewis Carroll's nonsense, for example), but we also consider reading as what Steven Pinker calls a moral technology, that is, a medium for exploring the minds of others, getting inside their skin, walking in their shoes, going inside their heads, and performing all the other strange empathetic acts that accompany our engagement with what are nothing more than black squiggles on a white page. Our students reward our efforts with attentive reading, understanding that many of these works enable them to go back in some way, yet also provide them with ignition power, the capacity to deepen and broaden their understanding of how we do things with words and narratives.

Our students often come to the course with a deeply personal relationship to the books we read, whether it is because their parents read them fairy tales by the Brothers Grimm at bedtime, or because they participated in a theatrical production of *Peter Pan*, or because they consider Harry Potter one of their most intimate friends. Consequently, we feel that we have a certain responsibility to keep alive the inventive enthusiasm they bring to the readings. Just as the experience of reading requires a collaboration between author and reader, so too the learning experience in the classroom can turn into a partnership between teachers and students. We all bring something to the narrative feast at our collective classroom table. And, what is more, we hope that what we read together becomes a *moveable* feast. We want our course to provoke, animate, and promote an appetite for stories. It is no accident that we begin our unit on fairy tales with the story about the girl in red and our unit on fantasy with *Alice's Adventures in Wonderland*, encouraging our students to wander off the beaten path into terrain where success depends on their own inquisitiveness, creativity, and courage. As Neil Gaiman writes in *The Ocean at the End of the Lane*: "Children use back ways and hidden paths, adults take roads and official paths" (Gaiman 2013, 113). We try hard to regress to those childlike ways.

We begin the semester-long course with fairy tales and, at midterm, we turn to fantasy literature. The rationale for this organization is twofold: First, it makes good chronological sense to begin with tales once told by the fireside and then to progress to literary texts in order for the students to witness how plots, characters, themes, and tropes migrate from times past into the contemporary narratives we use to make sense of our lives. We envision the two parts to the course as a diptych: each section complements the other, and, when taken together, they illuminate each other and promote a better understanding of literary works that move in the mode of the marvelous and uncanny. Our second reason for dividing the term is to demonstrate that the inflection point at which oral turns to literary, fairy tale turns into novel, and myth turns into history is less of a sharp break than it seems.

In the first half of the course, we read a variety of tale types ("The Children and the Ogre," "The Animal as Bridegroom," "The Princess on the Glass Mountain," "The Name of the Supernatural Helper," and others) in order to build a foundation for identifying cultural discourses, character types, landscapes, and motifs in myth and fairy tale. This method permits students to recognize how those elements come to be recycled in later fantasy texts, and it also introduces them to the concept of intertextuality and the broader network of storytelling. During the first half of the term, along with our primary fairy-tale and mythological texts we include secondary readings comprising various excerpts and full-length essays written by influential scholars who created the foundation for studying folklore and mythology. Vladimir Propp, Philippe Ariés, Claude Lévi-Strauss, Alan Dundes, Lewis Hyde, Bruno Bettelheim, and Robert Darnton offer a range of approaches to the material under consideration. We try to offer our students multiple perspectives on methodology so that they will emerge with a clear understanding of folkloristics as an academic discipline.

When we make the shift to fantasy literature, we position the narratives as part of a continuous category that requires examination from more than just the literary perspective. In the second half of the term, we read a number of novels and limit the amount of secondary material assigned, although we continue to challenge the students to develop an analytic apparatus for examining the stories by introducing new terminology, reading critical essays, and assigning excerpts from secondary sources. By employing this model we find that by the second half of the course, students are comfortable analyzing the primary and secondary texts that we assign without as much step-by-step guidance. As a result, they are able to generate class discussions and conduct their own independent investigations that form the basis of their final papers and projects.

We have found that the most effective pedagogical arrangement is to meet twice per week, once as a whole group for a formal lecture with the course instructor, and once in smaller groups for a discussion session with what our institution calls section leaders. In lecture, we offer an overview of the readings for the week and provide historical context, as well as background on how the tales have been analyzed and interpreted. We also present students with counterarguments to prevailing critical wisdom and encourage them to develop their own critical entry point through close readings of passages. In our unit on trickster narratives, for example, we introduce them to Lewis Hyde's study of male tricksters and note that he defines those figures in ways that exclude female counterparts. By examining tales like the German "Hansel and Gretel" and the Russian Baba Yaga tales like "Vasilisa the Fair," we try to identify a parallel tradition, showing how female figures develop a distinctive form of trickster identity, with a different set of priorities and domains of agency. In addition, through references to contemporary films, television programs, songs, visual culture, consumer products, and political satire, we show how these stories remain relevant and continue to build our social and cultural identities. In the second half of the term, we emphasize how the works we read figure as meaningful cultural touchstones. Whether looking at the critique of reality television and media violence in *The Hunger Games* or investigating the advocacy of reading and the promotion of social responsibility in *Harry Potter*, we work through the stories to discover how powerfully children's fantasy fiction mirrors our own cultural preoccupations and personal concerns. In lecture, we try to promote dialog as well as convey information. We give our students brief assignments each week to start them thinking about the material, and we encourage discussion through group brainstorming at the start of each lecture. For *Peter Pan*, for example, we asked students to bring to class three words to describe Neverland. For the unit on "Little Red Riding Hood," they came to class with one other version of the story they had encountered. "Who's your daemon?" we asked in the unit on *The Golden Compass*. We then continue the dialog initiated in lecture in section meetings and, in this way, we are able to dive right into discussion because the students are already engaged with the material.

Discussions in section are designed to help students navigate the secondary readings, to digest the content of lectures, and to explore the readings in a more informal environment. Given the size of the course (approximately thirty to thirty-five students), it is impossible for every student to participate in lecture. Section, which comprises a maximum of fifteen students, provides a more intimate space for questioning, debating, investigating, and digging deeper. We keep students engaged and enthusiastic about the material by providing some space for personal reactions and observations, but we also seek to provide a foundational understanding of folklore and fairy tales as well as interpretive tools for approaching children's fantasy literature. We are aware that students often choose our course over others because they imagine that it will be "fun" and "easy." As we tell our students, the stories we read in the course represent the simple expression of complex thought, and they are often more challenging to interpret than texts that seem to lend themselves more readily, on the surface of things, to decoding. We have discovered that we do not have to sacrifice rigor for pleasure, or vice versa. We maintain a high standard of critical thinking for our students and try to show how rereading stories from their own childhoods through a critical lens can be intellectually challenging and revelatory. Because many of the assigned readings will be familiar to the students, our suggested strategy for other teachers of fairy tales and fantasy literature is to approach each unit from an unexpected angle in order to encourage a more active engagement with the texts. Whether participating in a mental scavenger hunt to identify fairy-tale motifs in "Hansel and Gretel," refereeing a "caucus race" to determine the figure with the greatest authority in *Alice in Wonderland*, conducting a mock trial for Bluebeard's wife to debate the ethics of her decision to enter the Bloody Chamber, or drawing daemons to identify Pullman's criteria for these physical manifestations of a character's soul, students discover that exercising their critical faculties in a playful manner can lead to more sophisticated insights about concepts ranging from Paul Ricœur's notion of ontological vehemence to Elaine Scarry's understanding of how writers create vivacity. Our students respond enthusiastically to these nontraditional types of discussions, and we find that these experiences in the classroom promote innovation in the students' own independent research, papers, and projects.

In keeping with our aim to make the course an interactive experience and to encourage a free-flowing exchange of ideas from the outset, the section leader meets with each student for a one-on-one session. These meetings enable students to connect with the instructor and to ask questions about course requirements and expectations, while the instructor acquires a clear sense of the student's interests and aspirations. Most important, however, these meetings help to break the ice and to efface the invisible barrier that often exists between students and their instructors. It is, of course, impossible for students to forget entirely that their instructors are evaluating them, but what we emphasize during these initial conversations is that we value intellectual curiosity, courage, and creativity. We want students to focus less on being "right" and more on becoming "curiouser and curiouser," thinking critically and investigating deeply. Our goal is to establish an environment in which students feel secure enough to ask questions, test hypotheses, and speak spontaneously, even when a response might seem "obvious" or "controversial."

Our course requirements include a manifest commitment to class participation, brief weekly writing assignments (generally 150–200 words), a midterm paper (1,500–2,000 words), a two-hour final examination, and a choice of a final paper (3,000–3,500 words) or a final project. The section leader provides the class with a unit on how to write a paper for the course and meets with students individually to discuss their paper topics and proposal. Approximately two-thirds of the way through the course, we ask the students to submit a proposal for their final papers or creative projects. Since the students have investigated the cultural energy of fairy tales and fantasy literature in their multiple forms over the past two centuries, we require students to write a rationale for their creative work, one that demonstrates their understanding of the medium in which they are working as well as the question of cultural impact. With the final project, we hope to inspire the students to use the knowledge they have gained about the works we study to create something new. Projects have included picture book adaptations of traditional fairy tales; writing and illustrating an original fairy tale; writing a chapter of a fantasy novel; making an interactive web page for one of the texts studied in class; creating a build-your-own-adventure story based on themes, characters, and motifs we have come to associate with fairy tales and fantasy literature and setting up that interactive experience on campus; creating a film; making a stop-motion animation short film;

writing a television pilot or a short play; filming a series of movie trailers about one or more of the works we studied; creating a series of paintings, photographs, or other form of visual art inspired by the course readings; and creating a musical score, writing a song, or choreographing a dance interpretation of one or several of the stories. Assessment has its challenges, but we have found that measuring a student's intellectual investment in the project, as well as the time commitment devoted to it, is in general fairly straightforward.

When Michel Foucault declared that he dreamed of a "new age of curiosity," he situated curiosity firmly in the territory of wonder, defining it as "a readiness to find what surrounds us strange and odd" and as "a passion for seizing what is happening now and what is disappearing" (Foucault 1980, 325). The creative projects are another way for students to internalize what they have learned and to take the course with them out into the world. By engaging in the process of exploring their immediate environment and using the course readings to deepen skills they already have, they also make what we read their own. And they add their own fresh new ingredients to the constantly simmering cauldron of story.

"Fairy Tale, Myth, and Fantasy Literature" includes ten units, and the topics for each appear below:

"LITTLE RED RIDING HOOD": A STORY AND ITS HYPERTEXTS

We begin with a story that everyone seems to know (though we all have surprisingly different versions of it in our heads). We then turn to a number of fairy-tale hypertexts from Germany, France, and England and look at how they are culturally encoded and also at how they capture the so-called timeless universals. How are the tales transmitted, adapted, and appropriated? As we trace the path of Little Red Riding Hood from seventeenth-century France to the United States today, we engage in three-dimensional thinking, contemplating the intersection points of story, audience, and culture. We ask that the students bring to class a contemporary version of "Little Red Riding Hood" that is not included in their course readings, in an effort to demonstrate the ongoing pervasiveness of the fairy-tale tradition. Employing this familiar tale as the introductory text to the course has proven to be a successful way to acquaint our students with the important questions we will be investigating throughout the semester.

BEAUTIES AND BEASTS:
HEROINES, NICE AND NARCOTIZED

"Beauty and the Beast" is our cultural story about monstrosity and compassion. We turn to ancient sources to understand how the tale configures the nature/culture divide, and we also look to the insights of structural anthropology to understand what the story reveals about human nature. Why do animal grooms evolve from the seductively divine (Zeus) to the abjectly humble (frog prince), and how do mortal brides grow, over time, to become compassionate paragons of virtue? We also consider different cultural inflections of "Sleeping Beauty" and investigate the nexus of beauty, sleep, and death in versions of the tale. Many of these stories involve characters and actions that are morally reprehensible or, at the very least, morally ambiguous, thus we address the question: Why do morality tales so often lack morality? We examine various works of visual art with "sleeping beauties" and anthropomorphized beasts such as Titian's painting *The Rape of Europa*, Antonio Canova's sculpture *Cupid and Psyche*, and illustrations by Arthur Rackham, Warwick Goble, and Charles Robinson, in order to show our students how these stories appear and undergo transformation in other media.

TRICKSTERS AND HUNGER NARRATIVES:
OUTWITTING THE OGRE

Hospitality, or *Hostipitality*, to use Jacques Derrida's (2000) term, figures in our considerations of tricksters, those transgressive figures who both subvert the social order and ensure its survival. Functioning at the margins of the social order, they also incarnate the energetic intelligence required to maintain it. We consider how Little Thumbling, Jack, and Vasilisa test boundaries and use pretense, disguise, mimicry, and mischief to outwit giants and witches and to avoid becoming their next meal. We assign an excerpt from Lewis Hyde's *Trickster Makes This World*, which inspires our discussion about gendered trickery, and we read Anne Sexton's poem "Hansel and Gretel" to examine how the tale is reinflected in the twentieth century. This poem is particularly successful in conveying to our students the way that fairy tales transcend chronological and cultural boundaries by inspiring aesthetic innovation.

Hans Christian Andersen and the Cult of Beauty and Suffering

Hans Christian Andersen listened to folktales as a child and produced his own as a writer. What shifts take place as we move from oral storytelling cultures to literary tales? We explore Andersen's aesthetics and attention to surfaces even as we explore the minds of his characters. How does the offering or withholding of details by a text let the reader imagine beauty? What is the connection of beauty to suffering or pain? We read Michel Foucault's introduction to *Discipline and Punish* and discuss models of public torture and private punishment in conjunction with Andersen's cult of suffering and the Christian ritual of repentance. Andersen's literary tales provide us with a portal into the second half of the semester, as we fall down the rabbit hole into fantasy literature.

ALICE AND WONDERLAND: BOREDOM, CURIOSITY, NONSENSE, AND WONDER

Presented as a series of surreal adventures in which the notions of development and education are banished, *Alice's Adventures in Wonderland* opens up a world that not only contains wonders but also offers the promise of escape from the adult world of sense and meaning. What is the role of nonsense, and how does it serve as an antidote to the toxic conventions of children's literature from an earlier era? Is there a downside to Wonderland? What agents stifle curiosity in children's literature? Who has the ultimate authority in this text, the child or the adult? We talk in depth about the breakdown of language in Wonderland in relation to the linguistic theories of Ferdinand de Saussure (1998) and discuss how the arbitrariness of language in this novel indicates a larger loss of logic and a concern with mere sound and beauty rather than meaning.

PETER AND WENDY: MAPPING THE CHILD'S MIND

The philosophers John Locke and Jean-Jacques Rousseau both developed competing claims about the child's mind, but they were also committed to making the child the center of philosophical investigation. J. M. Barrie inaugurated a literary impulse that looked to the mind of the child rather than to the agendas of adults for its inspiration. We explore the discovery of childhood imagination and the tragedy of growing up through the cultural myth about Peter Pan and discuss Neverland as representative of a collective childhood imagination. Because the most prominent version of the Peter Pan story is a play about play, we read an excerpt from John Huizinga's *Homo ludens: A Study of the Play Element in Culture* in which he argues that play constitutes culture-building work. We see that when Peter Pan "breaks through" and "rents the film that obscures Neverland," he enables his magic to encroach on the reality of the nursery at Number 14. Play moves the Darling children from the world of phenomena (the realm of the everyday) to a second world (mythic, spiritual, and imaginative). We therefore ask if Neverland is simply an interlude, as play itself is an interlude, "secluded" and "limited" in time and space, or if Neverland can take up a more permanent residence in children's minds.

DAEMONS AND DUST:
GOLDEN COMPASSES AS MORAL COMPASSES

The French cultural theorist Jean-François Lyotard tells us that postmodernism is marked by incredulity toward metanarratives—the grand narratives and master narratives that once dominated the literary landscape. Have metanarratives found a comfortable home in children's literature? Is this the one domain that allows authors to take on the great existential questions about the meaning of life and what really matters? Philip Pullman's *His Dark Materials* trilogy is characterized by his cinematic style of writing, whether he is describing the aurora borealis or his heroine's escape into a wardrobe. We read Elaine Scarry's essay "On Vivacity," to help us understand how Pullman reproduces the deep structures of perception in his fantasy trilogy. Scarry's essay helps students to successfully envision the process of creating realness or believability in a fictional world.

DEATH IN CHILDREN'S LITERATURE

In conjunction with the novels we address in this unit, we also read an excerpt from Margaret Atwood's *Negotiating with the Dead: A Writer on Writing* in which she tells us: "All writers must go from *now* to *once upon a time*; all must go from here to there; all must descend to where the stories are kept; all must take care not to be captured and held immobile by the past" (Atwood 2002, 178). Atwood tells us that writers must bring the treasures of the dead—their stories—back into the land of the living, enabling them to enter "the realm of the audience, the realm of the readers, the realm of change" (Atwood 2002, 178). How have writers managed mortality in books for children? We begin with Wilbur's "I don't want to die!" in *Charlotte's Web* and investigate Neil Gaiman's *The Ocean at the End of the Lane*, a memorate (an oral narrative from memory relating a personal experience, especially the precursor of a legend) that documents an encounter with death. What is the memorate and why do authors choose this particular genre? How does Gaiman's text evoke amnesia and at the same time disavow it? How do water, memory, and immersion function in this autobiographical account? And can children cope with the issues Gaiman brings to the surface?

CHILD'S PLAY AS MORTAL COMBAT

We turn to dystopias in fiction for adults and for the young and investigate the troubling cathartic pleasures of the *Hunger Games* series. We read an excerpt from Mark Pizzato's (2005) *Theatres of Human Sacrifice* and apply his theories on melodrama and purging versus tragedy and catharsis to young adult novels. Suzanne Collins's trilogy enables us to explore issues ranging from the use of children in combat situations to mimetic violence. We debate whether Collins's critique of culturally sanctioned violence becomes complicit in perpetuating the glamour and attractions of violence. We also interrogate the *Hunger Games* films and their positioning of viewers as fascinated spectators engaging in voyeuristic delights even as those same viewers disavow the pleasure as part of their experience of the Games.

TURNING CHILDREN INTO READERS AND INTERPRETERS

Mircea Eliade (1957) tells us that myth and story can create ontologically rich places and that, in secular cultures, entertainment can serve a religious function. How has J. K. Rowling's series of books evolved and what has been its cultural impact? In what ways has the book taken advantage of hermeneutic puzzles and mythical materials to attract readers? We discuss moments of intertextuality throughout the seven-part "epic," where elements of fairy tales, myth, and fantasy literature are seamlessly bound together. We observe the ways in which Rowling's protagonist benefits from a tradition of heroic action that dates back to classical antiquity, but also recognize how Harry finds his mission and purpose in the twenty-first century. We examine J. L. Austin's (1975) work on speech-act theory and relate it to the structure and function of spells, the performative utterances peculiar to Rowling's universe. We analyze the embedded story, "The Tale of the Three Brothers," and demonstrate how Rowling employs this story to teach us about the crucial importance of children's books as tools that not only teach us how to create meaning, but also—as the "boy who lives" models for us—how to live.

ANIMATION AND IMAGINATION

In our final unit, we address questions about cross-writing and crossover fiction as we plunge headfirst into turn-of-the-century Paris, Georges Méliès's cinema of attractions, and the secret world of Hugo Cabret. Brian Selznick's books combine word and image in powerful and original new ways that challenge us to reconsider the relationship between the verbal and the visual. How does the reader's shared perspective with Hugo change the way we enter and maneuver our way through his story? We investigate how Selznick reenergizes fantasies about animation and explore how artifice operates within the text. What is the value of the talisman in children's literature and how does it develop new layers of significance in this book about personal remembrances and cultural memory?

TEXTS

J. M. Barrie, *Peter Pan*, Jack Zipes, ed., or *The Annotated Peter Pan*, Maria Tatar, ed.

Suzanne Collins, *The Hunger Games*

Neil Gaiman, *The Ocean at the End of the Lane*

Donald Grey, ed. *Alice in Wonderland*

Philip Pullman, *The Golden Compass*

J. K. Rowling, *Harry Potter and the Deathly Hallows*

Brian Selznick, *The Invention of Hugo Cabret*

Maria Tatar, ed. *The Classic Fairy Tales: Texts, Criticism*

E. B. White, *Charlotte's Web*

SECONDARY READINGS

Philippe Ariès, *Centuries of Childhood*

Margaret Atwood, *Negotiating with the Dead: A Writer on Writing*

Bruno Bettelheim, *The Uses of Enchantment*

Angela Carter, *The Bloody Chamber: And Other Stories*

Robert Darnton, "Peasants Tell Tales: The Meaning of Mother Goose," in *The Great Cat Massacre and Other Episodes in French Cultural History*

Michel Foucault, *Discipline and Punish*

Johan Huizinga, *Homo Ludens: A Study of the Play-Element in Culture*

Lewis Hyde, *Trickster Makes This World*

Claude Lévi-Strauss, *The Structural Study of Myth*

Elaine Scarry, "On Vivacity: The Difference Between Daydreaming and Imagining-under-Authorial-Instruction" in *Dreaming by the Book*

Anne Sexton, *Transformations*

Vladimir Propp, *Morphology of the Folktale*

REFERENCES

Atwood, Margaret. 2002. *Negotiating with the Dead: A Writer on Writing*. New York: Cambridge University Press.

Austin, J. L. 1975. *How to Do Things with Words*. Ed. J. O. Urmson and Marina Sbisá. Cambridge: Harvard University Press.

Calvino, Italo. 1986. *The Uses of Literature*. New York: Harcourt Brace.

Derrida, Jacques. 2000. "Hospitality." Translated by Barry Stocker. *Angelaki: Journal of Theoretical Humanities* 5 (3): 3–18.

Eliade, Mircea. 1957. *The Sacred and the Profane: The Nature of Religion*. Trans. Willard R. Trask. New York: Harcourt, Harvest.

Foucault, Michel. 1980. "The Masked Philosopher." In *Ethics: Subjectivity and Truth: The Essential Works of Michel Foucault 1954–1984*, vol. 1, ed. J. Faubion, trans. Robert Hurley., 321–28. Harmondsworth: Penguin, Allen Lane.

Gaiman, Neil. 2013. *The Ocean at the End of the Land*. New York: William Morrow.

Hanna. 2011. Directed by Joe Wright. Santa Monica: Focus Features.

Hard Candy. 2005. Directed by David Slade. Seattle: Vulcan Productions.

Lévi-Strauss, Claude. 1963. "The Structural Study of Myth." In *Structural Anthropology*, trans. Clair Jacobson and Brooke Grundfest Shoepf, 206–31. New York: Basic.

Nel, Phillip, and Lissa Pau. 2011. *Keywords for Children's Literature*. New York: New York University Press.

Pizzato, Mark. 2005. *Theatres of Human Sacrifice: From Ancient Ritual to Screen Violence*. Albany: State University of New York Press.

Pullman, Philip. 2000. *The Amber Spyglass*. New York: Random House, Yearling.

Ricœur, Paul. 1981. *The Rule of Metaphor*. Toronto: University of Toronto Press.

Rowling, J. K. 2007. *Harry Potter and the Deathly Hallows*. New York: Arthur A. Levine Books.

Rushdie, Salman. 1991. *Haroun and the Sea of Stories*. New York: Penguin, Granta Books.

Saussure, Ferdinand de. 1998. *Course in General Linguistics*. Edited by Charles Bally, Albert Sechehaye, and Albert Riedlinger. Translated by Roy Harris. Chicago: Open Court.

Tatar, Maria. 1998. "This Juniper Tree." In *Classic Fairy Tales*, ed. Maria Tatar, 190–96. New York: W. W. Norton.

Tolkien, J. R. R. 1966. "On Fairy-Stories." In *The Tolkien Reader*, by J. R. R. Tolkien, 33–99. New York: Ballantine.

Wynne-Jones, Tim. 1998. "The Survival of the Book." *Signal: Approaches to Children's Books* 87:160–66.

2

Teaching Fairy Tales in Folklore Classes

Lisa Gabbert

THAT THE BROTHERS GRIMM ARE AMONG THE FOUNDING fathers of folklore is a fact learned early on in most folklore studies. The Grimms, who collected their tales with the interest in promoting German language and culture, produced *Kinder- und Hausmärchen* (*Children's and Household Tales*, 1812), a scholarly but also wildly popular publication that served as a kind of handbook for tale-collecting enthusiasts in various European countries during the mid to late nineteenth century (Grimm and Grimm 1974). These enthusiasts included Alexandr Afansef in Russia, Joseph Jacobs in England, and Peter Christen Asbøjrnsen and Jørgen Moe in Norway. Across Europe, tales were documented, classified, and compared to those found in the Grimms' collection, starting what was to become essentially a database of tales stored in archives and the basis for the beginnings of the more formal discipline (Georges and Jones 1995).

I am a folklorist and/but not a fairy-tale scholar, and I offer a general overview to fairy tales of approximately two weeks in my Introduction to Folklore classes at Utah State University. The term *fairy tales* commonly is used in popular parlance, but the broader German term *Märchen* is the one I prefer, referring to those tales that fall within the old Antti Aarne and Stith Thompson (AT) tale type index between numbers 300 and 1,199 and in the new Aarne-Thompson-Uther (ATU) index between numbers 300 and 749, which are labeled in the ATU as "Tales of Magic" (Uther 2011). Introductory folklore classes at Utah State University fill general education requirements as well as basic requirements for English majors; most students are from English, education, engineering, the sciences, or business. The primary objectives of the course are (1) to learn basic disciplinary terminology and classification of folklore genres, (2) to learn fundamental

DOI: 10.7330/9781607324812.c002

principles in the discipline of folklore, and (3) to gain a broader understanding and appreciation of folk materials.

I begin the semester with fairy tales because, for a number of reasons,
they are useful in introducing students to the broader study of folklore.
First, fairy tales are already part of what most students expect to study
in folklore classes, so they fit students' preconceived notions. Because the
materials are familiar, they are easily used to lay the foundational characteristics for what is considered "folklore" more broadly; typical folklore characteristics include orality, traditionality, anonymity, and variation (Brunvand
1998). As the semester progresses, these characteristics are applied to materials that may not fit students' preconceived notions of folklore, such as
Internet email scams, practical jokes, and *latrinalia* (writing on bathroom
walls), all examples that they may encounter in any given folklore class. Fairy
tales are also useful because the kinds of analyses and interpretations done
on fairy tales—such as thematic analysis, comparative analysis, and structural analysis—are common ways of approaching other forms of folklore
as well. Students usually are familiar with the tales, but have not considered
them in a scholarly way, and I think familiarity with form and content makes
starting analysis easier for them. Finally, students are willing to comment
and participate in conversations involving fairy tales, establishing good rap-
port and participatory context right up front.

TEXTS, THEMES, STYLE, AND STRUCTURE

We begin the semester with a textual orientation by examining tale content.
Depending on whether the class is geared toward European or American
materials, we read selections from Alexandr Afanas'ev's (1945) *Russian Fairy
Tales*, Grimm and Grimm's (1974) *Kinder- und Hausmärchen,* Zora Neale
Hurston's (2008) *Mules and Men,* or Kirin Narayan's (1997) *Mondays on the
Dark Night of the Moon.* Drawing on anthropologist William Bascom's (1954)
"four functions of folklore" (sometimes we read the article and sometimes
I just offer an overview), I emphasize that, according to Bascom's functions, such tales were told not only for entertainment, but also as a form of
education, as an escape from the harsh realities of life, as a way of validat-
ing culture, and as a means of social control. That is, according to Bascom,
tales may perform a number of functions beyond mere amusement, including that of reinforcing social and cultural norms. Students frequently are
surprised by the violence found in some tales, as well as lessons taught
involving trickery, cleverness, deception, or mistrust of family. The tale
"The Robbers" from *Russian Fairy Tales*, for example, begins with female

protagonist Alionushka defending her house by chopping off a robber's head, cutting up his body, and hiding it in various bags. The robbers, seeking revenge, convince her family to give her to them, and Alionushka must figure out how to save herself. The violent content, stupidity, and betrayal of family, as well as the fact that a female protagonist saves herself, jar with the more sanitized, Disney-like fairy tales with which most students are familiar (e.g., the Disney movie version of Cinderella) and serve as a good jumping-off point for discussion of how tales change over time. Values and lessons emphasizing trickery, cleverness, and lying—illustrated in the Russian collection by "Emelya the Simpleton" for example—are considered morally questionable according to my students' modern middle-class standards. In this tale, Emelya frees a pike instead of eating it. The fish grants Emelya anything he desires as a reward for its escape. Emelya uses his wishes to escape work, thrash and beat an assembled mob, escape the king, and marry his daughter. This disjuncture segues into a brief discussion of the historical context of the tales, including how ideas about childhood have changed over time and the ways in which middle-class values have reshaped the tales over the past several hundred years, including editorial changes undertaken by the Grimms themselves.

Students are also fascinated by the closing formulas, since most of them have not heard of any beyond the basic "and they lived happily ever after." In the Russian collection, the most common closing formulas are variations of "I was there and drank mead and beer; it ran down my mustache but it never got into my mouth" (Afanas'ev 1945, 365). One of the longer and more complex versions is "I drank beer at their wedding; it ran down my lips but never went into my mouth. I was given a flowing robe to wear, but a raven flew over me and cawed 'Flowing robe! Flowing robe!' I thought he was crying: 'Throw the robe!' So I threw it away. I asked for a cap but received a slap. I was given red slippers, but the raven flew over me and cawed: 'Red slippers! Red Slippers!' I thought he was crying: 'Robbed slippers!' so I threw them away" (Afanas'ev 1945, 46). Students are baffled by this one, so we talk about not only the function of a closing formula as signaling the end of a story, but also as a way to move the audience from the tale world to the real one through an intermediary (Lüthi 1987, 50). There are also a number of closing formulas in *Mules and Men*, such as "step on a pin, the pin bent, and that's the way my story went" and "by that time a flea asked me for a shoeshine so I left" that provide opportunities for discussion.

To supplement the overview of tale content, I include a PowerPoint presentation containing a variety of well-known drawings by illustrators such as Walter Crane, George Cruickshank, John D. Batten, Dorothea Snow, Edwin

John Prittie, and others. Students love Baba Yaga, the Russian witch who lives in a house that stands on chicken legs, so I have many depictions of Baba Yaga, in both older and more modern versions. I include illustrators such as Francesco Francavilla (Italian illustrator for comic book superhero Hellboy) as well as Boris Zvorykin, who portrays Baba Yaga in a more traditional Russian style. Since we rarely read an entire tale collection, these visuals enhance the stories, and they are useful for illustrating Danish folklorist Axel Olrik's epic law "Use of Tableaux Scenes," which states that many tales contain a particular scene that evokes a strong visual image. According to Olrik, in such scenes actors may draw near one another and time seems to slow down or freeze. These scenes characterize a major event in the tale. These tableaux scenes frequently are those illustrators choose to draw.

The next topic addressed is pattern and structure. Sometimes we read selections from Max Lüthi's (1986) *The European Folktale: Form and Nature*— particularly the chapters on one-dimensionality, depthlessness, and abstract style—in order to discuss stylistic patterns. Sometimes we read selections from Vladimir Propp's (1968) *Morphology of the Folktale* in order to discuss structure. If the syllabus is too crowded and time is an issue (which it frequently is), we may address structure by reading Axel Olrik's (1965) essay "Epic Laws of Folk Narrative" (it is shorter and a little easier to grasp than Propp) and skip discussion of style.[1] In either case, most students have not encountered the concept of structure before and are surprised that many tales fit the patterns described in the essays. I do emphasize that these patterns are particular to European tales and not necessarily found globally; Native American tales such as told by the Navajo, for example, are an exception (Toelken 1996). As a hands-on exercise, I sometimes have students invent their own tales following these "laws" for a bit of fun, which is an exercise that works particularly well with Olrik. Students make up their tales, identify the laws they have used in their writing, and read them aloud in class. Together the class identifies the laws they recognize. This activity helps students better grasp the fundamental nature of folklore, which is that there is a traditional pattern that also allows for variation. These laws also invariably show up at exam time and make for good identification or application questions.

Lüthi's books are also useful in a number of ways. He distinguishes tales from legends based not on content but on style, and so his work is helpful for students seeking to understand comparative work based on other kinds of criteria. We discuss qualities such as one-dimensionality, depthlessness, and abstract style. According to Lüthi, one-dimensionality refers to the notion that all tale characters live in the same dimension or on the same plane; strange characters are marked by geographic distance rather than innate difference in being, as they are in legends (Lüthi 1986, 6–10). Depthlessness means that tale characters are entirely superficial; all that exists can be seen on their surfaces as they lack any underlying "depth" (Lüthi 1986, 11). And one way to understand abstract style is in terms of descriptions: sharp outlines and bright colors characterize the tales, rather than subtle shadings and organic, soft outlines typical of legends (Lüthi 1986, 24). We consider these ideas in relation to tales we have already read. I usually follow my unit on fairy tales with a unit on legends, and so Lüthi's work also offers a nice segue into those materials as well.

Considerations of context are important as well. Elliott Oring notes that "the entire sense of a folktale is not sandwiched between 'Once upon a time' and 'they lived happily ever after.' . . . The problem is not only to understand how a text 'hangs together,' but also to understand why a particular individual or group of people would find such a text meaning-ful, worthy of attention, or deserving of repetition" (Oring 1986, 134–35). In order to answer such questions, Oring introduces four types of con-texts according to which narratives have been commonly examined. These include individual context, social context, comparative context, and cultural context. Individual context refers to the preferences of a particular tale-teller, whereas social context refers to the situation in which the stories are told. Comparative context simply means comparing narratives to each other in order to glean more information than one otherwise would from look-ing at a single example, whereas cultural context takes into account cultural values and influences on a particular story. I address individual and social context in the second section of the fairy tale unit, and focus on cultural and comparative context in the first section of the unit.

Cultural and comparative context are easily integrated with the concept of tale type, even though the construction of tale types did not account for cultural nuances. Tale types are the basis of comparative research, referring to a cluster of stories with the same basic plot. In the nineteenth century, when the concept of a tale type was invented, many scholars presumed that stories with similar plots were genetically related to an original story; it was the task of scholars well into the twentieth century to collect as many variants as possible, suggest an outline of the tale's history, and postulate a hypothetical *urform*.[2] The concept of the tale type is useful because it under-scores the importance of variation in folklore, a fact I account for in class by emphasizing that many of the stories were originally told orally (I realize this is a contested point in some circles, but again this is an introductory class). I use "Cinderella" 510A as the example here, since it is one of the oldest and most widely known tales; Alan Dundes's (1988) *Cinderella: A Casebook* is a good source of background information, and I include a handout and a PowerPoint presentation on the *Types of the Folktale* (Thompson 1961) as well. I have the students read a number of examples of 510A, including Grimms' "Aschenputtel," Afanas'ev's "The Golden Slipper," Charles Perrault's "Cendrillon," Basile's "Cat Cinderella" (in which Cinderella murders her stepmother), and a Chinese version found by R. D. Jameson (1982) dating from approximately the ninth century. We discuss how the story changes according to time period and culture, focusing particularly on the persisting motif of a lost shoe (I may or may not introduce the formal concept of motif at this point) and idea of a persecuted heroine who in this case, is abused.[3] By comparing the same tale across time and space, we see the usefulness of "comparative context," discussing the kind of broader information one gains about a story by reading multiple variants. The usefulness of "cultural context" manifests itself in, for example, the likely inclusion of a fish the further east one goes, by discussing the role of fish in parts of Asia. Another example of cultural context is the name of the character "Ivashko Lie-on-the Stove," found in some Russian stories. Students can be baffled by the name until we talk about the fact that the stove was used to keep warm and that the name connotes a degree of laziness.

COLLECTORS, TELLERS, SETTINGS, AND PERFORMANCES

The second section of our unit on fairy tales deals with issues of social context, performer, and performance. In this section, we focus particularly on social and individual context. We read selections from fieldwork-based collections for this unit, such as Zora Neale Hurston's *Mules and Men*, Barry Jean Ancelet's *Cajun and Creole Tales*, Carl Lindahl's and Maida Owens's *Swapping Stories: Folktales from Louisiana* , or Kirin Narayan's *Mondays on the Dark Night of the Moon* (Hurston 2008; Ancelet 1994; Lindahl and Owens 1997; Narayan 1997). These collections emphasize the performative nature of tales, illustrating that the lessons or morals illustrated are frequently tied to social contexts in which they are told.[4] Some tales, for example, such as those found in the first half of Narayan's collection, may only be told in ritual contexts and the actions depicted in the tale are rewarded or punished according to whether the characters follow ritual prescriptions.

The influence of social context is quite obvious in *Mules and Men*. Hurston very purposefully integrates the performance of all kinds of folklore, including the telling of tales, into the setting. For example, "Why Women Always Take Advantage of Men" is a traditional tale about how men and women used to be equal in strength. The man wanted to be stronger than the woman to "make her mind," and so he asked God to give him more strength than the woman. God complied. Furious, the woman asked God to give her her strength back. God could not, since he had increased the man's strength, but had not decreased the woman's. The woman then went to the Devil for help, who told her how to obtain keys to the kitchen, the bedroom, and "his generations" (i.e., children) in order to make the man do her will. This story, while obviously about gender roles, also illustrates social context. *Mules and Men* utilizes a frame narrative in which author Zora Neale Hurston writes about her experiences collecting folklore. In the frame narrative, a verbal fight arises between a couple sitting near Zora; the above story is told by the woman as a way to put down her man. By pointing out this relationship between frame narrative and tale content, students come to understand that tales are intricately tied to the social contexts in which they arise. As another example of social context, in a different part of the frame narrative Hurston and her friends are listening to a preacher across the street. The group then proceeds to tell stories about preachers and churches. In a final example, Hurston follows a group out fishing. As they walk along, her companions tell various stories about the wildlife, origins of particular species, and the importance of not fishing on a Sunday. Such text/context interrelationships are evident throughout the book, illustrating concretely that stories are told in response to particular situations and to make particular points that "comment on" or frame the ongoing social context. I often assign students particular portions of the book and have them write out the specificities of these text/context interrelationships.

Zora Neale Hurston is also useful in discussing the process of documenting and collecting fairy tales and folklore more generally. As a student of noted anthropologist Franz Boas, Hurston was given the task of collecting African American folklore in Florida as part of her research. Hurston grew up in Eatonville, Florida, where her first bout of collecting takes place and where *Mules and Men* begins. Hurston left Florida as a teenager to obtain an education and became involved in the Harlem Renaissance in New York before returning to her hometown to begin fieldwork in the region. Hurston therefore exemplifies what Kirin Narayan (Narayan, cited in Abu-Lughod 1991, 161n1) calls a *halfie*; that is, a researcher who is both part of the community s/he studies but outside of it as well. *Mules and Men* not only contains the folklore that Hurston documented (leaving aside the thorny question of how and whether or not it was authentically replicated or heavily fictionalized), but also is a story of her own interactions with the community and her fieldwork-collecting experiences. When Hurston arrived in Eatonville with a car given to her by her patron Ms. Osgood Mason, for example, many people assumed she was running liquor and/or was in trouble with the law, as it was quite uncommon in 1927 for African American women to travel alone in their own car at that time. Throughout the book she refers to the suspicions of other women about her, and in the end she is literally run out of a juke joint by a woman looking to kill her. Having students attend to not only the various stories told in the book but also Hurston's own story of her experience as a halfie allows for a discussion about fieldwork collecting and documenting, and about problems of integrating into a fieldwork community.

The discussion about collecting is important in introductory folklore classes, since students conduct their own fieldwork as part of their final project. Students collect examples of folklore as it emerges in the students' everyday life and they frequently conduct interviews in order to gather their materials. While this is a very preliminary assignment, students do obtain the experience of collecting, documenting, classifying and interpreting folklore materials, and so discussions about fieldwork collecting are important. These student collections are then deposited in the Fife Folklore Archive at Utah State University and serve as primary archival materials for researchers and scholars (see Gabbert 2010).

Mondays on the Dark Night of the Moon is also a collection of tales with a frame narrative that offers opportunities for discussions about social context, cultural context, and fieldwork. Author/collector Kirin Narayan is American East Indian and therefore also a "halfie" as she returns to the district of Kangra in order to collect stories for her research as an anthropologist. In Narayan's case, she finds many people are troubled by her status as an unmarried adult woman, a situation she and her mother eventually address by explaining that in America, women marry late and that she has a car. Narayan's American mother, who lives in Kangra, plays an important role in her fieldwork by introducing her daughter to people in the village and even leading Narayan to her key informant, Urmilaji, whom Narayan confesses to not having wanted to work with originally, since her mother had found her.

The emphasis on Narayan's singleness, her family connections to the home village, and her sometimes frustrated relationship with her mother leads to a discussion of women's roles in India more generally (an example of cultural context), a major theme throughout the tales that Narayan collects. "First Sour, Then Sweet," for example, is a humorous tale in which a dutiful and hospitable daughter takes in a stranger (deity in disguise) and is rewarded with gold, while the selfish daughter refuses to serve him properly and is rewarded with celestial feces. The tale illustrates the religious dimension of the role of hospitality and the importance of feeding others for women. Another tale, called "Daughter My Little Bread" is about a mother who refuses to accept that her daughter is growing up and replacing her, tying into themes of intergenerational conflict and rivalry between women. In the story, a mother insists that her daughter eat the larger piece of bread, while she eats the smaller. As the daughter comes of age, she realizes that her mother does all the work and therefore should have the larger portion. The daughter eats the smaller piece, and her mother responds by insisting things remain as they are. When her daughter marries a king, the mother insists on visiting her, an inappropriate action according to tradition that incites her daughter to kill her. The story, which is complicated, emphasizes the importance of actions fitting to one's station in life and the maintenance of proper social relationships for women in India. Narayan skillfully aligns the story with actual social expectations in her discussions of tale meaning with Urmilaji.

Social context plays an important role in *Mondays on the Dark Night of the Moon*. The emphasis on women's social relationships in the stories parallels the emphasis on female social relationships that Narayan forges as she conducts her fieldwork. After her discussions with Urmilaji, she writes in the introduction, "I could also see and feel that stories were not just *about* social relationships; they also *made* relationships" (Narayan 1997, 3). Urmilaji's stories connect Urmilaji to people she remembers from the past, as well as to Narayan, who leaves Kangra having "stored the stories in [her] stomach." Narayan explains, "that is, they [the stories] had become a part of me. If the stories are part of me, that means, I think, that Urmilaji herself, and the impressions of past tellers, are in me too" (Narayan 1997, 21).

Narayan includes a discussion of Urmilaji's performance cues as well. She includes the word *bas*, which Urmilaji uses often and which means "that's it"—a kind of linguistic pause. Narayan also includes descriptions of Urmilaji ending a story with a gesture, a gentle bow of the head and writes that her tale-telling was exceptionally measured and soft spoken. These fieldwork-based collections help students understand that tales are not just stories to be read, but that in many cultures they can be profitably understood as oral performances.

TRANSCRIPTION AND TRANSLATION

Issues of transcription, translation, and orthography permeate the practice of collecting and recording stories from living people. Problems with orthography are most evident in *Mules and Men*, since Hurston writes in dialect. It's necessary to discuss dialect writing immediately when introducing the book, as many students have not encountered it previously, find the book difficult to read, (although it tends to become easier for them as they go along), and find the dialect writing off-putting. I explain that dialect writing was a popular though contested writing strategy at the time and a misguided attempt to render the aural qualities of speech in print. Dialect writing not only distorts sound but also makes people seem unintelligent. Since African American speech in the past frequently was rendered in dialect while the speech of other groups were not, dialect writing reinforces stereotypes and beliefs of Anglo-Americans about the perceived linguistic inadequacies of this group. After explaining these issues, I have students listen to the audiobook of *Mules and Men* read by actress Ruby Dee in order to show the qualities of speech that Hurston tried to capture. Dee quite successfully re-translates Hurston's writings back into speech form. Students read along in their books while listening to Ruby Dee as she performs aloud. In this way, students hear, for example, that the "de" in print is really a much softer sound, and they both understand what Hurston was trying to do as well as what the problems with dialect writing are concretely. As mentioned earlier, I do this up front when introducing the text as it also helps students read the rest of the book if they can capture Dee's voice in their mind. Dee's reading of *Mules and Men* also emphasizes the dramatic differences between tale text and tale performance, aiding in overall comprehension not only of the story content, but also of the nature of folklore more generally.

Cajun and Creole Tales by Barry Jean Ancelet is useful for both discussion of translation as well as the importance of individual tale-tellers. This book contains a collection of traditional tales, with the French version printed parallel alongside the English one. It also includes biographies of the tellers themselves, which allows for some discussion of individual context, that is, the ways in which a person's individual life history, beliefs, and values play out in the stories s/he might tell. Ancelet's French and English versions illustrate the oral quality of the tales and also makes the process of translation a bit more transparent. This book does not privilege one language over the other.

CONCLUSIONS

The study of fairy tales is an essential part of introductory folklore classes. Approaching the genre of fairy tales in the ways outlined above lays the foundations for explorations of not only other kinds of traditional folkloric narratives such as legends and ballads, but also for the study of other, non-narrative folklore genres, including traditional foods, ritual, various forms of material culture, and even festival. First, beginning with thematic analysis, the study of fairy tales helps students see these stories in ways that they have not thought about previously. Most students think of fairy tales as entertainment for children only, and they have not considered the fact that such "common" materials might have deeper meanings, teach morals, or reinforce cultural values. This lesson is emphasized when we broaden our investigations later in the semester to other kinds of "common" materials the study of folklore entails. Second, the study of tale type and variation is applicable to nearly all folklore materials, whether or not there exists an official "type index" for a particular genre. The Child Ballads, for example, which I cover in the American folklore class, also utilize the concept of "type," while the study of structure and style is particularly applicable to examinations of ritual and festival. I mentioned above that students invent their own fairy tales based on Olrik's laws; this assignment is repeated during our study of festivals, using Alessandro Falassi's (1987) ten festival "rites" as the structural model.[5] Finally, an understanding of context is crucial in the study of folklore. Framing some tales as oral performances vis-à-vis fieldwork-based collections orients students away from a tales-as-texts model to a more processual and action-oriented framework that focuses on storytelling situations and individual storytellers. This reorientation paves the way for a modern academic understanding of folklore as a traditional form of communication or social action that has meanings and consequences in the conduct of everyday life.

NOTES

1. Olrik suggests that *sagen* follow thirteen laws or "rules," which he outlines in the article. Examples include the "Law of Opening and Closing," which suggests that tales begin and end with a period of calm rather than (for example) *in media res*; the "Law of Three," in which repetition happen three times; the "Law of Two to a Scene," which states that only two characters may interact in a scene at one time; and the "Law of Twins," which says that two characters may function as the same person or as "twins."

2. The notion that variants of tale types are genetically related stems from the study of languages and refers to the hypothesis that tale variants had a single origin from which all other variants emerged. For background reading on this idea, see Robert Georges and Michael Owen Jones, *Folkloristics: An Introduction* (Georges and Jones 1995). For a classic sample study, see Stith Thompson's (1965b) "The Star Husband Tale."

3. For information on the concept of motif in folkloristics, see Stith Thompson's (1965a) *The Motif Index of Folk Literature* as a primary reference work and Robert Georges (1997), "The Centrality in Folkloristics of Motif and Tale Type."

4. For foundational texts, see Richard Bauman (1986), *Story, Performance, and Event: Contextual Studies of Oral Narrative*, and Albert B. Lord (1981), *The Singer of Tales* .

5. Falassi's ten festival rites, which may or may not be included in any single festival, include the following: "Rites of Valorization," "Rites of Purification," "Rites of Passage," "Rites of Reversal," "Rites of Conspicuous Display," "Rites of Conspicuous Consumption," "Rites of Ritual Drama," "Rites of Exchange," "Rites of Competition," and "Rites of Devalorization."

REFERENCES

Abu-Lughod, Lila. 1991. "Writing against Culture." In *Recapturing Anthropology: Working in the Present*, ed. Richard G. Fox, 137–62. Santa Fe: School of American Research Press.

Afanas'ev, Alexandr. 1945. *Russian Fairy Tales*. Trans. Norbert Guterman. New York: Pantheon Books.

Ancelet, Barry Jean. 1994. *Cajun and Creole Tales: The French Oral Tradition of South Louisiana*. Jackson: University Press of Mississippi.

Bascom, William. 1954. "Four Functions of Folklore." *Journal of American Folklore* 67 (266): 333–49. http://dx.doi.org/10.2307/536411.

Bauman, Richard. 1986. *Story, Performance, and Event: Contextual Studies of Oral Narrative*. Cambridge: Cambridge University Press. http://dx.doi.org/10.1017/CBO97805 11620935.

Brunvand, Jan. 1998. *The Study of American Folklore: An Introduction*. 4th ed. New York: W.W. Norton and Co.

Dundes, Alan, ed. 1988. *Cinderella: A Casebook*. Madison: University of Wisconsin Press.

Falassi, Alessandro. 1987. "Festival: Definition and Morphology." In *Time out of Time: Essays on the Festival*, ed. Alessandro Falassi, 1–7. Albuquerque: University of New Mexico Press.

Gabbert, Lisa. 2010. "Exploring Local Communities: Conducting Ethnographic Research in Folklore Studies." *CUR Quarterly* 30 (4): 37–42.

Georges, Robert. 1997. "The Centrality in Folkloristics of Motif and Tale Type." *Journal of Folklore Research* 34 (3): 203–8.

Georges, Robert A., and Michael Owen Jones. 1995. *Folkloristics: An Introduction*. Bloomington: Indiana University Press.

Grimm, Jacob, and Wilhelm Grimm. [1812] 1974. *Kinder- und Hausmärchen gesammelt durch die Brüder Grimm*. 3 vols. Frankfurt am Main: Insel. Grimm, Jacob, and Wilhelm.

Hurston, Zora Neale. 2008. *Mules and Men*. Harper Perennial Modern Classics.

Jameson, R. D. 1982. "Cinderella in China." Reprinted in *Cinderella: A Casebook*, edited by Alan Dundes, 71–97. Madison: University of Wisconsin Press.

Lindahl, Carl, and Maida Owens. 1997. *Swapping Stories: Folktales from Louisiana*. Jackson: University Press of Mississippi.

Lord, Albert B. 1981. *The Singer of Tales*. Cambridge, MA: Harvard University Press.

Lüthi, Max. 1986. *The European Folktale: Form and Nature*. Bloomington: Indiana University Press.

Lüthi, Max. 1987. *The Fairytale as Art Form and Portrait of Man*. Trans. Jon Erickson. Bloomington: Indiana University Press.

Narayan, Kirin. 1997. *Mondays on the Dark Night of the Moon: Himalayan Foothill Folktales*. Oxford: Oxford University Press.

Olrik, Axel. 1965. "Epic Laws of Folk Narrative." In *The Study of Folklore*, ed. A. Dundes, 129-41. Englewood Cliffs, NJ: Prentice-Hall. (Translated by Jeanne P. Steager from "Epische Gesetze der Volkdichtung," *Zeitschrift für Deutsches Altertum*, 51: 1–12.)

Oring, Elliott. 1986. "Folk Narratives." In *Folk Groups and Folklore Genres: An Introduction*, ed. Elliott Oring, 121–45. Logan: Utah State University Press.

Propp, Vladimir. [1928] 1968. *Morphology of the Folktale*. Translated by Laurence Scott. Bloomington: Indiana University Press.

Thompson, Stith. 1961. *Types of the Folktale: A Classification and Bibliography*. Bloomington: Indiana University Press.

Thompson, Stith. 1965a. *Motif-Index of Folk-Literature*. Bloomington: Indiana University Press.

Thompson, Stith. 1965b. "The Star Husband Tale." Reprinted in *The Study of Folklore*, ed. Alan Dundes, 414–74. Englewood Cliffs: Prentice-Hall.

Toelken, Barre. 1996. *Dynamics of Folklore*. Logan: Utah State University Press.

Uther, Hans-Jörg. 2011. *The Types of International Folktales: A Classification and Bibliography*. 2 vols. Helsinki: Finnish Academy of Science and Letters.

3

At the Bottom of a Well

Teaching the Otherworld as a Folktale Environment

Juliette Wood

THE NUMEROUS TALES BROUGHT TOGETHER BY THE BROTHERS GRIMM and other collectors provide a seemingly endless selection of folk narratives. Although early scholarship sought to situate the folktale within theoretical frameworks that could explain the evolution of culture, it also recognized the characteristically patterned nature of such tales and produced indexes concerned with mapping out the components of oral tales. The most notable and comprehensive indexes were undoubtedly those of Stith Thompson and Antti Aarne, which are still in use today (Aarne and Thompson 1961).

Interest in the folktale, especially the *Märchen*, or fairy tale, has undergone something of a renaissance in recent decades. Courses on the folktale now appear regularly as part of the syllabus in many humanities departments, and these courses have proved popular with students who are already familiar with fantasy literature, fantasy-adventure films, graphic novels, and role-playing games. One attraction of such "themed" courses is that because the material is familiar from other contexts, it is easier to engage students in broader theoretical issues. The main objective of the course "At the Bottom of the Well: The Otherworld as Folktale Environment" is to establish a method and set a tone using folktales drawn from various sources that will engage students as quickly as possible in these issues. The course, which usually takes place during a single semester, is taught through the medium of English and is open to students working on degrees in English literature, and European languages, as well as folklore and cultural studies. Students who attend this course are usually upper-level undergraduates, year two and above, or graduate students pursuing master's-level degrees.

 DOI: 10.7330/9781607324812.c003

Contemporary folktale scholarship still recognizes that the meanings of tales are ultimately conveyed through their narrative structures, and this course focuses on a key narrative theme in many folktales, namely, the journey to the Otherworld. This theme enables students to consider how the Otherworld topos functions within specific tales as a way to express fundamental human needs, desires, and anxieties through a narrated journey to an alternate environment. Max Lüthi's concept of "one-dimensionality" as applied to the Otherworld in folktales is a useful starting point to examine these questions. In his classic study of European fairy tales (1961; translated edition Lüthi 1982), Lüthi introduced the concept of one-dimensionality to characterize the function of the supernatural. Although the folktale Otherworld is located at a distance, its marvelous qualities are accepted as natural rather than alien or threatening. This approach reflects the contemporary, more nuanced understanding of the interface between elite and popular culture and between Western and non-Western narrative strategies. It also reflects the relationship between literary forms and their traditional analogues, gender issues, and the transformation of traditional folktales by new media.

The fairy tale is an important parent genre for fantasy, and traditional tales provide a perennial source for retellings and adaptations. Shifting motifs and outcomes in different versions and in different genres illustrate the consequences of narrative transformation. How were encounters between Otherworld beings and their human counterparts conceived? What is the function of the encounter in different contexts? What are the conditions or circumstances for the encounter? Were the encounters understood as historical, or possibly historical, events, or as pure entertainment? Are there differences connected with the different genres and times of composition? Other genres also make use of Otherworld elements. For example, in myths the journey can highlight important cultural realities such as death, and in contemporary fantasy writing, and spin-offs such as film and role-playing games, it can reinforce or critique cultural norms. In science fiction, such journeys become technological, and in travelers' tales they can produce anxiety at encountering something alien. Students will be encouraged to engage with these issues and to develop skills and insights that they can use both in their major college programs and in their personal worldviews.

For such a pervasive topos, studies of the Otherworld in the folktale are rather unevenly distributed. The emphasis has been on Western models, although this is changing. Some of the tales used in this course in which a journey to the Otherworld is a prominent feature include "The Star Husband," "Jack and the Beanstalk," "Frau Holle," "The Search for the Water of Life," "East of the Sun and West of the Moon," and "Oisín in Tír na nÓg." These stand out because of their cultural importance and because students relate to them easily. However, the content of any folktale course is flexible due to the range of material available, and it is possible to use other examples in order to present the Otherworld topos with an awareness of the diverse ways in which it was adapted to folktale environments in different cultural contexts and at different times.

Various sessions in such a course would examine the discourse surrounding interpretations of the Otherworld in folk narrative, for example, the degree to which Otherworld environments may reflect genres such as myth or the fictionalized experiences of foreign places known as travelers' tales, and the question of archetype as a way of understanding and explaining the Otherworld journey. The focus will be on texts, but attention will be given to the various approaches and tools used by scholars to address fundamental questions about meaning and origin. Through a course which presents different types of "Otherworlds," it becomes possible to establish a methodology that addresses cultural issues associated with traditional tales and their uses, such as the ones listed above, as they apply to concepts of folk narrative and to encourage students to apply critical thinking to material from different genres of literature and from different cultures. This module comprises ten course units of two hours each and combines lectures that incorporate discussion of texts with visual information and source criticism. Handouts highlighting key issues relating to the session topic and suggestions for further reading accompany each session. The course is assessed through an essay submitted at the end of the course and a task entitled "Your Very Own Otherworld." Constructing an "other" world allows students to put concepts into practice, either as a writing task in which students can write their own tale, or as weekly responses to a series of prompts introduced progressively through the course that takes students step by step through an "Otherworld" environment. The progressive nature of the task, distributed over several weeks, allows students to express themselves on a variety of issues, not just a single topic in a final essay, and allows tutors to monitor progress and to support students' individual needs.

SAMPLE TASK: YOUR VERY OWN OTHERWORLD

1. *Every tale needs a place to start.* Create a protagonist, for example, a projection of yourself, male, female, talking animal or object. What is his/its/her situation? Is the protagonist a prince or princess, a kitchen boy or girl, or something entirely of your own creation?

2. *Now that you have a main character.* Why does your character have to go on a journey? We looked at "far-off" places this week and the riches they contain. Create a far-off place for your character to visit and some hidden treasure that your character has to receive.

3. *You have set out the basic details* of your main character and something about the journey and what the character needs to accomplish. Up to this point your tale has been flexible, but once you assign your protagonist a clear *tale role*, then you have to follow through the fairytale structure you have chosen. What is the first adventure your character experiences on his/her/its journey? This is a pivotal stage in developing ideas, and it would be useful to encourage a discussion about why students have chosen a particular tale "pathway."

4. *You have set your main character on a journey* to success (or not). What are the dangers and opportunities in the Otherworld that your character will visit?

5. *Your folktale should reach a climax and/or a turning point* (i.e., the accomplishment of the main task). You may wish to create a "rule of three" version of the task—either three separate tasks concluding with the most important one or three tries at the same task. What "Otherworld" prize is the character seeking? Is it a product or a person or something intangible?

6. *Now it is time to conclude your tale.* You may wish to add an extra adventure to bring your protagonist home or set her/him/it on another adventure. Check over your tale and be sure your characters and plot follow the "logic" of the type of folktale you have chosen. Give your tale a title. Think about this in the light of what we have been discussing. Is your tale more like *The Seven Voyages of Sindbad the Sailor*? "The Kind and the Unkind Girls"? Give a brief explanation of why you chose your title.

Students can submit their responses every week for feedback or, if they decide to compose their own tale, submit the entire task at the start of unit 7. For the final essay, students can chose a topic that interests them, subject to consultation with the tutor, or write on an assigned topic; for example, a comparison of the similarities and differences in the depiction of the Otherworld in a traditional tale from the Brothers Grimm or similar collection and a literary tale, such as Hans

Christian Andersen or Angela Carter or a film. The two tasks provide a balance between the critical thinking needed for the final essay and a more flexible creative approach required by the "Otherworld" task.[1]

UNITS 1–2: SPATIAL OTHERNESS AND THE JOURNEY THROUGH OTHERWORLD SPACE

As a result of the popularity of genres such as fantasy literature, many students will already be familiar with the concept of an alternative world, and this shared background can provide an effective starting point for teaching the folktale. Typically the examples students present are drawn from films, fantasy and science fiction, and these two weeks are an opportunity to move the discussion toward folktale examples and consider how spatial distance, one-dimensionality, and concepts of the alien help to characterize Otherworld traditions. Many of the students who attend this course are familiar with Welsh literature and folklore and their examples reflect the Otherworld contexts of the medieval tales in the *Mabinogion* and its contemporary reworking in fantasy and film.[2] Although the objective of the course is to lead the students to an understanding of the cultural and literary debates as they apply to concepts of folk narrative, the important point at this stage is to encourage students to express what they think the Otherworld is, and perhaps to begin to design their own Otherworld as a task which can be carried throughout the course.

Many folktales, especially "wonder tales," or *Märchen*, typically involve traveling into an "other world" where the critical adventures of the tale occur and from which the main character emerges triumphant. The term Otherworld has been used as a collective description for these places in the critical literature, but this "other" place is less clearly defined in the tales themselves. However, it always presents both dangers and opportunities— generally as a series of tasks—and a prize, usually in the form of a spouse who brings riches and status. These arenas of test and resolution are therefore essential to understanding how tales work.

Another useful means of introducing the basic concept of spatial otherness is through a discussion of medieval *mappa mundi* as an example of a bounded, enclosed world in which elements, even monstrous ones, are part of a meaningful whole. Depictions of mermaids, dragons, strange plants, and unusual people on these maps (the *Hereford Mappa Mundi* [de Bello and Crone 1285–1954] is an excellent example) resonate with folktale themes. Geographical exploration of "new" worlds, how maps resolved new discoveries and tales of fictional islands, and how this influenced the genre of utopian literature that seeks to construct a new society in a "new" world can form the basis for a discussion about how Otherworld concepts change over time. The second unit also introduces passages from travel literature with folktale resonance, for example, the sections on the kingdom of Prester John and the dragon-daughter of Ypocras from *The Travels of Sir John Mandeville* or the historian Diodorus Siculus's description of the Amazons (Kline 2001).

UNITS 3–9: OTHERWORLD LOCATIONS AND STRATEGIES OF ENGAGEMENT

Stith Thompson notes in his seminal study *The Folktale* that directions to the Otherworld in folktales are often vague. Nevertheless the *Motif Index* classifies material under three general headings: an upper world, a lower world, and one on the same plane as the ordinary world (Thompson 1955–1958, motifs F1–199). The variation and complexity within these categories are together the focus of this course, with an emphasis on how differing geographical locations, characterizations, and means of entering and leaving the Otherworld affect meaning and significance (Thompson 1977, 147; Garry and El-Shamy 2005).

The character of the lower world is often identified in classical literature as the home of the dead and in religious literature as the place of the damned or those excluded from paradise. The journeys of Odysseus and Aeneas to Hades reinforce their standing as heroic figures, while Gilgamesh's descent into the Babylonian underworld, Demeter's search for Persephone, and Orpheus's attempts to reclaim Eurydice suggest the ultimate triumph of death. Odysseus and Aeneas descend into Hades through caves and lakes, and Persephone is warned not to eat in the Otherworld, motifs that overlap with visits to the world of supernatural beings in folktales collected by the Brothers Grimm and many others. Mythic and heroic narratives share motifs with folktales and this unit (unit 3) addresses the significance of Otherworld space through three texts: "Cupid and Psyche," "Orpheus and Eurydice," and the medieval romance, *Sir Orfeo* (Milton 1949; Bliss 1966).

"Cupid and Psyche" bridges the world of classical myth and the folktale. The characters are classical deities and the Otherworld is equated with Hades, but the narrative is a variant of a common folktale, the "Search for the Lost Husband" (Thompson 1955–1958, type 425A), in which a character undertakes a series of tasks before being restored to a spouse, initially lost through carelessness or the violation of some taboo. In Apuleius's account, Psyche is advised on how to navigate the perils of Hades and told to avoid certain foods. The classical myth of Orpheus and Eurydice and the medieval tale of *Sir Orfeo* illustrate how the same tale structure can be adapted to different cultural contexts, genres, and time periods. The addition of supernatural motifs frequently associated with fairy narratives in this medieval tale allows Sir Orfeo to rescue his wife from an Otherworld located on a lower plane, where the classical Orpheus loses her to the power of Hades (Hansen 2002). Students can bring their own experience to this section by identifying the basic pattern that underlies this tale—a search for a lost loved one—in other contexts. For example in the film *Poltergeist* (1982) a mother "descends' through the television set to rescue a child stolen by malevolent ghosts, or Jim Henson's *Labyrinth* (1986), where a rebellious young girl saves her baby half-brother from the Demon King.

The character of the "lower world" varies considerably and is not inevitably infernal. "Frau Holle" is a Teutonic deity associated with winter, but this famous tale from the Brothers Grimm is a version of "The Kind and the Unkind Girls" (Thompson 1955–1958, type 480) in which a girl is sent down a well in pursuit of a lost object and finds herself in a world of talking objects for whom she performs a number of domestic tasks. She also provides service for Frau Holle, who rewards her for her obedience and industry, whereas her uncooperative sister is punished for slovenliness. There are no overtones of death or damnation; rather, the characters encountered in these lower worlds, although powerful and potentially dangerous, reward and punish fairly.

The folktale of "The Kind and the Unkind Girls" provides a model for techniques needed to negotiate Otherworld space (unit 4). In Hans Christian Andersen's (1974) literary folktale "The Girl Who Trod on a Loaf," a proud and selfish female protagonist descends to the realm of the marsh woman, where she learns humility. In this tale, the "unkind" girl learns to be "kind," and the environment has clear Christian overtones. The many variants that exist in differing cultural contexts illustrate the wide variation on a core set of themes, which is an essential characteristic of traditional narrative (Roberts 1958). Encouraging students to identify and explain significant similarities or differences in tale variants and to identify similar patterns in fiction, film, and so on, can be an effective inductive task. For example Alice, like the girl in "Frau Holle," falls down a rabbit hole in Lewis Carroll's (1971) fantasy book and there are many other examples from fiction and film. Ofelia in Guillermo del Toro's (2006) *Pan's Labyrinth*, the characters who travel though Tolkien's (1954) Mines of Moria (*The Fellowship of the*

Ring) and the wizards in the second volume of the Earthsea Cycle (trilogy), *The Tombs of Atuan* (1971) all encounter dangerous Hades-like environments with very different results. Even when the supernatural elements are removed, as they are in science fiction works such as Jules Verne's (1864) *Journey to the Center of the Earth* or H. P. Lovecraft's (1964) Antarctic horror story *At the Mountains of Madness*, lower worlds can be dangerous.

Heavenly realms are accessible by climbing a tree or other natural feature, a ladder or rope, or by being transported through the air by a bird, supernatural being, or a natural phenomenon such as a cloud or a wind. There are tales in which the upper world is equated with Heaven, but it is also a place of test and opportunity, a characteristic it shares with other alternative world environments. Unit 5 contrasts the actions of two visitors to the upper world: Jack and the Star Husband's wife. In "The Star Husband," one of the best-known North American tales, a young woman marries a star and remains in the upper world until she breaks a taboo against digging, whereupon she sees the world from which she came and returns to it. The tale concerns loss of both supernatural spouse and a recognition that the stasis of a beautiful, unchanging Otherworld is problematic for ordinary mortals (Thompson 1953; Dundes 1965; Young 1978).

Jack enters the upper world by climbing a magic beanstalk. There are numerous oral variants of "Jack and the Beanstalk." The tale, which has become a children's classic, also appeared as a printed chapbook and has been animated and filmed several times (*Jack the Giant Slayer* 2013; *Jack and the Beanstalk* [with Abbot and Costello] 1952) (Lindahl 2001; Cruikshank 1860). The successful completion of Jack's adventures in the upper world depends on cleverness rather than strength. This could lead to a discussion of the "upper world" in science fiction, in which space travelers typically encounter seemingly superior beings who are brought under control by human ingenuity. If we accept that any world reached via a spacecraft is an upper world (and this would make a good discussion point), then science fiction offers a variety of possibilities that embody folktale characteristic of an Otherworld as an environment of opportunity with both dangers and benefits. For example, the reptilian aliens of the *Alien* franchise are defeated by heroic action and reversal of gender roles, while the planet Altaira, an early example of a self-contained science fiction world (*Forbidden Planet* 1956), is home to a hideous creature who emerges from the dark subconscious of the scientist who has created this seemingly perfect world.

Journeys to the edge of the known world are an important subclass of Otherworld tales (unit 6). "East of the Sun and West of the Moon" (from the nineteenth-century collection of Norwegian tales by Peter Christen

Asbjørnsen and Jørgen Moe) contains the Otherworld motifs of a lost spouse, a journey involving visits to progressively wiser and more distant informants, animal helpers, acquisition of magic objects, and the eventual need to outwit an opponent (Asbjørnsen and Moe 1960). Variants of "The Search for the Water of Life" exist in a number of folktale collections and offer comparisons with the apocryphal legend of Adam's son, Seth, and his journey to retrieve the Oil of Mercy. This connection will allow students to link earlier discussions about the world depicted in the mappa mundi with the lost-world genre of adventure and science fiction (see Quinn 1962).

The Celtic Otherworld (units 7 and 8) has attracted a great deal of comment both scholarly and popular (see Ó hÓgáin 2006; Lindahl 2000–2002). There are a number of themes which arise in connection with "Celtic" tales, and this section is best divided into two units.

In Irish tradition, the Otherworld is the home of the Tuatha Dé Danann and the fairies and has been identified as the realm of the dead or a pagan Elysium. For example, "The Voyage of St Brendan" can provide a context to discuss pagan versus Christian aspects of the Otherworld and link back to earlier discussions of exploration and the appearance of Brendan's Isle on maps. The Welsh tales of the Tylwyth Teg (the fair family), a poetic term that has come to be applied to the Welsh fairies, deal with the idea of passage between world and with concepts of liminality (see Turner 1967). Of the two twelfth-century Welsh tales, King Herla from Walter Map's *Courtier's Trifles* touches on the wild hunt motif and the liminal world, while "Eliodorus and the Fairies," from Gerald of Wales's *Journey in Wales* deals with the separation of worlds (Hillers 1993; Coulter 1925; Carey 1987). Shamanism can be introduced to a discussion of Oisín in "Tír na nÓg" (The Land of Youth), or this can be a separate session not linked to the Celtic Otherworld. However, many Celtic folktales are linked with shamanism because they evoke romantic images of mystical journeys and exotic cultures in which powerful magicians travel between human and spirit worlds (Nagy 1981; Harvey 2002).

The dangers attached to people and objects displaced from Otherworld contact are considered in unit 9. In the North American tales "The Bear Who Married a Woman" and "The Girl Who Married a Crow," and the Welsh variants on "The Fairy Bride," there is less emphasis on the Otherworld itself and more on the tensions generated by crossing boundaries. These tales offer an opportunity to discuss gender as the issues raised by the tales center on marriage and its failure (see Boas 1916, 1917; Wood 1992). Removing objects from the Otherworld also brings consequences such as a stolen fairy possession such as "The Luck of Edenhall," a decorated glass goblet now in the Victorian and Albert Museum, and perhaps the most famous displaced Otherworld object: the Holy Grail (see Wood 2012).

Previous sessions have examined the nature of the Otherworld and considered aspects of its origin, meaning, and function. The worldview of the folktale is the final topic (unit 10); this unit places the material in the context of folk narrative research and extends it into contemporary meanings relevant to students' lives. It can be difficult to access the personal attitudes of teller and audience to the Otherworld, but interviews with a Hungarian storyteller, Sandor Erdész, in the 1960s illuminated the worldview of his repertoire, and the ways in which this structured his perception of the world. These interviews, taken with examples of the tales themselves, provide answers to question such as "How is the world arranged?" and "How far is the edge of the world?," which combine popular, religious and elite perspectives on not just the location of the Otherworld but on the interplay between this worldview and the everyday experience of the storyteller and his audience (see Erdész 1961, 1963; Dégh 1978). Alan Dundes's introduction highlights some important metaphors about access, organization, and limitations of the Otherworld in the teller's description and how this particular worldview reflects the teller's perceptions of his place in it (see Dundes 1984).

Examples such as this provide an opportunity for students to consider ideas about "worldview" and its implications in other works with folktale characteristics. One possible way to address the idea of folktale cosmogony in contemporary settings is through film and related Internet fan sites and computer games. Modern media outlets play an increasingly important role as conduits for folklore. Sites explaining the geography, culture, and customs of James Cameron's *Avatar* (2009) abound, some produced as part of the general advertising, but many from devoted fans keen to expand, clarify, and comment on a favorite parallel world. The current course proposal focuses on developing student skills and insights through the prism of "otherness" embodied in the traditional otherworld of the folktale, but the ultimate aim of this course is to encourage students to apply critical thinking in other areas of their college curriculum and ultimately beyond.

NOTES

1. This essay is based on a course which is regularly taught to students at Cardiff University, and for this reason many of the choices are Welsh tales. Since the secondary literature on the folktale is so vast, the students are provided with an annotated bibliography. Sioned Davies (2007), trans., *The Mabinogion.* This is the most recent and authoritative translation with explanatory notes of this collection of medieval Welsh tales; William Jenkyn Thomas,

The Welsh Fairy Book. Thomas, Pogány, and Wood (1995) reworked these tales from earlier sources. My introduction and appendix to Thomas's study add references to articles and resources in the field of Welsh folklore studies on this material; Jeffrey Gantz (1981) trans., *Early Irish Myths and Sagas*. The selection of texts used in the course contains literary mythic and folk narrative elements from Irish manuscript sources; see Joseph Jacobs (1968), ed. *Celtic Fairy Tales*, whose twenty-six tales are edited versions of Irish, Welsh, Scottish, and Manx tales drawn from major collecting ventures in the nineteenth century.

2. Welsh students are aware of Anglo-Welsh fantasy writing such as the novels of Lloyd Alexander, Alan Garner, and Evangeline Walton as well as the Welsh and English film reworking of the first four tales of the Mabinogion, notably *Y Mabinogi* (2003, English title *Otherworld*, Derek W. Hayes et al.), and they will also recognize "Celtic" elements in modern fantasy films and novels, for example the Tolkien films (2001–3) and popular television dramas such as *Merlin* (BBC One 2008–2012).

REFERENCES

Aarne, Antti, and Stith Thompson. [1928] 1961. *The Types of the Folk-Tale: A Classification and Bibliography*. Helsinki: Suomalainen Tiedeakatemia.

Andersen, Hans Christian. 1974. *The Complete Fairy Tales and Stories*. Trans. Erik Christian Haugaard. Garden City: Doubleday.

Asbjørnsen, Peter Christen, and Jørgen Engebretsen Moe, eds. 1960. *Norwegian Folk Tales*. New York: Viking Press.

Bliss, Alan Joseph, ed. 1966. *Sir Orfeo*. Oxford: Clarendon Press.

Boas, Franz. 1916. *Tsimshian Mythology*. Washington, DC: United States Government Printing Office.

Boas, Franz. 1917. *Folk-Tales of Salish and Sahaptin Tribes. Memoirs of the American Folk-Lore Society*. Vol. 11. Lancaster: American Folk-Lore Society.

Carey, John. 1987. "Time, Space and the Otherworld." *Proceedings of the Harvard Celtic Colloquium* 7:1–27.

Carroll, Lewis. 1971. *Alice in Wonderland*. New York: W.W. Norton.

Coulter, Cornelia C. 1925. "The Happy Otherworld and the Fairy Mistress Themes in the Odyssey." *Transaction and Proceedings of the American Philological Association* 56:37–53. http://dx.doi.org/10.2307/282883.

Cruikshank, George. 1860. *George Cruikshank's Fairy Library: Hop-O'-My-Thumb, Jack and the Bean-Stalk, Cinderella, Puss in Boots*. London: Bell and Daldy.

Davies, Sioned. 2007. *The Mabinogion*. Oxford: Oxford University Press.

de Bello, Ricardus, and G. R. Crone. 1285–1954. *Mappa Mundi*. London: Royal Geographical Society.

Dégh, Linda. 1978. "The Tree that Reached up to the Sky (Type 468)." In *Studies in East European Folk Narrative*, ed. Linda Dégh, 263–316. Bloomington: Indiana University Press.

Dundes, Alan, ed. 1965. *The Study of Folklore*. Englewood Cliffs, NJ: Prentice-Hall.

Dundes, Alan, ed. 1984. *Sacred Narrative Readings in the Theory of Myth*. Berkeley: University of California Press.

Erdész, Sandor. 1961. ""The World Conception of Lajos Amí, Storyteller." *Acta Ethnographica* 10." In *Sacred Narrative Readings in the Theory of Myth*, ed. Alan Dundes, 327–44. Berkeley: University of California Press.

Erdész, Sandor. 1963. "The Cosmogonical Conceptions of Lajos Ami." *Acta Ethnographica* 12:57–64.

Gantz, Jeffrey. 1981. *Early Irish Myths and Sagas.* Introduction and notes by Jeffrey Gantz. Harmondsworth: Penguin.

Garry, Jane, and Hasan M. El-Shamy. 2005. *Archetypes and Motifs in Folklore and Literature: A Handbook.* Armonk: M.E. Sharpe.

Hansen, William. 2002. *Ariadne's Thread: A Guide to International Tales Found in Classical Literature.* Ithaca: Cornell University Press.

Harvey, Graham. 2002. *Shamanism: A Reader.* London: Routledge.

Hillers, Barbara. 1993. "Voyages between Heaven and Hell: Navigating the Early Irish Immram Tales." *Proceedings of the Harvard Celtic Colloquium* 13:66–81.

Jacobs, Joseph, ed. [1892] 1968. *Celtic Fairy Tales.* New York: Dover Publications.

Kline, Naomi Reed. 2001. *Maps of Medieval Thought: The Hereford Paradigm.* Woodbridge, Suffolk, Rochester: Boydell Press.

Lindahl, Carl. 2000–2002. *Medieval Folklore.* Oxford: Oxford University Press.

Lindahl, Carl. 2001. *Perspectives on the Jack Tales: And Other North American Märchen.* Bloomington: Folklore Institute and Indiana University Press.

Lovecraft, H. P. 1964. *At the Mountains of Madness, and Other Novels.* Sauk City, WI: Arkham House.

Lüthi, Max. 1982. *The European Folktale: Form and Nature.* Trans. John D. Niles. Folklore studies in translation. Bloomington: Indiana University Press.

Milton, Rugoff, ed. 1949. *A Harvest of World Folk Tales.* New York: Viking Press.

Nagy, Joseph Falaky. 1981. "Shamanic Aspects of the Bruidhean Tale." *History of Religions* 20 (4): 302–22. http://dx.doi.org/10.1086/462877.

Ó hÓgáin, Dáithí. 2006. *The Lore of Ireland: An Encyclopaedia of Myth Legend and Romance.* Woodbridge, Suffolk: Boydell Press.

Quinn, Esther C. 1962. *The Quest of Seth for the Oil of Life.* Chicago: University of Chicago Press.

Roberts, Warren E. 1958. *The Tale of the Kind and the Unkind Girls: AT 480 and Related Tales.* Berlin: De Gruyter.

Thomas, William Jenkyn. [1907] 1995. *The Welsh Fairy Book.* Illustrations by Willy Pogany, introduction and appendix by Juliette Wood. Cardiff: University of Wales Press.

Thompson, Stith. 1953. "The Star Husband Tale." *Studia Septentrionalia* 4:93–163. Also in Alan Dundes, ed., *The Study of Folklore,* 414–74.

Thompson, Stith. 1955–1958. *Motif-Index of Folk-Literature: A Classification of Narrative Elements in Folktales, Ballads, Myths, Fables, Mediaeval Romances, Exempla, Fabliaux, Jest-Books and Local Legends.* Revised and enlarged edition. Copenhagen: Rosenkilde and Bagger.

Thompson, Stith. 1977. *The Folktale.* Berkeley: University of California Press.

Tolkien, J. R. R. 1954. *The Fellowship of the Ring.* New York: Ballantine.

Turner, Victor. 1967. "Betwixt and Between: The Liminal Period in Rites de Passage." In *The Forest of Symbols,* 93–111. Ithaca, NY: Cornell University Press.

Verne, Jules. 1864. *Journey to the Center of the Earth.* Trans. Scott McKowen. New York: Sterling.

Wood, Juliette. 1992. "The Fairy Bride Legend in Wales." *Folklore* 103 (1): 56–72. http://dx.doi.org/10.1080/0015587X.1992.9715829.

Wood, Juliette. 2012. *The Holy Grail: History and Legend.* Cardiff: University of Wales Press.

Young, Frank W. 1978. "Folktales and Social Structure: A Comparison of Three Analyses of the Star-Husband Tale." *Journal of American Folklore* 91 (360): 691–99. http://dx.doi.org/10.2307/538921.

Part II
Sociopolitical and Cultural Approaches to Teaching Canonical Fairy Tales

4

The Fairy-Tale Forest as Memory Site

Romantic Imagination, Cultural Construction, and a Hybrid Approach to Teaching the Grimms' Fairy Tales and the Environment

Doris McGonagill

Teaching undergraduate courses in German Studies I have had the opportunity to prepare several courses and smaller teaching units on the Grimms' folk and fairy tales, but each time I find myself facing the same question: How should I structure my material? There are some obvious choices—chronological, regional, thematic—each with its own advantages and limitations. Structuring principles based on thematic similarities and related plot elements—the folklorists' tale types—can provide a basic infrastructure, along with specific character constellations, motifs, and topoi. Thus your groups may include tales about family conflict and gender relationships ("child victims," "bad dads," "wicked stepmothers," "sibling rivalry," "monster bridegrooms" and so forth). You may have groups focusing on specific types of journeys, tasks, events, or heroes ("Seekers," "Tricksters," "Metamorphoses," "Animal Tales"). Your categories may include selected thematic constellations ("Forbidden Chambers," "Wish Fulfillment," "Abandonment," "Tales about Spinning") or follow structural oppositions such as "Reward and Punishment," "Prohibitions and Transgressions," or "Isolation and Overcoming Confinement." The great challenge with each of these approaches—even if you choose a mixed format to bring out the cross-cultural connections between different tales—is the question of progression. How do you ensure that your syllabus design is not merely additive? How do you continue to deepen your topic, progressively making it richer, not just broader? How do you ensure that students are moving up the learning curve, employ and enhance their critical faculties to make this a truly transformative classroom experience?

DOI: 10.7330/9781607324812.c004

Instead of a generic survey design that opts for a terminological/typological overview followed by selective—but necessarily superficial—samplings of different tales and the most influential critical approaches in fairytale scholarship, I propose a syllabus that pairs up the study of fairy tales with an approach that is notably underrepresented in traditional fairy-tale scholarship: Ecocriticism, the focus on nature, and questions of the interaction of humans and the environment. In particular, I suggest focusing on the representation of trees and forests in the Grimms' tales. It has often been noted that trees and forests loom large in the Grimms' fairy tales, literally and metaphorically (Zipes 1987, 67; Harrison 1992, 155; Schama 1996, 107). As themes and motifs, they dominate the narrative patterns of many tales. In woodland realms, beyond the bounds of the familiar world, protagonists get lost, have unexpected encounters, and undergo transformations. Under trees they find help, protection, and comfort. Protagonists hide in and under trees—and trees are used to hide them (Grimm and Grimm 1857, *Kinder- und Hausmärchen* [KHM, *Children's and Household Tales*] 3, 9, 12, 15, 21, 31, 49, 51, 60). Their fruits, leaves, branches, trunks, or roots can decide the fate of characters (KHM 12, 17, 24, 50, 53, 60, 87, 130, 133). Trees act as mediators to the departed and are used to transmit magic capabilities (KHM 21, 123). Some fairy-tale characters are transformed into trees or their fate is inexplicably (symbiotically) connected to trees and plants (KHM 31, 88, 123, 161, 203). Trees save the lives of characters (KHM 17, 88, 123) and play key roles in bringing characters back to life (KHM 47, 60). Characters who deliberately damage trees or manipulate nature are invariably punished (KHM 13, 15, 53, 161). "No one ever gains power over the forest, but the forest possesses the power to change lives and alter destinies. In many ways it is the supreme authority on earth and often the great provider" (Zipes 1987, 66). But the function of trees and forests transcends that of natural protagonist and space of initiation. My curriculum design follows the trail into the woods as a path to social memory and examines the role of trees and forests in the Grimms' tales as constructions, expressions, and repositories of the collective cultural imagination.

At the beginning and end of my courses, I present students with a catalog of questions concerning fundamental concepts: nature and environment; narrative, fairy tales, and folklore; and collective memory. Such questions might include the following: What does "nature" mean? Is there a difference between "nature," "environment," and "landscape?" How do we relate to nature/environment? How do/did other cultures/civilizations relate to nature? What role do trees and forests play in our society? In past societies? In what forms do cultures represent/pass on such knowledge?

What role does this knowledge/memory play in our collective imagination? What types of narratives about trees/forests/nature are you familiar with? What forms of symbolism lie embedded in these narratives? What advantages might narratives (in the forms of myth, folklore, fairy tales) have over/against strictly conceptual ways of preserving knowledge? By comparing the responses triggered by this catalog at the beginning and end of the teaching unit (noted down on index cards or presented on a digital tool such as Blackboard or Canvas and thematically arranged for classroom display), it becomes apparent just how far students have progressed in mastering facts and concepts, becoming acquainted with multiple traditions and in-depth discourses concerning the environment and folkloric traditions and honing their critical faculties by creating a theoretically informed and productive dialog between these discourses.

A hybrid teaching approach that pairs fairy tale studies with an interest in the physical environment as a lens to examine cultural memory suggests several distinct lines of synchronic and diachronic investigation that both focus and enrich the textual and contextual analysis of fairy tales. Some of these lines of investigation I outline below. The approach allows for the design of challenging, student-oriented curricula that draw on multiple disciplines (e.g. green studies, memory studies, Romanticism studies, anthropology, mythology and ideology criticism) to promote a deeper appreciation of the tales' historical specificity while simultaneously serving as an introduction to discourse criticism, which unfolds "naturally" from critical discussion of the Germanic mystification of the forest and the disconnect between imaginary construct and historical reality. Within the broader context of German identity formation, classroom analysis of the historical, social, and political contexts in which sylvan and arboreal images were shaped and of the philological and philosophical sources that—consciously or unconsciously—inform their symbolic presentation, offers profound insights into the Grimms' Romantic project of reclaiming the German cultural memory as a contribution to the national unification process. On a yet more abstract level, this approach also highlights the Grimms' attempt to compensate for experiences of longing and loss (of the alleged unity of traditions, community, laws, customs, language, economy, institutions, beliefs, modes of thought, religion, national character, and popular wisdom) with the nostalgia of literary imagination.

But beyond serving as a theoretically informed introduction to the German Romantic fairy-tale tradition, the strength of this approach lies in its flexibility and adaptability to numerous contexts, discourses, and disciplines; its compatibility with a wide range of interactive teaching/

learning approaches; and its easy implementation into digital environments. Although I have used this approach only in upper-division German studies classes (with many readings and classroom discussion in the target language), the principal course design and most readings easily translate into other contexts, in particular, classes in comparative literature, folklore studies, modern history, or general humanities. This approach may serve as a window into German history, culture, and popular traditions from the nineteenth century through the twenty-first (the path to a unified nation state, Nazi and GDR exploitation of the Grimms' tales, the formation of the Green movement, the fight against *Waldsterben* (forest dieback), and the creation of BUND citizens' movement for environmental protection). The approach may open up to a discussion of contemporary German institutions and initiatives, including cultural and recreational phenomena and habits (such as the German obsession with woodland adventure walks, rope forest parks, canopy pathways, and forest kindergartens). Most important, in times of decreasing enrollment in German studies, this hybrid approach combines for the classroom three of the discipline's particular strengths and attractions: the "evergreen" of the German fairy-tale tradition, the contemporary interest in nature/the physical environment, and the topical field of memory studies.

Accordingly, the suggested three-pronged approach draws on three different types of sources: The first, providing the intellectual framework, is rooted in the history of ideas and examines forest and trees as memory metaphors (Blumenberg 2012; Harrison 1992; Schama 1996). The second is rooted in fairy-tale studies that focus on the role of nature and the interaction of fairy-tale characters with the natural environment (Zipes 1987, 2002; Murphy 2000; Bottigheimer 1987). The third connects with contemporary ecocriticism discourse and attempts to find new ways of making the tales relevant to contemporary cultural and personal questions (Buell 2011; Heise 2006; Glotfelty and Fromm 1996). Drawing on a combination of backgrounds allows for an interdisciplinary/multidisciplinary approach to teaching the traditional fairy-tale canon. This approach engages students at all levels in innovative close readings of individual tales, topical contextualizations, and sociohistorically sensitive and informed discussions concerning philosophical, mythological, cultural, and environmental perspectives. On an advanced level, the approach facilitates critical discussions of the problematic Germanic mystification of forests as sanctuaries of origins and community and its ideologically tendentious remnants in contemporary discourse. It sensitizes students to both accomplishments and pitfalls of "deep ecology" (what Buell dubbed "first-wave Ecocriticsm," steeped in

Heideggerian thought), and stimulates discussion of contemporary ecological questions and perspectives that broaden and transcend the horizon of narrowly defined German studies.

FOREST AND TREES AS MEMORY METAPHORS

The philosophical background and theoretical framework in the areas of memory theory, general literary criticism, and art history are provided by Hans Blumenberg's (2012) concept of memory metaphors, Robert Pogue Harrison's (1992, 155–95) discussion of "Forests of Nostalgia," and Schama's discourse on collective memory and the forest birthplace of the German psyche (Schama 1996, 21–242, esp. 75–134). Blumenberg interprets myth and metaphors, the invention of metaphysical and cultural systems, as forms of coping with reality that offer orientation and regulative ideas, thus providing frameworks for thought, without delimiting it completely. I suggest reading the Grimms' representation of trees and sylvan landscapes in light of Blumenberg's theory as memory metaphors. Similarly, Harrison observes that "as forests were once everywhere in the geographical sense, so too they [are] everywhere in the fossil record of cultural memory" (Harrison 1992, x). Harrison's argument about the Romantic imagination and the Grimms' philological mystification of forests hangs on the assertion "that forests have the psychological effect of evoking memories of the past; indeed, that they become figures for memory itself. They are enveloped . . . in the aura of lost origins." Between forests and origins, according to Harrison, exists a form of correspondence "through the medium of recollection, and . . . the former provide a sort of correlate, or primal scene, for poetic memory itself" (Harrison 1992, 156 and 164). Schama's and Harrison's works discuss the German mystification of the forest (as authentic native homeland; quasi-extension of the Hercynian and Teutoburg Forests; and living natural sanctuaries) and the "disconnect" between imaginary construct and historical reality. Contemporary forestry manuals reveal that the Grimms' sylvan landscapes—foils for utopian primitivism, the myth of origin, social equality, and communal possession—contrast starkly with the economic realities of private forest ownership and timber profiteering during early capitalism (Schama 1996, 102; Harrison 1992, 176–77; Zipes 1987, 73). With respect to a possible classroom classification of forests in fairy tales, Harrison offers three categories I found helpful in designing a typology: forests as spaces of unity, community, and restoration. Other readings that have assisted me in the construction of the intellectual framework include Richard Hayman's *Trees:*

Woodlands and Western Civilization (Hayman 2003, esp. 97–110), Laura Rival's
The Social Life of Trees (Rival 1998, 1–36), and Kim Taplin's *Tongues in Trees*
(Taplin 1989, 13–26). Although this segment of the teaching unit is theoretically ambitious, students in upper-division courses, drawing on previous
coursework and some background knowledge in the field of German and/
or Romanticism studies, tend to be intrigued by this form of contextualization. And even if such an approach—or the discourses and methods it
involves—are entirely new to students, in my experience they react well and
respond by making sense of the theoretical content on a personal level: by
recalling favorite trees of their childhood, by commenting on the "sanctity"
of certain trees of their youth that were good for climbing, and by remembering trees planted for them (or their siblings) by their parents. That trees
and forests are specially charged with memories and nostalgia is intuitive
to many students and resonates with their own experiences. Students recall
childhood hiking or camping experiences and report on the gratitude they
felt toward trees for the protection they afforded during severe weather.
And they recall their grief at the loss of special trees to storm, disease, old
age, building developments, or the simple fact that their families were moving. Sometimes, the associations students share are mediated through the
lens of literature: Shel Silverstein's (1964) *The Giving Tree* and Joyce Kilmer's
(1914) poem "Trees" are frequently mentioned (Kilmer's famous first lines,
"I think that I shall never see / A poem lovely as a tree" also tends to come
up and offers a nice springboard for a discussion of "artificial"/"cultural"
vs. "natural" beauty [180]). Also, poems by American poet Wendell Berry
(1998) have been mentioned by students, for example, the opening poem
of Berry's collection *A Timbered Choir*, capturing the sensation of venturing
into primeval forests ("I go among trees and sit still" [5]), or the title poem
of the same collection ("Slowly, slowly, they return / To the small woodland
let alone: / Great trees, outspreading and upright, / Apostles of the living
light" [83]). Glancing at these (or similar) texts with which students might
be familiar can also help to carry them through the intimidation implicit in
the introduction of theoretical abstraction, and (re)connects philosophical and historical reflection with tangible experience. A similar strategy
for grounding theoretical discourse in greater immediacy is the analysis of
visual materials. I have included in my lesson plans images (by Albrecht
Altdorfer, Caspar David Friedrich, or Anselm Kiefer) and film clips (from
the forest cathedrals in Fritz Lang's *Die Nibelungen* [1924] to the heart trees
in *Game of Thrones* [2011]), and the ensuing discussions were always lively
and instrumental in illustrating some of the subtler theoretical points.

THE INTERACTION OF FAIRY-TALE CHARACTERS
WITH THE NATURAL ENVIRONMENT

Fairy-tale scholarship has frequently thematized the interaction of fairy-tale characters and the natural environment, yet a systematic examination is still outstanding—as is an annotated (English-language) edition of tales focusing on this particular topic. Zipes lists several textual examples of protagonists entering the forest, but is not concerned with concrete arboreal imagery or how specific characters relate to the forest environment (Zipes 1988, reprinted with minimal revisions in Zipes 2002). The forest is primarily of interest as the locale of enchanted encounters. Zipes makes three important distinctions that provided useful categories for my classroom typology of the role of trees and forests: First, the Grimms' forests are rarely themselves enchanted, but are the *sites* where enchantment takes place. Second, the forest as site of the enchanted encounter is a *seat of justice*. A place removed from society and its conventions, "[the forest] is the source of natural right, thus the starting place where social wrongs can be righted" (Zipes 2002, 67).[1] Third, the forest as *communal possession* belongs to all and levels social distinctions, and is therefore a privileged site for *changes of destiny* (Zipes 1987, 70).

Brief but helpful is Zipes's discussion of *Altdeutsche Wälder* (Old German Forests), the Grimms' journal designed to assemble diverse materials pertaining to German vernacular culture and language. The journal's name alludes to the nearly forgotten connotation of "forests" (or *Wälder/silvae*), meaning unstructured materials or unruly complexity in the sense of Quintilian, Martin Opitz, and Johann Gottfried von Herder (Weyergraf 1987, 13), and was singularly apt to convey the Grimms' particular interest in the vestigial customs, rituals, knowledge, laws, tales, and language of a culture that had forgotten its "natural" origins. By offering a trail into old German forests (consisting of fables, legends, poetry, songs, proverbs, anecdotes, fairy tales, philological commentary, and notes on the folklore of trees and flowers), the Grimms wanted to help the German *Volk* reclaim their heritage at a time when the German-speaking lands were politically divided and dominated by their powerful French neighbor. In order to convey to students the crucial connection between the Grimms' *Altdeutsche Wälder* and their fairy-tale collection, both part of *one* overarching political rescue-project, the teaching unit I propose includes early-on readings from the journal's foreword with particular attention to arboreal metaphors.

G. Ronald Murphy's *The Owl, The Raven, and the Dove* follows the remnants of ancient faith embedded in the Grimms' tales, reading them as syncretic amalgamations of classical Greco-Roman, Norse-Germanic, and biblical elements. Chapters 4 through 8 (Murphy 2000, 45–152) are dedicated

to in-depth interpretation of the spirituality and mythological influences
in KHM 15, 21, 26, 50, and 53, and comment extensively on the role of
trees and forests. These chapters make excellent readings for a class focusing on representations of trees and sylvan spaces as they trace the tree
as diachronic symbol, highlighting the influences of Germanic pagan religion on the Grimms' tales, in particular of the world tree *Yggdrasil* (58–59).
In classes I have taught, students celebrated these readings as "real eye-
openers." Especially illuminating is Murphy's discussion of "Hansel and
Gretel" (KHM 15) with its summary of the myth of *Yggdrasil* opening up
its trunk to admit the last boy and girl during *Ragnarök*, the Twilight of the
Gods (45–65). Murphy outlines how the tree as magical aid to miraculous
survival and human salvation lives on in the Christmas tree and its symbolic decorations. As an extension of this discussion, I also assign Murphy's
Appendix C: "Yggdrasil, the Cross, and the Christmas Tree" (171–77). This
appendix expands on the complex interaction of fairy tales, religious customs, and popular beliefs and traditions (including Christmas carols from
"The Holly and the Ivy" to "O Tannenbaum"), and explains the power
of the tree trunk and the concept of salvation by being "within the tree"
in connection to a wide range of phenomena.[2] For my typology I derived
from Murphy's examination of spiritual continuities associated with trees
two further categories. First, "Giving Trees": trees as the privileged paradigm of nature in league with the supernatural act as agents, bestowing
salvation, life, or magical aid (donors). Second, the mortification of trees
and manipulation of nature as principles opposed to life.[3] When teaching an
upper-division unit on fairy tales and mythology, I complement Murphy's
readings with excerpts from two other texts: Lesley Gordon's chapter "Man
and Tree," which offers a succinct overview of universal mythological
interconnections (Gordon 1985, 8–19), and Françoise Meltzer's "Reviving
the Fairy Tree: Tales of European Sanctity" (Meltzer 2009). Meltzer inter-
sects with Murphy in two main points: like Murphy, she is interested in
the palimpsestic character of popular rituals, rites, and traditions. Also like
Murphy she argues that this folkloric knowledge—including the spirituality
of Romantic fairy tales with their added ingredients of Rousseauean figures
of thought and the philosophical speculation of *Frühromantik*—does not
differentiate between magic and religion.[4]

A third approach from traditional fairy-tale studies that I integrate into
my teaching takes an entirely different direction. Ruth B. Bottigheimer urges
a gendered perspective on the interactions of humans and the natural environment in the Grimms' tales. The third and tenth chapters in *Grimms' Bad
Girls and Bold Boys* document the implications of gender issues particularly

well and make good class readings (Bottigheimer 1987, 24–39, 101–11). Bottigheimer comments on the preponderance of trees in spells, the trees' association with female characters, and the trees' association with precious metals (gold and silver) connecting them back to ancient Western mythological traditions (45). Her analysis references the imagery employed by the Grimms in the prefaces to the First Edition (translated in Tatar 1987, 204–22; 2004, 401–6). In these prefaces, Wilhelm Grimm famously defends the collection as *Naturdichtung* (nature poetry), and maintains with an eye to future child-audiences, "Nothing can protect us better than Nature itself." Together with the programmatic foreword to *Altdeutsche Wälder*, these prefaces make a great opening to the teaching unit.

In complicating our perception of the forest by pointing to the negative experiences female protagonists have in the wooded realm, Bottigheimer focuses less on the threatening or taxing aspects (encounters with witches, wolves, robbers or the task of providing food), but rather on moments of loneliness and tedium characteristic of the female experience in the sylvan solitude. Her discussion culminates in the conclusion that—for female protagonists—the forest embodies a dark *locus separatus*, associated with societal isolation, uncertainty, waiting, and noncommunity (Bottigheimer 1987, 102–3). In my courses, students have productively discussed (and challenged) Bottigheimer's approach—especially her generalizing claims about the forest, dwelling place of Germanic spirituality, being in league with the male—in the context of close readings of the above-mentioned tales and in juxtaposition with Murphy's spiritual interpretations. For the purposes of my classroom typology, Bottigheimer provides the categories "Trees as Hiding/Dwelling Places," and "Isolation and Solitude."[5]

Situated at the borderlands of the scholarly and the mainstream are Sara Maitland's (2012) *From the Forest: A Search for the Hidden Roots of Our Fairy Tales* and Djamila Jaenike's (2010) *Baummärchen aus aller Welt*. Part travelogue, part folklore, Maitland's volume gathers twelve modern retellings of popular Grimms' tales (KHM 12, 15, 17, 26, 27, 37, 49, 50, 53, 55, 89) and combines these retellings with (autobiographical) recollections of Maitland's own journeys into the British forests. Idiosyncratic and performative, arguing that both forests and fairy tales are under threat by our contemporary urban lifestyle, the collection is stimulating, but does not translate into classroom use without contextualization (e.g., by Buell 2011) that points out the problematic aspects of this example of sentimental "deep-ecology" (Maitland 2012, esp. 8–9). Presenting exclusively fairy tales about trees, tree spirits, and tree metamorphoses from different cultures (but leaning heavily toward the European and German-speaking), Jaenike's volume, on the other hand, supplied to my instructional matrix four more categories: "Advice by Tree and Forest Spirits," "Enchanting Trees," "Humans Conjured in Trees," and "Trees as Mediators to the Dead."

CONTEMPORARY ECOCRITICISM DISCOURSE

Contemporary Ecocriticism discourse serves in my approach as the third way of contextualizing the Grimms' tales and making them relevant to contemporary cultural (and personal) questions. Instructors of courses on fairy tales and the environment should consider including in their curricula at least one of the following texts: Cheryll Glotfelty's landmark introduction to the *Ecocriticism Reader*, in which she defines the project of "Ecocriticism" as "the study of the relationship between literature and the physical environment" (Glotfelty and Fromm 1996, xv–xxxvii, here xviii); Ursula Heise's "Hitchhiker's Guide to Ecocriticsm," which explains the term *Ecocriticism* "as a convenient shorthand for what some critics prefer to call environmental criticism, literary-environmental studies, literary environmentalism, or green cultural studies" (Heise 2006, 506); or, the most up-to-date and detailed overview by Lawrence Buell, "Ecocriticsm: Some Emerging Trends," which provides "a usable narrative of that initiative's evolution and present agendas," and comments that major European literary cultures (including the German one) as yet are relatively underexplored (Buell 2011, 88, 92). In upper-division or graduate courses, I include selections from Laurence Coupe's *The Green Studies Reader*, in particular seminal texts by Max Horkheimer and Theodor Adorno ("The Logic of Domination" from *Dialectic of Enlightenment* and "Nature as 'Not Yet'" from *Aesthetic Theory*) and contributions by Kate Soper, Patrick D. Murphy, and Karla Armbruster on ecofeminist criticism, which I find helpful in contextualizing (and historicizing) Bottigheimer's interpretations (Coupe 2000, 77–83, 139–43, 193–203).

Approaching fairy tales from the perspective of questions concerning the environment can be complemented by selected background readings outlining the intellectual horizon of the Romantic reconceptualization of nature, to which the Grimms are indebted.[6] James McKusick (2000) and Catherine Rigby (2004) suggest useful categories that instructors can bring to bear on the study of fairy tales.[7] The same applies to Timothy Morton's introduction to *The Ecological Thought* (Morton 2010, 1–19), and the chapter dedicated to teaching approaches and learning strategies in *Philosophical Foundations for the Practices of Ecology* (Reiners and Lockwood 2010, 155–93). Axel Goodbody's (2002, 2007) publications engage with the ecology movement in Germany and environmental awareness in public, political, social, literary, and filmic discourses.[8] I assign short student presentations on several of these background texts, which serve as springboards for general classroom discussions on topics such as concepts of nature/landscape; domestication, aestheticization, exploitation, and protection of nature; literary and artistic representations of trees and forests; modes/methods of environmental education, ecology versus economy; the nature-culture divide; German versus North American environmental politics and sensibilities. Reading assignments heavy on the history of ideas I complement with more "hands-on" treatments of practical questions concerning, for example, medicinal properties of trees or the relationship of forests, climate change, and sustainability.[9] In many of these discursive contexts, students who have spent time in a German-speaking environment can supplement class discussions with their own impressions and experiences. Thus students in my classes observed that the derogatory American epithet "tree-hugger" lacks a direct German equivalent or that numerous German proper names contain etymological references to "wood," "tree," or "forest" (*Holz, Baum, Wald*, etc.).

Three helpful resources for the German cultural context (not available in English translation) are Hansjörg Küster's (1998) *Geschichte des Waldes*, Bernd Weyergraf's (1987) *Waldungen: Die Deutschen und ihr Wald*, and Ute Jung-Kaiser's (2008) *Der Wald als romantischer Topos*. Küster offers an extensive cultural history of the forest ecosystem from the ice age to modernity with multiple references to the Grimms.[10] Weyergraf's and Jung-Kaiser's collections both assemble a series of insightful essays and are particularly helpful for instructors planning to "branch out" from fairy tales to the discussions of trees and forests in the contexts of religion, art, architecture, literature, music, popular discourse, and recreational habits. All three volumes consist of self-contained chapters/essays, which I assign, based on course emphasis, dynamics, and particular interest, either for general reading or selected student presentations.

PRACTICAL PERSPECTIVES:
CLASS ORGANIZATION AND REQUIREMENTS

The last part of this chapter outlines my implementation of this approach with respect to methods, formats, assignments, and assessment. I organize my fairy-tale classes in a combination of short lectures, student presentations, group assignments, partner work, and reading-based general discussions. I aim to facilitate a blended learning/teaching approach that is interactive and challenging, yet flexible enough to integrate any special interests and background students may bring to the classroom. In the context of my hybrid teaching approach that combines the study of fairy tales with environmental criticism and questions of the interaction of humans and the environment, my main objectives are to promote reflection questions, student-invested debate, open-ended and self-directed learning, and the transfer of newly acquired knowledge to different areas. I particularly strive to stimulate curiosity for comparative and interdisciplinary examination— of literary, mythological, folkloristic, and environmental phenomena and debates—and awareness of the interconnectedness of different knowledge-producing discourses in ecology/green studies, folklore, and literary studies.

Overall, my courses move from a more closely scripted and directed to a more open format, in which students increasingly take responsibility for their own learning. I try to reconcile two opposing trajectories: on the one hand, my instructional design aims to move from a discussion format that invites brainstorming, free associations, and direct personal responses to a format designed to solicit more theoretically informed, sophisticated, and research-based treatments of specific topics. It is, for example, only in the second half of the course that I encourage students to develop concept maps, which require a firm conceptual grasp of the interrelation of specific phenomena: the relationship of Norse mythology and fairy-tale elements in specific tales; the migration of specific motifs from one cultural/linguistic context (Italian or French) to another (German); or the comparative analysis of the gendered interaction of female/male protagonists with trees and forests. On the other hand, I aim over the course of the teaching unit to move away from supplying students with precise guiding questions for partner work, group assignments, or general discussions (I supply these typically at the beginning of the term) to more open formats, in which students are expected to develop their own questions out of the material, determine research strategies, and establish connections and dialog with topics discussed earlier.

At the beginning I invite personal and anecdotal contributions designed to draw students in and make them see the topic's relevance in terms of their own background/experience (ranging from the above-mentioned childhood climbing trees to contemporary forest adventures in form of zip-lining, treetop obstacle courses, and geocaching). A brainstorming exercise at the opening of the "mythology" segment might solicit contributions addressing the role of trees and forests in popular culture, books, or films students are familiar with. Typically, students bring up examples from fantasy literature: Tolkien's Middle-earth narratives (The Old Forest, Old Man Willow, Lothlórien, Mirkwood, Fangorn, Treebeard, Ents, Huorns, Saruman's destruction of trees, the White Tree of Gondor); the *Harry*

Potter series (Forbidden Forest, Whomping Willow, Forest of Dean); and the Percy Jackson books (Thalia's tree in *The Lightning Thief* and the tree in the garden of the Hesperides from *The Titan's Curse*). Once students have gleaned a personal connection to the topic, as an instructor you have struck gold, because from that moment on students are self-motivated to think about the forms and functions of tree/forest metaphors and how they draw on myth, folklore, and fairy-tale motifs. In my experience, this personal investment then easily translates into curiosity about other forms of narrative. Another successful discussion starter that taps into students' immediate interests involves brainstorming about the symbolic signification of trees/wood(s) in religious and secular contexts. This catalyst, in past courses, ignited conversations about the cultural history of the Christmas tree and its contentious career in puritan North America.

Toward the end of the course, I open up the format to include special projects and creative work: for example, students produce fairy tales that center on the role of trees/forests/nature or write a critical commentary contextualizing a current topic, discourse, or news item that addresses the role of trees/forests and the environment. In order to facilitate these types of projects, I do not completely spell out the syllabus for the last two weeks. Instead, I reserve this window for student presentations, which allows for enough flexibility to take into account a given group's special interests and for the opportunity to develop an inductive general review of our materials and approaches. Popular topics for such projects engage with discourses in contemporary North American society and include the history of National Forests; North American versus German politics of classification, land management, environmental protection, and conservation; comparative discussion of the use of forest resources; and conflicts between special-interest groups and environmentalists. Students with a particular interest in the mythological/religious significance of trees have in the past prepared presentations on the sanctity of trees in various cultural contexts, for example in Native American communities. All projects, creative or more directly research based, need to be informed by our critical discussions and reflect the students' ability to apply what they have learned to different/broader contexts. On occasion, these projects have developed into contributions to a student newspaper or the local public radio station.

In order to monitor students' progress throughout the term I assign short-response papers documenting students' engagement with and understanding of the course materials. These (weekly) contributions are prepared in advance of each meeting and—as a basis for classroom discussion—posted on the course website. The grades students receive for these postings (based on content and, in classes with a language component, on linguistic proficiency) make up a significant percentage of the final grade (50 percent), followed by the percentage for participation (30 percent), and students' classroom presentations and final projects (each 10 percent). The response papers reflect the course's general movement from more closely directed to more open formats. In the beginning, I supply guiding questions, signaling to students the kind of comparative investigation I want to encourage. Later in the term, students determine themselves what aspects of the readings they consider worth commenting on. Because every student is expected to read everybody else's contributions, classroom conversations offer ample opportunity for peer input, which translates into a higher level of both student engagement and sophisticated reflection.

When we compare students' responses to the same questions that were presented at both the beginning and the end of the semester, it becomes clear how much the students have learned. Tracing representations of trees and forests conveys to students important insights into the centrality and multilayered symbolism of environmental imagery in fairy tales, folklore, and the romantic imagination in general. More important, paradigmatic focus on the portrayal of trees and sylvan landscapes and the many mythical qualities they retain proves a productive gateway to the examination of what could be dubbed "the substratum" of many aspects of historic and contemporary German society, self-understanding, and everyday life. A powerful metaphor of cultural memory, studying the forest/tree trope provides students with a meaningful approach to a topic that draws on their interests and background knowledge from many disciplines, encourages student investment in learning, and is well suited to the examination of the interconnectedness of imaginary constructs, the real-life public sphere, and discursive space.

NOTES

1. His interest in social types leads Zipes to examine particularly the encounters of soldiers in the forest (KHM 100, 101, 116, 125, 199). But the observation that the forest is a place of natural justice where society's wrongs are righted applies to many other tales (KHM 11, 13, 15, 31, 65, 93, 123, 130).

2. These phenomena include the origin of pine coffins, sanctuary portals in Norwegian stave churches, and the design of Gothic cathedrals.

3. Murphy develops the inversion of the traditional "Tree of Life" metaphor in his reading of "Hansel and Gretel," where he interprets the misleading noise of the "dead tree" (the branch that the protagonists' woodcutter father uses at the tale's beginning to soothe their fears about abandonment) as a dangerously false signal (56). Murphy's other discussions of trees include from "Little Red Riding Hood" the hazel hedges and oak trees (along with

ash and evergreen sacramental in Germanic mythology); from "Cinderella" the pear tree that serves as a hiding place and the tree-grave with the magical hazel motif; from "Sleeping Beauty" the rose hedges of the heroine's thorn-surrounded sleep, contextualized by mythological references to the Valkyrie Brynhild (Murphy 2000, 34–35, 67–112, 100–103, 141).

4. Although the cultural context of Meltzer's contribution is primarily French, her commentary on the syncretic character of cultural memory and the survival of ancestral religious beliefs (such as the Celtic belief in the transmigration of souls through nature) on the margins of culture, particularly in popular tales, is helpful for reading the Grimms' tales.

5. In Bruno Bettelheim's psychoanalytical reading, fairy-tale forests symbolize the unconscious, and the passage through the forest signals the emergence of a more developed personality (Bettelheim 1991, esp. 94). Although psychoanalytical analysis of fairy tales has fallen out of favor with many interpreters, I find a short, historicizing portrayal of this influential approach helpful to convey to students a more accurate and keenly developed sense of the changing field of fairy-tale studies.

6. Keith Thomas' classic *Man and the Natural World* is a great resource (Thomas 1983, esp. 192–204, 212–23, 243, 254–57).

7. McKusick's study is primarily geared at English Romanticism, whereas Rigby's comparative ecocritical reconsideration of British and German Romanticism discusses literary and philosophical examples invested in the Romantic conception of nature as living organism.

8. Goodbody's 2002 collection includes a didactic essay by Dagmar Lindenpütz on form, function, and literary value of children's literature as a medium of environmental education (187–201). Goodbody's 2007 monograph offers an instructive overview of theoretical perspectives (particularly 3–41).

9. Useful for opening up classroom conversation to larger environmental issues is Diana Beresford-Kroeger's (2010) *The Global Forest*. This somewhat impressionistic collection brings together short essays about folkloric tree symbolism with traditional plant-lore studies and chapters on forest ecology.

10. Küster (1998, 112, 132, and 181).

REFERENCES

Beresford-Kroeger, Diana. 2010. *The Global Forest*. New York: Viking.

Berry, Wendell. 1998. *A Timbered Choir: The Sabbath Poems, 1979–1997*. Washington, DC: Counterpoint.

Bettelheim, Bruno. 1991. *The Uses of Enchantment*. London: Penguin.

Blumenberg, Hans. 2012. *Quellen, Ströme, Eisberge: Beobachtungen an Metaphern*. Berlin: Suhrkamp.

Bottigheimer, Ruth B. 1987. *Grimms' Bad Girls and Bold Boys: The Moral and Social Vision of the Tales*. New Haven: Yale University Press.

Buell, Lawrence. 2011. "Ecocriticism: Some Emerging Trends." *Qui Parle* 19 (2): 87–115. http://dx.doi.org/10.5250/quiparle.19.2.0087.

Coupe, Laurence, ed. 2000. *The Green Studies Reader: From Romanticism to Ecocriticsm*. New York: Routledge.

Glotfelty, Cheryll, and Harold Fromm, eds. 1996. *The Ecocriticism Reader: Landmarks in Literary Ecology*. Athens: University of Georgia Press.

Goodbody, Axel, ed. 2002. *The Culture of German Environmentalism: Anxieties, Visions, Realities*. New York: Berghahn Books.

Goodbody, Axel. 2007. *Nature, Technology, and Cultural Change in Twentieth-Century German Literature: The Challenge of Ecocriticsm.* New York: Palgrave-Macmillan. http://dx.doi.org /10.1057/9780230589629.

Gordon, Lesley. 1985. *The Mystery and Magic of Trees and Flowers.* Exeter, UK: Webb & Bower.

Harrison, Robert Pogue. 1992. *Forests: The Shadow of Civilization.* Chicago: Chicago University Press. http://dx.doi.org/10.7208/chicago/9780226318059.001.0001.

Hayman, Richard. 2003. *Trees: Woodlands and Western Civilization.* London: Hambledon and London.

Heise, Ursula K. 2006. "The Hitchhiker's Guide to Ecocriticm." *PMLA* 121 (2): 503–16. http://dx.doi.org/10.1632/003081206X129684.

Grimm, Jacob, and Wilhelm Grimm. 1857. *Kinder- und Hausmärchen.* Göttingen: Dieterische Buchhandlung.

Jaenike, Djamila, ed. 2010. *Baummärchen aus aller Welt.* Lützelflüh, Switzerland: Mutabor.

Jung-Kaiser, Ute, ed. 2008. *Der Wald als romantischer Topos.* Bern: Peter Lang.

Kilmer, Joyce. 1914. *Poems, Essays, and Letters in Two Volumes. Volume One: Memoir and Poems.* New York: George H. Doran Company.

Küster, Hansjörg. 1998. *Geschichte des Waldes: Von der Urzeit bis zur Gegenwart.* Munich: Beck.

Maitland, Sara. 2012. *From the Forest: A Search for the Hidden Roots of Our Fairy Tales.* Berkeley, CA: Counterpoint.

McKusick, James C. 2000. *Green Writing: Romanticism and Ecology.* New York: St. Martin's Press. http://dx.doi.org/10.1007/978-1-349-38629-1.

Meltzer, Françoise. 2009. "Reviving the Fairy Tree: Tales of European Sanctity." *Critical Inquiry* 35 (3): 493–520. http://dx.doi.org/10.1086/598812.

Morton, Timothy. 2010. *The Ecological Thought.* Cambridge, MA: Harvard University Press.

Murphy, G. Ronald. 2000. *The Owl, the Raven, and the Dove: The Religious Meaning of the Grimm's Magic Fairy Tales.* New York: Oxford University Press.

Reiners, William A., and Jeffrey A. Lockwood. 2010. *Philosophical Foundations for the Practices of Ecology.* Cambridge: Cambridge University Press.

Rigby, Catherine E. 2004. *Topographies of the Sacred: The Poetics of Place in European Romanticism.* Charlottesville: University of Virginia Press.

Rival, Laura, ed. 1998. *The Social Life of Trees: Anthropological Perspectives on Tree Symbolism.* Oxford: Berg.

Schama, Simon. 1996. *Landscape and Memory.* New York: Vintage.

Silverstein, Shel. 1964. *The Giving Tree.* New York: Harper and Row.

Taplin, Kim. 1989. *Tongues in Trees: Studies in Literature and Ecology.* Bideford, UK: Green Books.

Tatar, Maria. 1987. *The Hard Facts of the Grimms' Fairy Tales.* Princeton: Princeton University Press.

Tatar, Maria, ed. 2004. *The Annotated Brothers Grimm.* New York: W.W. Norton.

Thomas, Keith. 1983. *Man and the Natural World: Changing Attitudes in England 1500–1800.* New York: Oxford University Press.

Weyergraf, Bernd. 1987. *Waldungen: Die Deutschen und ihr Wald.* Berlin: Akademie der Künste.

Zipes, Jack. 1987. "The Enchanted Forest of the Brothers Grimm: New Modes of Approaching the Grimms' Fairy Tales." *Germanic Review* 62 (2): 66–74. http://dx.doi .org/10.1080/00168890.1987.9934193.

Zipes, Jack. 1988. *The Brothers Grimm: From Enchanted Forests to the Modern World.* London: Routledge.

Zipes, Jack. 2002. *The Brothers Grimm: From Enchanted Forests to the Modern World.* New York: Palgrave-Macmillan.

5

Grimms' Fairy Tales in a Political Context
Teaching East German Fairy-Tale Films

Claudia Schwabe

Alle sozialistischen Märchen beginnen mit: "Es wird einmal . . ." (All socialist fairy tales begin with: "Once upon a time there will be . . .").

—Zarko Petan (1979), *Mit leerem Kopf,* 11

ONE OF MY GERMAN STUDENTS ONCE STUMBLED UPON several fairy-tale film adaptations by the *Deutsche Film-Aktiengesellschaft* (DEFA), the state-owned film studio of the former German Democratic Republic (GDR), and inquired: "Are these movies very different from the Grimms' original fairy tales?" This question inspired me to design a German fairy-tale class that ties students' interest in fairy tales and films to a significant and fascinating part of Germany's recent history. Although the Grimms' *Märchen* (fairy tales) are firmly embedded in courses and syllabi in German language, literature, folklore, culture, history, narrative theory, and fairy-tale studies, they are rarely discussed in a particular political context other than that of Romantic nationalism. Teaching the Grimms' fairy tales in conjunction with East German films offers students the opportunity to examine how a socialist country has used fairy tales as vehicles for anticapitalist propaganda. In this course, I seek to help students understand the sociopolitical connections between folk and fairy tales and the political messages that are subliminally conveyed in East German fairy-tale films.

These are some of the driving questions I devised: To what extent do DEFA fairy-tale films promote socialism? In what way does the diegesis of the films vary from the Grimms' tales? What has been added, deleted, or modified, and how do we interpret these alterations? How do the films

DOI: 10.7330/9781607324812.c005

portray characters and archetypes such as the figure of the hero or heroine? Who is represented in a predominantly positive or negative light? What are the films' messages regarding gender roles and family relationships? What sense of justice do the films convey? What kind of values and virtues do the films emphasize? By analyzing the mise-en-scène, what is noticeable about the settings, costumes, props, and sound?

The structure and organization of the course are determined not only by the number of students in the class and the number of hours available per week but also by the background of the students and their reactions to the material. Depending upon the desired time frame, the course can be taught in three to four weeks or for an entire semester. Since the films and texts covered require an advanced level of German-language proficiency, the instructor may choose to teach primarily in German. I recommend consulting a number of relevant publications related to DEFA and DEFA fairy-tale films prior to the course, including *Zwischen Marx und Muck: DEFA Filme für Kinder* (König, Wiedemann, and Wolf 1996), *East German Cinema: DEFA and Film History* (Heiduschke 2013), "'Keep the Home Fires Burning': Fairy Tale Heroes and Heroines in an East German Heimat" (Fritzsche 2012), *The Enchanted Screen* (Zipes 2011), "The First DEFA Fairy Tales: Cold War Fantasies of the 1950s" (Silberman 2007), *The Politics of Magic: DEFA Fairy-Tale Films* (Shen 2015), and "Barometers of GDR Cultural Politics: Contextualizing the DEFA Grimm Adaptations" (Shen 2011).

During the forty-six years of its existence, DEFA produced about 750 feature films; 180 were feature-length productions for children made between 1946 and 1990 (Berghahn 2005, 10, 43), and more than 25 were fairy-tale films made between 1950 and 1989 (Zipes 2011, 342).[1] While not all films are available for purchase and few feature English subtitles or have been dubbed in English, many films are accessible via YouTube.[2] Films that I have used in this course are *Das tapfere Schneiderlein* (1965, *The Brave Little Tailor*); *Das Zaubermännchen nach dem Märchen Rumpelstilzchen* (1960, *The Magic Dwarf*, with the working title *Rumpelstiltskin*); *Das hölzerne Kälbchen* (1961, *The Wooden Calf*), *Schneewittchen* (1961, *Snow White*); *Rotkäppchen* (1962, *Little Red Riding Hood*); *Frau Holle* (1963, *Mother Holle*, 1963); *Die goldene Gans* (1964, *The Golden Goose*); *Dornröschen* (1970, *Sleeping Beauty*); *Sechse kommen durch die Welt* (1972, *Six Make their Way through the World*), *Drei Haselnüsse für Aschenbrödel* (1973, *Three Nuts/Wishes for Cinderella*); and *Schneeweißchen und Rosenrot* (1979, *Snow White and Rose Red*). For a shorter teaching period, an instructor could screen selected scenes instead of the entire films. As the screening schedule allows a certain degree of flexibility, further films can be added to the list. In addition, the instructor can include DEFA films based on other fairy-tale authors, such as Wilhelm Hauff, Theodor Storm, and Hans Christian Andersen.

During the first two weeks, our classroom discussions centered on exploring how the Grimms' tales reflect the sociopolitical conditions of feudalism in a precapitalist Germany of the eighteenth and early nineteenth centuries. In addition, I asked my students to read "Breaking the Magic Spell: Politics and the Fairy Tale" by Jack Zipes (1975) to learn about the difference between *Volksmärchen* (folk tale) and *Kunstmärchen* (literary fairy tale) and about the connections between fairy tales, folk, politics, and class struggle. My students first examined the text individually and in small groups and then shared their results with the rest of the class. By asking simple bell-ringer questions at the beginning of class, such as "What are fairy tales?," "Why do people tell fairy tales?," or "Why are some fairy tales more popular than others?," I was not only able to assess students' level of knowledge but also aimed at increasing their interest in the topic. Bell ringers were answered in writing, and I collected them for a weekly participation grade. As a creative homework assignment, I prompted my students to invent their own fairy tales (one to two pages) but to make it more challenging, they also had to incorporate current social, political, economic, or environmental issues into their tales. The students enjoyed this assignment a lot and demonstrated a great deal of imagination and humor by composing tragic, comedic, suspenseful, and outrageous stories. I highly recommend encouraging students to read their papers out loud because it helps to break the ice during the first week and fosters a positive classroom atmosphere. Since the Grimms' (1812) *Kinder- und Hausmärchen* (KHM, *Children's and Household Tales*) constitutes one of the main readings for this course, every student should own a copy and bring it to class. I worked with the Insel edition of 1974 (Grimm and Grimm 1974).

The next two weeks we covered the history of the GDR (depending upon students' level of knowledge, the first two weeks can also serve as a review). This history review is needed to lay the groundwork for the rest of the semester. Although the focal points are up to the teacher, I recommend discussing some (or all) of the following topics with the students: the end of World War II and the development under the conditions of the Soviet occupational zone; the founding and collapse of the GDR; the rise and fall of the power of the Sozialistische Einheitspartei Deutschlands (SED; Socialist Unity Party of Germany); the uprising of June 17, 1953; the erection and fall of the Berlin Wall; the formation of the so-called welfare dictatorship in the 1970s; the methods of the Staatssicherheitspolizei ("Stasi"; State Secret Police); censorship and surveillance; culture, art, music, theater, and DEFA films; everyday life in the GDR; the communist

youth movement Freie Deutsche Jugend (FDJ; Free German Youth); possibilities and limits of the consumer society; the failure of the East German
centrally planned economy; the Peaceful Revolution / Monday demonstrations in 1989 and 1990; and the way to reunification and Die Wende (The
Change). If students have access to computers, they can access the interactive website *Zeitklicks*, which is a very useful online resource for exploring
GDR history and learning more about some of the topics stated above.[3]

During the rest of our fifteen-week semester (three hours a week), I
devoted each week to reading, discussing, film screening, and analyzing one
selected fairy tale. At the beginning of each week, the students read the preas-
signed fairy tale in the Grimms' *Children's and Household Tales* either together in
class (especially if it is a shorter tale) or as a homework assignment. When I
assigned a reading for homework, I always reminded my students to take notes
and write down their reflections and questions for discussion ahead of time.
If I did not stress this particular approach, as I quickly discovered, only a few
students would come prepared for class. Sometimes, I additionally assigned
questions for the students to answer in writing or asked for short position
papers of one to two pages. I was careful though, never to assign too much
homework at a time, so that the students would not feel overburdened. Based
on my experience, it is worth spending the time to reread important parts of
the tales together in class for three reasons: to refresh students' memories,
to practice German reading and pronunciation skills, and to draw out the
quiet students and encourage them to participate. I based the final grade on
class participation, homework assignments, three to four written film analyses
(four to five pages each), student presentations, and one final reflective essay
(five to seven pages) in response to a thought-provoking statement or subject,
for example, "Compare the treatment of one of the following themes in the
Grimms' tales and DEFA's film adaptations: gender equality, punishment and
reward, social classes" or "Discuss the term 'socialist realism' in the context
of DEFA fairy-tale films." All written assignments should be in German if
the class is taught as a German-language fairy-tale class.

My aim throughout the course was to communicate to the students that
fairy tales and their adaptations are the looking glass of society, or in other
words, the cultural signifiers of a country at a particular time. In fact, fairy
tales reveal to some extent a society's cultural traditions and mores, values
and virtues, and accepted gender norms and roles, and may indicate philosophical beliefs, religious views, ideological convictions, moral sensibilities,
and attitudes toward life. Whenever a country and its people undergo a
significant transition, as, for instance, a new form of government, cultural
artifacts such as fairy-tale adaptations can reflect those changes.

I recommend screening the DEFA fairy-tale films in chronological order, although other screening sequences are possible, such as following the order of the tales as they appear in the Grimms' *Children's and Household Tales* or arranging the films by directors. Helmut Spieß's *The Brave Little Tailor* is the first DEFA adaptation based on the tales by the Brothers Grimm. In their film analyses, my students readily noticed the negative and risible portrayal of the nobility, ministers, and courtiers: Prince Vanity (Eitel), Princess Lovely (Liebreich), King Grouch (Griesgram), Treasurer Greed (Gier), and Valet Squeamish (Zimperlich). The students grasped that the film ridicules every aristocratic figure in different ways. Prince Vain is discourteous, loutish, cowardly, and arrogant. His miserly nature is revealed when he does not pay for a fine tailoring job but extends his princely gratitude instead. The rude prince is a suitable match for the haughty princess, who verbally and physically harasses her maidservant Traute, the daughter of the gardener Summer (Sommer). In sharp contrast to her name, Princess Liebreich is grabby, wasteful, greedy for gold and power, scheming, and ruthless. The relationship with her father is cold and full of hate. Many students reacted with amusement when they discovered that the two-faced king hides an onion in his hand to pretend that the tears he cries for the sake of his people and their distress are real.

The main focus in this adaptation of *The Brave Little Tailor* is on the small man who can still make a big difference in life and reach his goals by using his brains and courage. During our class discussion, students compared the little tailor of the story to other underdog characters, such as J.R.R. Tolkien's hobbit Frodo Baggins, or J. K. Rowling's young wizard Harry Potter. This is also a great moment to divide the students into small groups and ask them to generate a list of what they perceive to be heroic traits. In my class, the students then explored together fundamental questions, such as: What makes a hero a hero? Are heroes born or made? What are the differences and similarities between leaders and heroes? Who are today's heroes and heroines? Can fairy-tale heroes or heroines embody a political ideology? I used the discussion as scaffolding to draw my students' attention to the fact that the success of the little tailor in the DEFA story is not defined by the acquisition of wealth or a royal marriage as in the Grimms' tale. He turns into a socialist hero, a man who represents the common people and does not care about royal etiquette or dressing in aristocratic clothes. The agrarian crowd, which has been added to the diegesis, celebrates the Warrior Seven with One Strike as folk hero by carrying him on their shoulders. It is only fitting for a socialist adaptation that the hero chooses a maidservant as his bride (Figure 5.1). Together they rule as king and queen from the

Figure 5.1. *Das tapfere Schneiderlein* ©DEFA-Stiftung, Erich Günther.

lower class over the peasantry; however, they do so without crown, imperial insignia, or status symbols. Furthermore, the tailor remains true to his craft until the very end of the film, when he stitches the sleeve of his servant-bride. While the Grimms' version is already "conveniently crafted to signal class conflict and the liberation of the proletariat," the DEFA adaptation by comparison "heralds an absolute overhaul of the political system" (Shen 2011, 74). *The Brave Little Tailor* is only one example of many East German fairy-tale films that disparage nobility and the rich. Throughout the course students will discover that the image of a perpetually negative and selfish upper class is a recurring trope in DEFA adaptations.

There are striking parallels between the films *The Brave Little Tailor* and *The Golden Goose*. My students loved this adaptation, not least because of the wonderful music. During our class discussion, I seated the students in a circle and used the "Two Cent Method," a great pedagogical approach to encourage equal contributions to the debate.[4] Similarly to the first film we watched, I asked the students to analyze the portrayal of the aristocracy, the

Figure 5.2. *Die goldene Gans* ©DEFA-Stiftung, Roland Dressel

lower class, and the hero, and compare their findings to the portrayal (of the aristocracy, the lower class, and the hero) in KHM 64. In the Grimms' *Märchen* the protagonist of "The Golden Goose" is called Dummling (Simpleton), and his character is not described in detail. In the woods he encounters a magical helper who completes the king's challenges for him to gain the princess's hand. The DEFA film *The Golden Goose* added the name Klaus and his specific job occupation as cobbler. Similar to the valiant tailor, Klaus is kindhearted and shrewd and lives among people who treat him poorly (his two brothers). I reminded my students to pay particular attention to the mise-en-scène and the colors of the film. The students had no problems identifying and describing the bright, intense colors used, which some of them compared to the 1939 American musical fantasy *The Wizard of Oz.* They agreed with me that the "Agfa" colors contribute to a kitschy image, complementing the already joyful music and happy atmosphere of the DEFA film. These features, combined with a physical labor scene that has been added to the diegesis (the joined lifting of a gigantic treasure chest for the king), are reminiscent of socialist-realism artworks and propaganda materials, glorifying proletarians as a working collective to achieve the common goal of socialist progress (Figure 5.2).

To illustrate the similarity between DEFA film scenes and socialist-realism art, I showed my students socialist propaganda posters and paintings available online, such as Ivan Bevzenko's *Young Steel Workers* (1961), Valentine Ilich Dudin's *Women's Factory Brigade* (1961), and the *Women of the Kolkhoz* by an unknown Ukrainian artist. In contrast to the Grimms' version of "The Golden Goose," the DEFA film features the villain "Troublemaker" and folkloristic dancing scenes, in which a distinctive separation between the classes remains until the final scene. While the king is only concerned about his riches and assiduously counts his gold coins, the royal advisor visibly disapproves of the celebrating community by shaking his head. In response, the lower class laughs at him for being chased out of the room by the Golden Goose. The princess alone joins the dancing crowd, indicating that she prefers to be among commoners and thus symbolically lowers her royal status to Klaus's proletarian level. This transformation of classes sheds a positive light on her character.

At times I stopped the screening of a film to ask my students about their expectations of how the story of the East German production might unfold. When we watched Christoph Engel's *Rumpelstiltskin,* for example, I paused the film at the cliff-hanging moment when the young queen guesses the dwarf's name correctly and had students speculate about the ending. I used this exercise several times throughout the semester to check if students understood DEFA's socialist approach, such as the censoring of violence and the emphasis of socialist values and ideals, and to demonstrate how certain fairy-tale characters had undergone a profound "socialist makeover." In the literary version from 1857, Rumpelstiltskin tears himself into two pieces, whereas in the version from 1812 he runs away angrily and never comes back. Although the two endings of the Grimms' tale are different, the dwarf remains an uncanny and wicked character that finally dies or vanishes for good. The DEFA film, however, portrays Rumpelstiltskin as a socialist-driven role model for young viewers, who lectures the king and queen wisely about the temptations of gold and greed (Figure 5.3). True to Marxist-Leninist convictions, the dwarf despises the accumulation of wealth and riches. In fact, he considers himself to be the victim of a deceiving and money-grubbing society, which robbed him of all his assets despite his help in times of need. His reason for stealing the baby from his mother is a socialistic-pedagogical one: he wants to raise the infant in the woods away from society so that "it may not know the corruptive power of gold."

The film depicts Rumpelstiltskin as a caring and nurturing figure, who spares no effort to build the most beautiful cradle for the stolen child. The hermitic and alternative lifestyle he plans to offer his foster child seems flawed, however, given the fact that the boy would grow up isolated and socially impoverished and without human contact, friends of the same age,

Figure 5.3. *Das Zaubermännchen* ©DEFA-Stiftung, Josef Borst.

or a female reference figure. Only after the dwarf considers the inexperi-
enced king to be healed from his greed for gold and after his wife, the miller's
daughter Marie, has fulfilled her task of name guessing, is Rumpelstiltskin
willing to leave the newborn in the care of his biological parents and return
to his hideout. By deploring the rich and the lazy (represented by the avari-
cious treasurer and the mendacious miller) and by praising the honest, diligent working class (represented by Marie, the miller's apprentice Hans, and
Rumpelstiltskin), the film repeatedly promotes socialist ideals and morals,
such as hard work, truthfulness, modesty, and material restraint. As punishment, the parasitic treasurer gets banned from the kingdom and is replaced
by kindhearted Hans, while the miller has to resume the work in his mill
and, for each of his lies, donate a bag of flour to the poor. Hence, the
director's final message hints at the restoration of the economic and social
balance in the GDR.

Of paramount importance for a Workers' and Peasants' State (*Arbeiter-
und-Bauern-Staat*) is the emphasis on industriousness and a hardworking
labor force. Some students observed that already the collection by the
Brothers Grimm underscores assiduity and condemns idleness. I explained
that in the DEFA films, however, the merits of diligence and a devoted
workforce have to be examined against the political background of postwar

reconstruction and the creation of a socialist state. Qinna Shen remarks in her essay, "While West Germany, buttressed by the Marshall Plan, boasted an 'economic miracle' and attracted thousands of East Germans before the building of the Berlin Wall in 1961, the GDR government preached against the corrupting power of gold. As it fell behind economically, the socialist state waged psychological warfare by contrasting socialism and capitalism in terms of the fairytale dualism of good and evil" (Shen 2011, 78). Later in the course, I asked students to create a timeline that places the films in their specific historical contexts. Such a timeline stimulates students' critical thinking skills and highlights connections between the DEFA works, contemporary political developments in East Germany, communist principles laid down by the SED, and the aesthetics of socialist realism. Based on personal feedback, this exercise facilitated students' comprehension of the historical, political, and cultural interconnections of the materials covered. With the benefit of hindsight, I believe it would be even more constructive to prime students with this exercise at the beginning of the semester before watching the films.

Fairy-tale films of the 1960s and early 1970s, such as Gottfried Kolditz's *Snow White* (*Schneewittchen* 1961) and *Mother Holle* (*Frau Holle* 1963) and Walter Beck's *King Thrushbeard* (*König Drosselbart* 1965) and *Sleeping Beauty* (*Dornröschen* 1970), heavily promote industrious protagonists. A princess, for instance, could only function as a positive role model for a socialist audience when she was not above such menial tasks as cooking, cleaning, serving, and spinning. In *Snow White* the socialist slant is especially noticeable in the portrayal of the characters: the dwarfs, the royal servants, and the princess herself are depicted as diligent and cheerful workers throughout the film (Figure 5.4). Their smiling faces and their constant singing and whistling convey the idea that labor is always fun. Therefore, it seems only natural for Snow White to help the kitchen staff and assist the head chef with food preparations for the royal banquet (Figure 5.5). When she enters the banquet hall as a serving girl, the prince immediately falls in love with her and ignores the narcissistic queen completely. The dominating motif of the film is obvious: charm through manual labor. The dwarfs, who live secluded but in harmony with nature (similar to Rumpelstiltskin), represent an idealized socialist work collective and commune. Their solidarity and spirit of "comradeship," to use the GDR terminology, give viewers a picture of a better world and way of living. As most of my students were already familiar with Disney's *Snow White and the Seven Dwarfs* (1937), I drew on the Disney version for comparison. During the classroom discussions, I also focused on political parallels and read with my students several excerpts from Jack Zipes's (2005)

Figure 5.4. *Schneewittchen* ©DEFA-Stiftung, Karin Blasig.

essay "Breaking the Disney Spell." He argues that Disney's ever-joyful, hard-working dwarfs can be interpreted as the humble American workers, who pull together during the Depression of the 1930s (Zipes 2005, 37). One really fun assignment that resonated with the students and kept them highly engaged was the translation and examination (and even singing) of the dwarfs' work songs. Whereas Disney's lyric has a capitalistic undertone ("It ain't no trick to get rich quick if you dig dig dig with a shovel or a pick in a mine! . . . Where a million diamonds shine!"), DEFA's song does not center on monetary gains and jewels but rather on making the job more enjoyable ("Deep in the mine, blow upon blow, the bright day awakes outside, if we sing a light ditty, then the work goes twice as fast").[5]

The socialist influence in Beck's adaptation of *Sleeping Beauty* is already evident in the opening scene. The first camera shot depicts a workroom with five barefoot peasant women spinning wool into thread on spinning wheels, all singing cheerfully about the virtue of industriousness. Since the previous translation exercise went so well, I prompted my students to investigate the song more closely and attempt to translate the German text into English: "Twine the entanglement to yarn, spin assiduously without respite, finally you see, diligence accomplishes more than haste. If you have work to do, get it done, because diligence and skill are loved by everyone."[6] Unfortunately, many of the students struggled with this translation exercise

Figure 5.5. *Schneewittchen* ©DEFA-Stiftung, Karin Blasig.

due to the old-fashioned German vocabulary so that I had to provide additional assistance and point them in the right direction. In the film, the king and queen host a grand celebration in honor of the birth of princess Rosalinde. They invite twelve fairies, who present the princess with positive traits. Since the king disdains industriousness and considers the trait to be a useless gift for a princess, he does not invite the thirteenth fairy, the Fairy of Diligence. The affronted fairy, whose gift is symbolized in a spinning wheel, admonishes the king publicly to honor her trait and emphasizes that only diligence sustains his land. In the Grimms' "Sleeping Beauty," there is no relation between the virtue of diligence and the thirteenth "wise woman." Further, the king lacks detail and remains a vague character. The GDR version, however, turns the royal figure into an irascible, obstinate man who is obsessed with power and wealth. He personifies the capitalist system in conjunction with imperialistic exploitation and totalitarian control.

In extended scenes, the DEFA adaptation expands significantly on the king's order to destroy all spindles in the realm and thus focuses on evoking an emotional response in the viewer. On penalty of death the king forbids every man, woman, and child to own, hide, or even think of spindles. The burning of a massive pile of spindles, which the royal soldiers forcefully robbed from the working class, evokes the Nazi book burnings (Figure 5.6).

Figure 5.6. *Dornröschen* ©DEFA-Stiftung, Lothar Gerber.

To my surprise, many of the students had already made the connection to Nazism and the book burnings in their minds before I pointed it out to them. Shen also associates this episode with the communists' antifascist struggle and therefore aligns the film with proletarian revolutionary cinema (Shen 2011, 80). Indeed, the desperate men and women, whose livelihood depends on spinning, come across as rebellious resistance fighters. While some workers oppose the royal order by secretly hiding spindles, others curse the king loudly: "This king plunges us all into misery, he ruins people and country. The king should be cursed. He should be cut like grass. He should wither like green weed. He should be like chaff before the wind. He should be exterminated." At the end of the film, the Fairy of Diligence places a spinning wheel in front of Rosalinde on her throne, asking her to give the people a demonstration of how to spin (Figure 5.7). The young queen thus becomes the epitome of socialist principles: abolition of class boundaries, equal work production, distribution of wealth, and unity.

There are obviously multiple socialist messages in DEFA fairy-tales pictures, such as the triumph of love over wealth, the penalty for hoarding treasures and laziness, the rewards for diligence and courage, the adverse depiction of royalty as allegoric representation for capitalism and imperialism, the positive portrayal of the proletariat, and the basic concept of

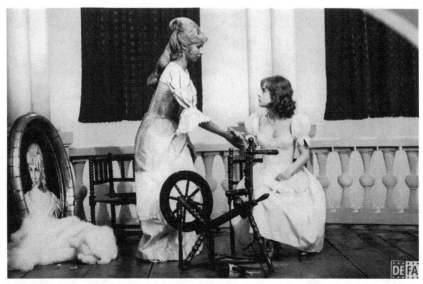

Figure 5.7. *Dornröschen* ©DEFA-Stiftung, Lothar Gerber.

promoting identification with the oppressed, working-class hero or heroine.
Another overriding theme in the films is gender equality and the advocacy
of strong female characters. In order to help students better grasp why
female emancipation and gender equality are essential tropes, I found it
useful to include a minilecture on the economic situation of the GDR and
the everyday working life. Socialist ideology and a severe economic need
pressuring the GDR government were major forces behind the attempt to
integrate women into economic life and encouraged women to participate
in the labor force. Therefore, it is hardly surprising that the East German
adaptations place significant emphasis on resolute and resilient women, on
female characters cross-dressing to appear and act as men, and on equal
rights for both sexes. In stark contrast to the Grimms' tale, Götz Friedrich's
Little Red Riding Hood presents a bold and resourceful girl, one who knows
how to defend herself against the assaults of an insidious fox and the big
bad wolf. The production, partially based on a Russian play by Jewgeni
Lwowitsch Schwarz, features Little Red Riding Hood living with her parents
in the forest. Her friends are a rabbit and a bear, and her foes are a fox and
a wolf. One day the girl is alone at home and has to defend her geese with
a large stick against the disguised fox (Figure 5.8). On her way to visit the
sick grandmother, Little Red Riding Hood encounters the wolf but manages to drive him away with a good load of snuff that she blows into his
face. The sly fox resorts to a trick: he sprinkles white chalk over the wolf's

Figure 5.8. *Rotkäppchen* ©DEFA-Stiftung, Karin Blasig.

fur so he can pass as a white dog and sneak into the grandmother's house. Alarmed by the rabbit, the mother and father and even the bear come to the rescue. After saving Little Red Riding Hood and the grandmother, they do not, however, fill the wolf's belly with rocks, as stated by the Brothers Grimm. Remarkably, the father passes his rifle on to the grandmother to keep the wolf at bay, which accentuates once more the empowerment of women and advocates sexual equality. Befitting a socialist ending of toned-down violence, the wolf does not fall dead but is carried away and put into a cage for good.

A film that stands out for gender cross-dressing and resists conforming to the Grimm hypotext of "Cinderella" is *Three Nuts/Wishes for Cinderella*, a Czech-German DEFA coproduction by Václav Vorlíček. A brief class survey by raise of hands revealed this film to be my students' favorite. Based on a fairy tale by Božena Němcová, the emancipated heroine of this socialist-inspired version is a diligent young woman who humbly serves her wicked stepmother and spoiled stepsister. My students immediately detected that the director endowed the production with a powerful feminist edge. Unlike the Grimms', Charles Perrault's, or animated Disney portrayals, Cinderella is not depicted as a passive wallflower but rather as an active, resourceful spirit full of guile and wit. In the woods she has her first encounter with an unconventional prince who prefers hunting with his friends rather

Figure 5.9. *Drei Haselnüsse für Aschenbrödel* ©DEFA-Stiftung, Jaromír Komárek.

than attending to his studies or court business. This headstrong and playful prince defies royal etiquette as well as the king's views on marriage by
comparing the traditional ball to look for a wife with a "hunt." The rebellious prince finds his equal in the perky Cinderella. As a modern and spritely
woman, Cinderella does not simply fall into the prince's arms but shows
that she is quite capable of making a fool of the king's son. Disguised as a
hunter, she defeats the prince in sharpshooting, plays hard to get at the royal
ball, and challenges him with witty riddles upon his first marriage request
(Figure 5.9). Throughout her encounters with the prince, Cinderella takes
on three personas, highlighting the complexity of her figure: she impersonates a child, a man, and a woman. First, she displays her childlike nature by
throwing a snowball at the prince, by running away, by playing catch, and by
climbing up a tree. She then cross-dresses as a man in tights and becomes
"king of the hunt" in a hunting contest between the prince and his followers.
Finally, she appears as an attractive, sophisticated, and mysterious woman
at the royal ball who charms the prince and his entourage. Cinderella turns
the prince's first marriage request down, to make him realize that her true
identity is multifaceted and that she is emancipated and skilled. Only once
the prince understands that his future bride is in fact no wealthy princess
but a hardworking and poor *Aschenbrödel* (Cinderella from French *Cendrillon*,

Figure 5.10. *Sechse kommen durch die Welt* ©DEFA-Stiftung, Klaus Goldmann; Waltraud Pathenheimer.

which translates to "little ash girl") does the orphaned girl accept his proposal.[7] As a socialist heroine, Cinderella also protects oppressed servants from her stepmother's rage and, in return, is loved and supported by all workers on the family estate. From the beginning to the end of the film, she remains an independent figure who rides on her horse, Nicolas, to the ball and who marries out of love and not out of necessity.

When I will teach this class again, I may tie the topics of female to male cross-dressing, which also occurs in *Six Make their Way through the World*, empowerment of women, and the portrayal of the socialist heroine in DEFA fairy-tale films to a larger debate on gender roles and equality of the sexes in modern society (Figure 5.10). I would like to span this bridge at the end of the semester by demonstrating how relevant some of the messages communicated by East German fairy-tale films are to contemporary political and social issues. If time allows, I would also discuss DEFA fairy-tale films in connection with the contemporary topic of Germany's *Ostalgie* (Ostalgia) phenomenon, a term which refers to nostalgia for aspects of life in East Germany. Students might be surprised to learn that some DEFA fairy-tale films, especially *Three Nuts/Wishes for Cinderella*, enjoy a large following in today's Germany. In fact, they have become a staple in German television culture and air annually during the Christmas season.

NOTES

1. Jack Zipes's number presumably refers to feature-length live-action fairy-tale films only. Qinna Shen states that DEFA produced twenty-three feature-length live-action films for children based on tales by the Brothers Grimm from 1956 to 1989. "This count does not include animation films, silhouette films, and particular Grimm adaptations shown only on television" (Zipes 2011, 70). Joachim Giera, in contrast, refers to about 130 fairy-tale films from 1950 to 1990, a number which includes animation films (Giera 2002, 293).

2. The three DEFA fairy-tale films that have been dubbed in English are *The Story of Little Mook* (*Die Geschichte vom kleinen Muck*, 1953), *The Golden Goose* (*Die goldene Gans*, 1964), and *Who's Afraid of the Devil?* (*Wer reißt denn gleich vor'm Teufel aus*, 1977). In addition to these dubbed versions, three subtitled fairy tales are available: *The Singing, Ringing Tree* (*Das singende, klingende Bäumchen*, 1957); *Rumpelstiltskin* (*Das Zaubermännchen nach dem Märchen Rumpelstilzchen*, 1960); and *Snow White* (*Schneewittchen*, 1961).

3. For details, see www.zeitklicks.de.

4. I slightly altered the "Two Cent" method from the original approach: every student receives two cents and one single white sheet of paper is placed in the middle of the circle. When a student wants to speak, he or she tosses a coin in the middle. This fun game continues until all students are out of coins. The student who manages to land a coin—or two—on the paper, which is rather difficult, wins the game.

5. "*Tief im Bergwerk Schlag auf Schlag, draußen wacht der helle Tag, singen wir ein Liedchen hell, geht die Arbeit doppelt schnell.*"

6. "*Zum Fadenzwirn ist das Gezause, spinnet emsig ohne Pause, schließlich seht ihr, dass der Fleiß mehr als Eil zu schaffen weiß. Hast du Arbeit frisch daran, Fleiß und Kunst liebt jedermann.*"

7. *Brödeln* or *putteln* was a Middle High German verb, which meant "to dig, to dig in the sand, to rummage." *Aschenbrödel* and *Aschenputtel* were nicknames given to both men (scullions) and women, who did lower chores around the household, mainly the kitchen.

REFERENCES

Berghahn, Daniela. 2005. *Hollywood behind the Wall: The Cinema of East Germany*. Manchester: Manchester University Press.

Fritzsche, Sonja. 2012. "'Keep the Home Fires Burning': Fairy Tale Heroes and Heroines in an East German Heimat." *German Politics and Society, Issue 105* 30 (4): 45–72.

Giera, Joachim. 2002. "Vom Kohlenmunk-Peter, dem kleinen Muck und seinen Leuten . . . Märchenfilme aus den DEFA-Filmstudios." In *Die Kunst des Erzählens: Festschrift für Walter Scherf*, ed. Helge Gerndt and Kristin Wardetzky, 293–300. Potsdam: Verlag für Berlin-Brandenburg GmbH.

Grimm, Jacob, and Wilhelm Grimm. [1812] 1974. *Kinder- und Hausmärchen gesammelt durch die Brüder Grimm*. 3 vols. Frankfurt am Main: Insel.

Heiduschke, Sebastian. 2013. *East German Cinema: DEFA and Film History.* New York: Palgrave Macmillan. http://dx.doi.org/10.1057/9781137322326.

König, Ingelore, Dieter Wiedemann, and Lothar Wolf. 1996. *Zwischen Marx und Muck: DEFA Filme für Kinder.* Berlin: Henschel Verlag.

Petan, Zarko. 1979. *Mit leerem Kopf nickt es sich leichter: Satirische Aphorismen.* Graz: Styria.

Shen, Qinna. 2011. "Barometers of GDR Cultural Politics: Contextualizing the DEFA Grimm Adaptations." *Marvels & Tales* 25 (1): 70–95.

Shen, Qinna. 2015. *The Politics of Magic: DEFA Fairy-Tale Films.* Detroit: Wayne State University Press.

Silberman, Marc. 2007. "The First DEFA Fairy Tales: Cold War Fantasies of the 1950s." In *Take Two: Fifties Cinema in Divided Germany,* ed. John Davidson and Sabine Hake, 106–19. New York: Berghahn Books.

Zipes, Jack. 1975. "Breaking the Magic Spell: Politics and the Fairy Tale." *New German Critique, NGC* 6 (6): 116–35. http://dx.doi.org/10.2307/487657.

Zipes, Jack. 2005. "Breaking the Disney Spell." In *From Mouse to Mermaid: The Politics of Film, Gender, and Culture,* ed. Elizabeth Bell, Lynda Haas, and Laura Sells, 21–42. Bloomington: Indiana University Press.

Zipes, Jack. 2011. *The Enchanted Screen: The Unknown History of Fairy-Tale Films.* New York: Routledge.

FILMOGRAPHY OF DEFA FILMS BY DATE OF PRODUCTION

Die Geschichte vom kleinen Muck (The Story of Little Mook). 1953. Directed by Wolfgang Staudte. East Germany: Deutsche Film AG.

Das tapfere Schneiderlein (The Brave Little Tailor). 1956. Directed by Helmut Spieß. East Germany: Deutsche Film AG.

Das singende, klingende Bäumchen (The Singing, Ringing Tree). 1957. Directed by Francesco Stefani. East Germany: Deutsche Film AG.

Das Zaubermännchen nach dem Märchen Rumpelstilzchen (The Magic Dwarf Based on the Fairy Tale Rumpelstiltskin). 1960. Directed by Christoph Engel, Erwin Anders. East Germany: Deutsche Film AG.

Das hölzerne Kälbchen (The Wooden Calf). 1961. Directed by Bernhard Thieme. East Germany: Deutsche Film AG.

Schneewittchen (Snow White). 1961. Directed by Gottfried Kolditz. East Germany: Deutsche Film AG.

Rotkäppchen (Little Red Riding Hood). 1962. Directed by Götz Friedrich. East Germany: Deutsche Film AG.

Frau Holle (Mother Holle). 1963. Directed by Gottfried Kolditz. East Germany: Deutsche Film AG.

Die goldene Gans (The Golden Goose). 1964. Directed by Siegfried Hartmann. East Germany: Deutsche Film AG.

König Drosselbart (King Thrushbeard). 1965. Directed by Walter Beck. East Germany: Deutsche Film AG.

Dornröschen (Sleeping Beauty). 1970. Directed by Walter Beck. East Germany: Deutsche Film AG.

Sechse kommen durch die Welt (Six Make their Way through the World). 1972. Directed by Rainer Simon. East Germany: Deutsche Film AG.

Drei Haselnüsse für Aschenbrödel / Tři oříšky pro Popelku (Three Nuts for Cinderella). 1973.
    Directed by Václav Vorlíček. East Germany / Czechoslovakia: Deutsche Film
    AG / Barrandov Studios.
Wer reißt denn gleich vor'm Teufel aus (Who's Afraid of the Devil?). 1977. Directed by Egon
    Schlegel. East Germany: Deutsche Film AG.
Schneeweißchen und Rosenrot (Snow White and Rose Red). 1979. Directed by Siegfried Hart-
    mann. East Germany: Deutsche Film AG.

OTHER FILMS

Snow White and the Seven Dwarfs. 1937. Directed by David Hand. Burbank, CA: Walt Disney
    Productions.
The Wizard of Oz. 1939. Directed by Victor Fleming. Metro-Goldwyn-Mayer.

6

Teaching Charles Perrault's *Histoires ou contes du temps passé* in the Literary and Historical Context of the Sun King's Reign

Christa C. Jones

MY UNDERGRADUATE FRENCH LITERATURE AND CIVILIZATION class is a communication and writing-intensive class that discusses Charles Perrault's (1697) *Histoires ou contes du temps passé*, excerpts from other seventeenth-century literary and historical texts, and contemporary fairy-tale adaptations, both onscreen and literary. One of my main goals is to enable students to enjoy studying the original French text, which can be challenging for students who read a seventeenth-century text for the first time. To this end, I encourage an intertextual approach: my hope is to "hook" students on Perrault's tales by anchoring his tales in the cultural background of his time and by introducing students to selected works of historians; key seventeenth-century writers; and prominent contemporary actors, musicians, and directors. Over the course of a fifteen-week semester with two class periods per week, my students have ample opportunity to practice their reading, writing, oral, and analytical skills through close readings of primary- and secondary-source materials, in-class discussions, weekly two-page writing assignments, an oral presentation, and, finally, conference participation.[1] Throughout the semester, our discussions investigate the magnetism and longevity of Perrault's tales and why they "stick" (Zipes 2006) in France, even today. In class, we discuss the development of various folktale types and gender stereotypes and then examine how these stereotypes are being perpetuated or undermined today, for example in fairy-tale parodies such as *Hoodwinked!* (*La véritable histoire du Petit Chaperon Rouge* 2005) *or Happily N'Ever After* (*Cendrillon ou le prince pas trop charmant* 2007). We examine to

DOI: 10.7330/9781607324812.c006   99 what extent Perrault's tales reflect or reinforce gender stereotypes and how they are constantly refashioned, and often call into question entrenched gender stereotypes in order to better reflect contemporary trends or to project possibilities for societal change. We do this, for instance, by comparing Perrault's Cinderella with her sexually adventurous counterpart in Catherine Breillat's adaptation *The Sleeping Beauty*, by examining gender role changes in Olivier Dahan's screen remake of Perrault's "Little Thumbling" (*Le Petit Poucet* 2001), or by discussing Belgian novelist Amélie Nothomb's (2012) emancipated heroine in *Barbe bleue*, her take on Perrault's classic tale.

On the first day of class, I walk students through the syllabus and explain course requirements and expectations (i.e., materials covered, class structure, attendance policy, homework, participation, oral presentation, two graded five-page essays written in French, two weekly two-page non graded essays written in French, and a ten-page conference paper, also written in French).[2] I hand out a bibliography with key primary and secondary sources and I meet with students individually to discuss their respective research projects, which have covered topics such as "Sleeping Beauty: From Basile, to Perrault, Grimm, Disney to Catherine Breillat," "Genies and Djinns in the *Arabian Nights*," "Monsters in Fairy Tales," "The Importance of Transformations in Fairy Tales," and "Cinderella and Its Chinese Counterparts." Several students proudly presented their research at the institution's annual departmental student research symposium which takes place every spring term. During the semester, I invited colleagues to guest-lecture on German, Chinese, and medieval French tales and we visited the Special Collections and Archives unit of Utah State University's Merrill Cazier Library, which claims to boast the largest Little Red Riding Hood collection (books, LPs, drawings, and various other artifacts) nationwide. At the library, students particularly appreciated their discussions with two folklore librarians who readily shared their insights into the field of folklore and fairy-tale studies and offered fresh ideas, suggestions, source materials, and feedback for students' research projects.

In the first five weeks of class, my main focus is to establish a framework for Perrault's tales by introducing students to the concepts of French absolutism and classicism, the imposing figure of Louis XIV, the spectacle of court life at Versailles, the roles of aristocratic women, the literary scene of seventeenth-century France, and the life of Charles Perrault.[3] In class, we read and discuss excerpts from Jean-Christian's Petifils's *Louis XIV expliqué aux enfants* (2007) as well as Evelyne Lever's (2002) *Marie-Antoinette: Journal d'une reine*. To familiarize students with seventeenth-century France, I lecture on the reign of the Sun King (referring to François Lebrun's [2007]

Louis XIV: Le roi de gloire), the importance of the Académie Française, which Perrault joined in 1671, and the dispute between the ancients and the moderns. I also introduce students to other key literary figures, including playwrights Pierre Corneille, Jean-Baptiste Racine, and Jean-Baptiste Poquelin (Molière); moralists Jean de La Fontaine, François de La Rochefoucauld, and Jean de La Bruyère; novelist Madame de Lafayette; and poets and critics Nicolas Boileau and Jacques-Bénigne Bossuet. I explain the impact of the phenomenon of salon culture in France (focusing on figures such as Catherine de Rambouillet, the Marquise du Plessis-Bellière, Madame de Scudéry, and Madame de Lafayette). Drawing on La Rochefoucauld's (1665) *Réflexions ou Sentences et maximes morales* (the entries pertaining to women, virtue, integrity, and society), La Bruyère's (2010) *Les Caractères ou les mœurs de ce siècle* (the entries "Of Women" and "Of the Court,") and Madame de Lafayette's *La Princesse de Clèves* (Lafayette 1678), we discuss key concepts such as civility, love, and the truly good man (i.e., *honnête homme*). In this context, Lafayette's novel *La Princesse de Clèves* or her novella *La Princesse de Montpensier* (Lafayette 1662)—adapted to the screen by Bertrand Tavernier in 2010 (*La Princesse de Montpensier* 2010)—can be assigned as oral presentations. Both discuss the ideal of courtly love and portray the devastating impact of love in an aristocratic, patriarchal society, and the required strict adherence to codes of conduct, such as civility and propriety for aristocratic women. In Lafayette's *La Princesse de Clèves*, female characters do not marry for love but to strengthen family ties or foster political alliances. We also discuss the origin of the terms *contes de fées*, coined by Marie-Catherine d'Aulnoy in 1697 (Aulnoy 2004, originally published in 1697; Zipes 2002, 22), as well as terms such as *le merveilleux* (marvelous) and *la morale* or *moralité*. In Perrault's texts, the ideal of French classicism, so prominent in the seventeenth century, is tempered by the introduction of the marvelous, magic, enchantment and the storyteller's performance, which is rooted in the medieval oral tradition (Génetiot 2005, 448). Turning to selected fables by Jean de La Fontaine (1693)—"The Ant and the Grasshopper," "The Wolf and the Lamb," and "The Frog and the Ox"—we discuss the socioeconomic and political divide (clergy, the aristocracy, and the commoners) of seventeenth-century France, and we briefly discuss the Sun King's foreign policy. In this context, students generally are astonished to learn that the personal reign of Louis XIV (1661–1715) was marred by twenty-six years of war.

Starting week 6, we devote two consecutive weekly class periods to close readings and discussions of Perrault's individual tales, to fairy-tale films of his work, and to students' oral presentations. To study Perrault's tales, I have found the *Petits Classiques Larousse* edition of his *Contes* particularly useful

(Perrault 2009a). This edition is indeed widely used in French middle and high schools.[4] In my experience, using a French scholastic edition is a very efficient didactic tool, because it provides much needed grammar and vocabulary explanations in the target language. Undoubtedly, students will at first be deterred by the omnipresence of the *passé simple* (literary past tense) in Perrault's text, so a quick grammar review is needed before delving into close readings. The Larousse edition contains a comprehension and discussion section after each fairy tale. Further, it has essay topics, in-depth appendices about Perrault and his contemporaries, a fairy-tale glossary, and valuable additional source materials and secondary readings such as excerpts from Vladimir Propp's (1968) *Morphology of the Folktale*, a bibliography, and a filmography. The Larousse "mini-anthology" contains "Sleeping Beauty," "Little Red Riding Hood," "Bluebeard," "Puss in Boots," "The Fairies," "Cinderella," "Riquet with the Tuft," and "Little Thumbling." In addition, I provide students with a prose version of "Donkey Skin," (Perrault 2009b) which we compare with Jacques Demy's musical comedy (*Peau d'âne* 1970), and I make supplementary readings, exercises, and films available in the language lab and/or online (on Canvas, the online teaching tool used at Utah State).

In my quick PowerPoint lectures, which I offer before students delve into discussion about individual tales, I draw on contemporary fairy-tale research by scholars such as Maria Tatar, Jack Zipes (which, conveniently is available in French: *Les contes de fées et l'art de la subversion* [Zipes 2007]), Phillip Lewis, and others. I also refer to David Ruffel's (2006) *Les contes de Perrault illustrés par Gustave Doré*, which provides supplementary literary readings, a historical and cultural context, illustrations, a synopsis, and analyses of all of Perrault's fairy tales, and I find the *Greenwood Encyclopedia of Folktales and Fairy Tales* (edited by Donald Haase 2008) very useful in providing students with definitions of recurring topoi such as cannibalism, incest, magic, metamorphosis, and so forth. Before delving into Perrault's tales, I point out that his tales seek to educate and entertain both children *and* an adult audience. As a refresher to what they already learned at the beginning of the semester, I assign students to read pages 6–27 ("Fiche d'identité de l'œuvre," "Biographie," "Contextes," "Tableau et chronologie," and "Genèse de l'œuvre") in the Larousse edition of Perrault's *Contes* that we use in class. Finally, I introduce the term *intertextuality* (using Tiphaine Samoyault's [2005] *L'intertextualité: Mémoire de la littérature*, but of course Julia Kristeva's [1969] definition could be used as well). The concept of intertextuality (which my students were not yet familiar with) works as a door opener to students' understanding of fairy tales, especially as they begin to identify and compare common and recurrent motifs and variants of fairy tales and fairy-tale films, and as they start to distinguish between men- and women-centered fairy tales. In *Fairy Tales and the Art of Subversion*, Jack Zipes states that little girls and women are the target audience of "Sleeping Beauty," "Little Red Riding Hood," "Bluebeard," "The Fairies," and "Cinderella," whereas "Puss in Boots," Riquet with the Tuft," and "Little Thumbling" target above all a male readership, an assertion that we examine throughout the semester.

When discussing Perrault's tales, I regularly divided students into small groups (four to five students each) for group discussions based on a catalog of questions I gave them. After fifteen minutes of discussions, they would share their insights with the class. In their evaluations, students pointed out that they benefitted from these group discussions. Starting out with Perrault's "Cinderella," which stresses the importance of gracefulness and the role played by fairy godmothers, we watch Georges Méliès's two shorts: *Cinderella* (1899) and *Cinderella or The Glass Slipper* (1912)—both are available on YouTube or in *Georges Méliès: Trente chefs-d'œuvre de George Méliès remastérisés tournés entre 1896 et 1912* (2008)—and we discuss various special effects such as apparitions and disappearances, which reflect Perrault's use of magic and metamorphosis. *Cinderella* (1899) is a rapid succession of twenty scenes or tableaux with Méliès participating in the shape of a gnome popping out of a clock to alert Cinderella that it is time to leave the dance. Méliès's longer, second remake no longer captured the public's interest and was a complete flop. Interestingly, Perrault's "Cinderella" is a rather active female character who knows what she wants and how to get it: she cries when she is told she cannot go to the dance and she (purposely?) forgets her glass slipper on the steps. Students are generally amused by Méliès's shorts and enjoy discussing his cinematic techniques.

Turning to Jean Bacqué's *Cendrillon*—part of a mini television series titled *Si Perrault m'était conté* (1966) starring Claude François as prince charming and Christine Delaroche in the role of Cinderella—we note that this pre-May 1968 Parisian Cinderella is wealthy, but she appears lethargic and initially less emancipated than Perrault's. Unlike Perrault's Cinderella, Bacqué's heroine is very well to do. She is reticent to marry the man deemed to make a good husband: a dreary, snobbish, and tedious but rich bourgeois. Finally, she has the courage to go out and meet her prince charming whom she will marry: in this case the popular singer Claude François, who plays himself and projects his pre-disco and pre-Claudettes perfect son-in-law image. Still more recently, Paul J. Bolger's *Happily N'Ever After* (*Cendrillon ou le prince pas trop charmant* 2007) presents a much more outspoken, emancipated, and rebellious twenty-first century Cinderella, who opts for the underdog Ricky and rejects the narcissistic, self-centered, and swanky prince. Cinderellas of both the twentieth and twenty-first centuries must choose between heart and reason, as "Cindy" in Bolger's film puts it: "Is this the goal in life? To marry a prince?" In contrast to Perrault, where the prince literally is a prince, in the contemporary versions, the prince becomes a malleable personalized concept. Students pointed out that the prince represents no longer a figure of authority or wealth but rather a customizable commodity: a prince can be anyone the heroine considers to be her prince.

Perrault's short tale "The Fairies" can be discussed in conjunction with Cinderella," "Donkey Skin," and Jeanne-Marie Leprince de Beaumont's (1866, originally 1740) "Beauty and the Beast," which the students generally adore. As in "Cinderella" and in "Beauty and the Beast," the power vacuum attributable to the absence of fatherly authority leads to a dangerous imbalance. As expected, the young and beautiful heroine is mistreated and exploited, but she ends up getting revenge on her arrogant older stepsister. In "The Fairies," the young and virtuous heroine is rewarded for giving water to a fairy in disguise. In de Beaumont's "Beauty and the Beast" Belle sheds tears of diamonds, while the girl in Perrault's "The Fairies" has roses, pearls, and diamonds gushing out of her mouth every time she speaks. As in Perrault's "Donkey Skin," where the princess runs away from her father's incestuous desires and seeks refuge in the woods, the heroine in "The Fairies" meets a prince who takes her to his father's kingdom and marries her. In "The Fairies," the pretentious sister is punished: she spits out snakes and toads for refusing to offer water to a fairy disguised as a princess and ends up dying alone in the forest. The lessons according to Perrault are that sweet words (*douces paroles*) are more important than diamonds and that integrity (*l'honnêteté*) will always be rewarded, whereas arrogance will be punished. Clearly, my students pointed out, these morals are meant to instill good behavior in children, teaching them to be well behaved and not to lie. However, the prince is not seduced just by the heroine's beauty but also by the fact that she sheds gems. The tale's materialist aspects contradict the morals. As in "Donkey Skin," the prince does not merely wed a beautiful princess. More important, he acquires a golden ass to cement his power. Given Perrault's salon readership, the message to readers might be that wealth and social status are paramount when it comes to marriage.

Perrault's "Donkey Skin" problematizes the "incest averted" motif (Jorgensen 2008, 483), which also appears in "Beauty and the Beast." In Perrault's tale, the fairy godmother helps the princess to hide from her father who intends to marry her and, as expected, she meets the prince she ends up marrying. We discuss the tale against Jacques Demy's eponymous musical comedy, which stars Catherine Deneuve in the role of the princess and Delphine Seyrig as the fairy godmother. In "Donkey Skin," Cinderella's "sister tale" (Lewis 1996, 154), the orphan heroine's stark metamorphosis— Perrault uses the term *souillon* (sloven), which could translate to impure, suggesting that the girl's reputation has been tarnished by her father's inces- tuous desire—symbolizes her father's monstrous desires. The tale which contains ATU 510B ("The Dress of Gold, of Silver, and of Stars") conveys "a sexually abused girl's movement from victimhood to empowerment, as when she sheds her animal-skin disguise for a magical dress, signaling that she is ready to marry" (Jorgensen 2008, 484). As in "Beauty and the Beast" where Belle subsequently sees her dying father and an agonizing Beast when she looks in the magic mirror, the mirror motif in Perrault's "Donkey Skin" reinforces the heroine's awareness of her temporarily regained sense of virtue but also her awareness of her own beauty, an attitude that hinges on narcissism (see Perrault 2009b, 43). In his adaptation, Jacques Demy adds rivalry between the godmother and the daughter, both of whom desire the father. Unlike in Perrault's original, Demy's heroine does not seem opposed to marrying her father. Demy's use of anachronism (notably a telephone and a helicopter scene) along with the sumptuous costumes and locations (Château de Chambord, Château du Plessis-Bourré, and Château de Neuville), anchors the tale both in seventeenth-century classicist and in 1970s France. Demy also pays homage to the French poet and painter Jean Cocteau, when the king cites "L'Ode à Picasso" to seduce his daughter, as well as to the poet Guillaume Apollinaire in the song "L'Amour, l'amour," beautifully interpreted by Catherine Deneuve.

Turning to Perrault's "Sleeping Beauty," we discuss motifs such as sleep, cannibalism, anthropophagy, transformations, and the concept of rites of passage, in particular the transition from childhood to adolescence and adulthood. I show students excerpts from Catherine Breillat's *The Sleeping Beauty* (*La belle endormie* 2010). Breillat's heroine, Anastasia, pricks her finger on a spindle and falls into a deep sleep. During her sleep, she lives out the fantasies of a little girl and young woman. Anastasia is far removed from the passive, victimized model portrayed by Perrault who waits to be awoken by her prince. She is already liberated before she meets her prince, a French high school graduate called Johan, and she has tested out taboo models of behavior, including bisexuality. Even though she runs away after Johan impregnates her, they meet again and she makes it clear that she is his equal.

Perrault's "Little Red Riding Hood" is his shortest tale and can easily be read out loud and performed in class, which is what we did. Students love the dramatic aspect of the tale and the devouring of the grandmother. Perrault himself stressed the theatrical character of his tales in the introduction to his 1695 manuscript. The performance of the original French text, which can appear quaint stylistically, makes the text come alive to students. I usually have one student narrate the story while three more students perform the tale in front of the class. This tale also lends itself to creative rewritings. For instance, one of my students wrote a final paper in which he retold the fairy tale from the wolf's perspective. The same student eagerly shared his knowledge of the Grimms' version of the tale, which is less cruel. I also assigned a two-page essay comparing Perrault's tale with the contemporary remake *La véritable histoire du Petit Chaperon Rouge (Hoodwinked!)*.

"Bluebeard" is another cautionary tale. I was astonished to learn that none of my students had ever read this tale, which turned out to be one of their favorites. The figure of Bluebeard is supposedly inspired by a man called Gilles de Rais (also spelled Retz), who was "one of the darkest and most mysterious figures" (Grimaud 2012, 85) of the Middle Ages. Born in 1404 north of the Loire River, he gained notoriety for carrying out "horrible crimes on children" (Grimaud 2012, 85): child abuse and beheading of his victims. After a valorous start in his youth (he distinguished himself by fighting alongside Jeanne d'Arc) and following an inheritance, he became immensely rich and retreated to a castle where he lived in pomp and indulged in the practice of sorcery and murder. As the editors of *Fairy Tale Films: Visions of Ambiguity* note, this tale targets an adult readership, because it uses AT 312 ("Maiden-Killer [Bluebeard]," previously "The Giant-Killer and His Dog"), the murder motif (Greenhill and Matrix 2010, 184). Bluebeard's young wife is saved from being murdered in the nick of time by her brothers. In his first moral Perrault suggests that women are particularly prone to curiosity, and in his second moral he downplays the detrimental consequences of curiosity by saying that such cruel husbands are a thing of the past and that women generally gain the upper hand over their husbands, whatever their foils or weaknesses might be. I have students discuss "Bluebeard" along with Jeanne-Marie Leprince de Beaumont's "Curiosity" and La comtesse de Ségur's "The Little Gray Mouse," which are both available in *Trois contes sur la curiosité* (edited by Nicolas Saulais 2013). Instructors may assign comparative papers on Angela Carter's (1979) tale *The Bloody Chamber* and Margaret Atwood's (1986) *Bluebeard's Egg*. One of my students indeed wrote a research paper comparing Perrault's tales with the rewritings of Carter and Atwood. For future projects, it would be interesting to compare Perrault's tale to Amélie Nothomb's feminist adaptation. "Bluebeard" is a good example of fairy tale diffusion, a tale derived from oral tradition. Interestingly, the Grimms' version, titled "Blaubart," and published in *Kinder- und Hausmärchen* (Grimm and Grimm 1812–1815), is identical. As Jacques Barchilot and Peter Flinders note: "We tend to believe that the tale of the cruel husband may well be an original invention of Perrault. However, two elements come from earlier popular tradition: the motif of the forbidden chamber, and the magical key with the indelible spot of blood" (Barchilot and Flinders 1981, 93–94). It is also a story of sexual transgression as visualized by the bloody chamber and the bloody key (Bettelheim 1977, 302). The indelible stain on the key lends itself to a discussion of symbolism, as keys often are "symbolic representations of initiation and knowledge" (Cirlot 1962, 167). Traditional interpretations claim that the bloody key symbolizes disobedience, adultery, or both a moral and sexual transgression and that it "marks the heroine's 'irreversible loss of her virginity'" (Tatar 1992, 111). Yet, one wonders what Bluebeard does during his two absences, when he is supposedly on business trips? Certainly most husbands today would not punish infidelity by dismemberment. However, marital infidelity can be disguised under the pretense of "business trips," which gives this classic tale a contemporary twist. In class, we discuss *Bluebeard* (*La Barbe Bleue* 2009), Catherine Breillat's sumptuous remake of female empowerment and cruelty (the older sister is killed by her younger sister while she is reading Perrault's tale to her in the attic). The film ends with a shot of the heroine caressing Bluebeard's severed head, which rests on a silver tray (inspired by Lucas Cranach's *Judith with the Head of Holofernes*, ca. 1530). This provocative image illustrating the beheading of the serial killer underlines that today, traditional gender-defined roles of victimizer (man) and victimized (woman) can be reversed, as Amélie Nothomb illustrates in her feminist rewriting of the tale.

The discussion of "Puss in Boots" can be combined with a viewing of Pascal Hérold's 2009 animated version *The True Story of Puss 'N Boots* (*La véritable histoire du Chat botté* 2009). Alternatively, Jean Bacqué's musical *Le Chat botté* (in *Si Perrault m'était conté* 1966) offers an interesting take on 1960s French youth, the so-called yé-yé (yeah yeah) generation. In Bacqué's film, Perrault's bucolic countryside setting has been replaced by a Parisian urban landscape. Likewise, the hero is no longer male but rather a young Parisian woman named Cabotine (Anne Béranger) who lives in a rooftop apartment in fashionable Saint-Germain-des-Prés. Cabotine is, as her name indicates, a fairy even though her powers do not immediately become apparent. She inherits a white tomcat from her deceased aunt and is amazed to find out that he can morph into a human figure (Jacques Chron) who proclaims that Perrault's cat was his ancestor. Cabotine, who is pretty but lacks any ambition, tells the tomcat that she has no money. The latter promises to find a rich and handsome husband for her. Unlike Perrault's miller, who obeys the cat's orders, the girl appears unworthy of the cat's services: she is not even motivated enough to find her prince charming who might rescue her from her financial strife. The cat then sets out to find a young man who fits the bill. The ensuing courtship leads Cabotine, who now calls herself Charlotte, to get engaged to a pretentious and rich guitarist who has no time for her. Charlotte/Cabotine eventually leaves her fiancé and confesses her love to the cat whom she wants to marry (even though he is twice her age and has no possessions), because he is good, brave, and generous, and because she loves him. She then morphs into a cat so that she may marry the cat. The lesson here is not unlike Perrault's original morals. Despite her poverty, the girl possesses the necessary beauty and charm to seduce the cat. She also has the magical power to transform into a cat so that she may become his companion. While the cat in Perrault's tale is rewarded by becoming a nobleman, Bacqué's tomcat gets the 1960s princess: a girl whose only wealth are her beauty and admiration of her husband. The unexpected ending echoes Bacqué's *Cendrillon* (*Si Perrault m'était conté* 1966), which also ends with a love marriage that transcends socioeconomic class barriers. In both cases, the female characters free themselves from social conventions and choose their husbands rather than agreeing to a marriage of convenience.

Perrault's "Little Thumbling" can be discussed against Olivier Dahan's adaptation *Le Petit Poucet* (2001) and against the Grimms' "Hansel and Gretel," which also features the themes of parental abandonment, children's ingenuity, and social advancement. Unlike Perrault, who makes mention of a famine, Dahan adds war to his script to justify the repeated parental abandonment of five sons—Perrault's version has seven sons—in the forest. Also, the king is replaced by a queen (Catherine Deneuve), to give the tale a more contemporary twist. In addition, Dahan's Poucet falls in love with Rose, one of the ogre's five rebellious daughters who refuses to become an ogress and turns out to be a fairy with magic powers. Unlike in Perrault's tale, where the ogre kills all of his daughters, Rose escapes with the five boys. Poucet delivers an important message to the queen that puts an end to the war. He is nominated to the post of queen's messenger and ends up marrying Rose. Students noted that whereas Perrault's version is a men-centered tale, focusing on the importance of courage and prowess in the face of adversity, Dahan's contemporary remake features three strong and clever female characters to appeal to contemporary female viewers. Whereas in Perrault's story the ogre's wife is old, faceless, submissive, and mute, in Dahan's adaptation she is young, pretty, and pleads with her husband to spare the boys' lives. Likewise, Rose, who is intelligent and good, takes on an active role and accompanies the boys as they flee the ogre's house.

Perrault's "Riquet with the Tuft" is part of the patriarchal cycle of fairy tales, inspired by "Cupid and Psyche" and Giovanni Francesco Straparola's sixteenth-century tale "Re Proco" (Zipes 1983, 65). An earlier variation of the tale was published by Catherine Bernard (1979) in her novella *Inès de Cordoue* and could be assigned as an oral presentation. Perrault's tale stresses that aristocratic women should not seek beauty in men but rather intelligence and ambition. The tale echoes with "Bluebeard," where the heroine is blinded by Bluebeard's wealth and decides that he is an honorable man and not so ugly after all. Perrault's two morals emphasize the power of love over reason and nature and yet the text hints that reason and critical thinking are the driving forces behind the princess's decision to marry Riquet. The miraculously transformative power of love diminishes the hero's physical imperfections; yet, it is reason (*la raison*) that convinces the princess to marry him. Riquet reflects the courtly ideal of the *honnête homme* and therefore deserves to be loved in spite of his imperfections, which turn out to be rather charming features and make him all the more lovable. Much like Lafayette's *La Princesse de Clèves* (Lafayette 1678), the tale stresses the superiority of virtue, reason and dignity over love.

In conclusion, by studying Perrault's tales in the cultural and sociohistorical contexts of French absolutism and today, and by discussing them in connection with remakes and textual variants, students gain an appreciation and a better understanding of the original French text. By juxtaposing Perrault's late seventeenth-century social and ideological context with the legacy and adaptation of his tales across time and cultures, students learn not only about France today and in the past, but hopefully also expand their own worldview. This is indeed the feedback I have been given by one of my former students, a French major, who said he learned immensely from this course and now uses Perrault's fairy tales when teaching intermediate French. Finally, my aim as a French language and literature instructor is to ensure that our student generation—infatuated with smartphone, twitter, and social media—learns to analyze and appreciate Perrault's tales in their cultural and historical contexts and after engaging with Perrault's complex tales in the original language leaves the classroom informed of seventeenth-century France. With this in mind, my chapter offers interdisciplinary teaching suggestions and readings based on his tales and other key texts and films. Again, it cannot be stressed enough that apart from studying French fairy tales and their impact today, students truly enjoy reading out loud and performing Perrault's tales. Over the course of the semester, students come to understand the impact that tales such as "Little Red Riding Hood" continue to have in French low and high culture today (and indeed worldwide), given the unabated flow of variants, such as Joël Pommerat's (2005) play *Le Petit Chaperon rouge*, Nicolas Charlet's and Bruno Lavaine's 2013 comedy *The Big Bad Wolf* (*Le grand méchant loup* 2013), and more recently French Moroccan novelist Tahar Ben Jelloun's (2014) rewriting, *Mes contes de Perrault*. Most important, by studying Perrault's tales, students acquire essential knowledge familiar to most children in France, and thus considerably develop their intercultural competency.

NOTES

1. Grading percentages are as follows: attendance, participation, homework, and weekly position papers: 30 percent; oral presentation: 20 percent; 2 five-page graded essays: 20 percent, final ten-page research paper: 30 percent.

2. The main objectives for this course are to develop critical thinking and analytical skills by close readings and critical assessment of fairy tales and film adaptations in their historical and contemporary contexts; to present ideas clearly in French through oral presentations, writing assignments, class activities, and group discussions; to transform theoretical comprehension into creative and scholarly expression.

3. To prepare my PowerPoint lecture about Perrault's life and work, I have found Marc Soriano's (1990) edited collection, entitled *Charles Perrault*, very useful. This collection contains a number of insightful essays by prominent Perrault scholars, including Marc Soriano, Pierre Gripari, Louis Marin, Jack Zipes, and others.

4. In France, an astounding variety of annotated scholastic editions of Perrault's fairy tales are available from Paris-based publishers such as Gallimard Flammarion, Hachette, Hatier, Magnard, and Nathan.

REFERENCES

Atwood, Margaret. 1986. *Bluebeard's Egg and Other Stories*. Boston: Houghton Mifflin.
Aulnoy, Marie-Catherine Jumelle de Berneville, Comtesse d'. [1697] 2004. *Madame d'Aulnoy: Contes des Fées suivis des Contes nouveaux ou Les Fées à la Mode*, ed. Nadine Jasmin. Paris: Champion.
Barchilot, Jacques, and Peter Flinders. 1981. *Charles Perrault*. Boston: Twayne Publishers.
Ben Jelloun, Tahar. 2014. *Mes Contes de Perrault*. Paris: Seuil.
Bernard, Catherine. [1696] 1979. *Inès de Cordoue: Nouvelle espagnole*. Geneva: Slatkine Reprints.
Bettelheim, Bruno. 1977. *The Uses of Enchantment: The Meaning and Importance of Fairy Tales*. New York: Vintage Books.
Carter, Angela. 1979. *The Bloody Chamber, and Other Adult Tales*. New York: Harper and Row.
Cirlot, J. E. 1962. *Dictionary of Symbols*. New York: Philosophical Library.
de la Bruyère, Jean. [1688] 2010. *Les Caractères ou les mœurs de ce siècle*. Paris: Petits Classiques Larousse.
de La Fontaine, Jean. 1693. *Fables choisies, mises en vers par M. de la Fontaine*. Amsterdam: D. de la Feuille.
de La Rochefoucauld, François. 1665. *Réflexions ou Sentences et maximes morales*. Paris: Claude Barbin.

Génetiot, Alain. 2005. *Le classicisme.* Paris: Presses Universitaires de France.

Greenhill, Pauline, and Sidney Eve Matrix, eds. 2010. *Fairy Tale Films: Visions of Ambiguity.* Logan: Utah State University Press.

Grimaud, Renée. 2012. *Secrets d'histoire de France de l'Antiquité au Moyen Âge.* Issy-les-Moulineaux: Prat Editions.

Grimm, Jacob, and Wilhelm Grimm. 1812–1815. "Blaubart." In *Kinder- und Hausmärchen,* 285–89. Berlin: Realschulbuchhandlung.

Haase, Donald, ed. 2008. *The Greenwood Encyclopedia of Folktales and Fairytales.* Westwood, CT: Greenwood Press.

Jorgensen, Jeana. 2008. "Incest." In *The Greenwood Encyclopedia of Folktales and Fairytales,* ed. Donald Haase, 481–3. Westwood, CT: Greenwood Press.

Kristeva , Julia. 1969. *Sèméiotikè: Recherches pour une sémanalyse.* Paris: Seuil.

Lafayette, Marie Madeleine Comtesse de. 1662. *La Princesse de Mon[t]pensier.* Paris: Billaine.

Lafayette, Marie-Madeleine Pioche de La Vergne. 1678. *La Princesse de Clèves.* Paris: Claude Barbin.

Lebrun, François. 2007. *Louis XIV: Le roi de gloire.* Paris: Gallimard.

Leprince de Beaumont, Jeanne-Marie. 1866. *Contes de fées, tirés de Claude Perrault, de Mme d'Aulnoy et de Mme Leprince de Beaumont.* Paris: Hachette.

Lever, Evelyne. 2002. *Marie-Antoinette: Journal d'une reine.* Paris: Laffont.

Lewis, Phillip Eugene. 1996. *Seeing through the Mother Goose Tales: Visual Turns in the Writings of Charles Perrault.* Stanford: Stanford University Press.

Nothomb, Amélie. 2012. *Barbe bleue.* Albin Michel.

Perrault, Charles. 1697. *Histoires ou Contes du Temps Passé.* Paris: Claude Barbin.

Perrault, Charles. 2009a. *Contes.* Paris: Petits Classiques Larousse.

Perrault, Charles. 2009b. "Peau d'Âne." In *Les Contes de Perrault,* 33–53. Paris: Atlas.

Petitfils, Jean-Christian. 2007. *Louis XIV expliqué aux enfants.* Paris: Seuil.

Pommerat, Joël. 2005. *Le Petit Chaperon rouge: Théâtre.* Arles: Actes Sud-Papiers.

Propp, Vladimir. 1968. *Morphology of the Folktale.* 2nd rev. ed. Ed. Louis Wagner and Alan Dundes. Trans. Laurence Scott. Austin: University of Texas Press.

Ruffel, David. 2006. *Les contes de Perrault illustrés par Gustave Doré.* Paris: Hatier.

Samoyault, Tiphaine. 2005. *L'intertextualité: Mémoire de la littérature.* Paris: Armand Colin.

Saulais, Nicolas, ed. 2013. *Trois contes sur la curiosité.* Paris: Poche.

Soriano, Marc. 1990. *Charles Perrault.* Paris: Europe and Messidor.

Tatar, Maria. 1992. *Off with their Heads! Fairy Tales and the Culture of Childhood.* Princeton: Princeton University Press.

Zipes, Jack. 1983. *Fairy Tales and the Art of Subversion. The Classical Genre for Children and the Process of Civilization.* London: Wildman Press.

Zipes, Jack. 2002. *The Irresistible Fairy Tale: The Cultural and Social History of a Genre.* Princeton: Princeton University Press.

Zipes, Jack. 2006. *Why Fairy Tales Stick: The Evolution and Relevance of a Genre.* New York: Routledge.

Zipes, Jack. 2007. *Les contes de fées et l'art de la subversion.* Paris: Petite Bibliothèque Payot.

FILMOGRAPHY

La belle endormie (The Sleeping Beauty). 2010. Directed by Catherine Breillat. France: Arte.

Cendrillon ou le prince pas trop charmant (Happily N'Ever After). 2007. Directed by Paul J. Bolger. United States: Lions Gate.

Georges Méliès: Trente chefs-d'œuvre de Georges Méliès remastérisés tournés entre 1896 et 1912. [1896] 2008. Directed by Georges Méliès. France: Studio Canal.

La Barbe Bleue (Bluebeard). 2009. Directed by Catherine Breillat. France: Flach Film.

La Princesse de Montpensier (The Princess of Montpensier). 2010. Directed by Bertrand Tavernier. United Kingdom: Studio Canal.

La véritable histoire du Chat botté (The True Story of Puss 'N Boots). 2009. Directed by Pascal Hérold. France: MK2 Productions.

La véritable histoire du Petit Chaperon Rouge (Hoodwinked!). 2005. Directed by Cory Edwards. Australia: Roadshow Entertainment.

Le grand méchant loup (The Big Bad Wolf). 2013. Directed by Nicolas Charlet and Bruno Lavaine. France: Mars Distribution.

Le Petit Poucet. 2001. Directed by Olivier Dahan. France: Studio Canal.

Peau d'âne (Donkey Skin). 1970. Directed by Jacques Demy. France: Marianne Productions.

Si Perrault m'était conté. 1966. Directed by Jean Bacqué. France: Office de Radiodiffusion Télévision Française.

7

Lessons from Shahrazad
Teaching about Cultural Dialogism

Anissa Talahite-Moodley

Sɪɴᴄᴇ ᴛʜᴇ ʙᴇɢɪɴɴɪɴɢ ᴏꜰ ᴛʜᴇ ᴇɪɢʜᴛᴇᴇɴᴛʜ ᴄᴇɴᴛᴜʀʏ, the stories of the *One Thousand and One Nights*—also known as *The Arabian Nights*—have exercised a particular fascination on the Western imagination. Whether it is in the context of the Orientalist construction of an exotic Eastern "Other" or the more recent feminist and postcolonial rereadings of the tales, the *Nights* is a text that has generated numerous critical responses as well as a wealth of literary, musical, artistic, and cinematographic adaptations, some of which are examined in this chapter.[1] In this respect, it constitutes an ideal text for college students to explore some of the key concepts of literary, cultural, and historical studies, particularly as they pertain to the interdependent and complex relationship between East and West, and the question of the exoticized cultural or gendered "Other." As students taking Humanities Studies courses in North American universities are increasingly being drawn toward the study of signifying practices that have historically shaped understandings of non-Western culture—whether it is from a historical, gender, cultural or race perspective—a text such as the *Nights* offers many opportunities to teach about how cultural meanings are created and re-created in a dialogical way. This chapter offers ideas and suggestions for exploring the frame story of the *Nights*—Shahrazad's story—in the humanities classroom in order to better understand the dynamics of gender, agency, and the female voice in the context of cultural difference and intercultural dialog. More particularly, it looks at some of the ways in which Shahrazad's story has been reinterpreted and rewritten through a variety of media—such as ballet, painting, literature, and cinema—and suggests methods through which these diverse interpretations of the frame story can be used

DOI: 10.7330/9781607324812.c007

as teaching tools for exploring issues relating to cultural dialogism that is to say, the process through which cultural meanings are created through the semiotic interaction between different texts and interpretations.[2] In other words, the complex intercultural and intertextual dialogues that underpin the *One Thousand and One Nights* as a text that is contingent on its many adaptations will serve as an entry point into understanding and acknowledging the idea that cultures are relational and interdependent. This approach will in turn make the students aware of the shortcomings of cultural essentialism, especially the problematic assumption that cultures are homogenous, autonomous, and essentially impermeable to one another. The main objective of this task will be to appreciate the ways in which cultural dialogism can be a useful tool to deconstruct the "us-versus-them" mindset.

INTRODUCING THE CONTEXT

Initiating a response from the students and introducing the essential elements of background and context of the *Nights* that are necessary to be able to appreciate and interpret the significance of the frame story of King Shahrayar and Shahrazad are the two main objectives of the first introductory session. I have found that it is useful to allow the students to interact with a text prior to introducing them to its cultural context, which could in some cases create a distance between the readers and the text, more often the case when discussing Arab/Muslim culture in a North American classroom. Thus, in order to avoid the "us" and "them" binary that might arise in such situations, it seems important to offer the students an opportunity to identify and engage with the text at a personal level before discussing its background. Asking the group for their immediate responses to the story of King Shahrayar and Shahrazad can do this. The *Nights* opens with the story of two kings, Shahzaman and his brother Shahrayar, both of whom are betrayed by their wives. Together, they decide to roam the world in search of someone more unfortunate than they, whom they eventually identify in the form of a giant *jinni*. The jinni appears suddenly while the brothers are hiding and unlocks a chest from which emerges a beautiful woman. After the jinni falls asleep, the woman explains that he captured her on her wedding night and has kept her locked inside the chest since then. She orders the two brothers to make love to her and threatens to wake the jinni up if they refuse. The two brothers obey the woman, who then takes their rings and places them in a purse along with the ninety-nine others she had kept from other men with whom she had slept. Following this encounter, the brothers return home, convinced that women are fundamentally malicious and treacherous beings. They order their unfaithful wives to be killed. King Shahrayar not only executes his wife but also decides to marry a new bride every day and orders her execution the day after to make sure she is not unfaithful to him. In order to stop this cycle of violence, Shahrazad, the vizier's daughter, volunteers to marry King Shahrayar with a plan in mind. By telling him a story every night, she hopes to be able to postpone her execution until the king can eventually change his mind. Her sister Dinarzad is part of this plan: she accompanies Shahrazad to the king's chamber on her wedding night and, as instructed by her, waits under the bed until the marriage has been consummated before asking Shahrazad for a story. At this point, Shahrazad starts telling her stories until dawn when she interrupts herself and promises the king to tell an even more wonderful story the following night if her life is spared. Captivated by Shahrazad's tales for one thousand and one nights, the king eventually lets her live having learnt "to trust and love her" (Haddawy and Mahdi 1990, 518).[3] By then, Shahrazad has borne King Shahrayar three children.

In order to engage with the text, the students need to share their immediate responses to some of the most striking aspects of the story, such as Shahrayar's uncompromising attitude, the jinni's captive and her desire for revenge, Shahrazad's generous act to save womankind, the presence of Shahrazad's sister under the bed, and the rather explicit references to sex. In her online teaching guide to the *Nights*, Sofia Samatar includes a section with "resources on the Issue of Explicit Language/Content in the Classroom" while observing that "the bawdy nature of some of the stories is likely to provoke surprise in students who have a view of Islamic societies as puritanical and sexually repressed" (Samatar 2010, 6). Listening to the students' responses and encouraging them to reflect on whether the story is close to what they imagined it to be is an important entry point into the narrative. Once the students have established a connection with the text, its plot, the characters, the language, and the style, they can be invited to address wider questions, such as: What is the value of Shahrazad's story for a modern reader? Why read the *Nights*? What can be gained from reading and understanding stories that have been handed down to us through generations? These questions will then form the basis for a discussion about the significance of telling and transmitting stories within and across cultures. Storytelling has traditionally been regarded as a reflection of a nation's cultural heritage and collective consciousness. Moreover, stories that have traditionally been transmitted orally from generation to generation—as is often the case with traditional storytelling, including fairy tales—are often seen as the repository of social and cultural values that survive the passing of time. In the context of colonialism, traditional folktales are often associated with what the colonial imagination saw as the timeless magic of the "Orient" or the mystery of "Africa." When translated into European languages, traditional folktales became part of the colonial project of textualizing oral folklore. Sadhana Naithani describes the transcription and translation of Indian traditional stories as "the transformation of orality not just into written words, but into the written words of another language. As Indian folklore has been textualized, it has moved from dialects to foreign language(s). The reason for and the implication of this were the same: the published collections were not meant for those who had told the stories, but for British and other European readers" (Naithani 2006, 19). Students need to be aware that the same process is at work in the *Nights*. As Haddawy explains, "From Galland to Burton, translators, scholars, and readers shared the belief that the *Nights* depicted a true picture of Arab life and culture at the time of the tales and, for some strange reason, at their own time" (Haddawy and Mahdi 1990, xxvi). This is all the more surprising when we find out that many stories contain supernatural creatures and events. In this sense, non-Western traditional folktales have often been and continue sometimes to be interpreted as a space of cultural otherness founded on the idea of atemporal, unchanging and far away places, such as the exoticized image of "Arabia." This is why it is important, early in the course, to invite the students to consider the role of traditional folktales. Is the role of storytelling to preserve the past or alter its meaning and understand the present? While they might appear as fixed and unchanging, stories are dynamic as they acquire a new meaning each time they are interpreted in a particular context. By establishing a dialog between the past and the present, the act of storytelling questions the border between historical objectivity and the collective imaginings of community, nation, and culture, an aspect that is necessary to emphasize when examining a text such as the *Nights*. One way of inviting students to reflect on how traditional folktales have the power to adapt, change, and acquire new meanings depending on the new contexts they inhabit is by looking at the history of the various transcriptions and translations of the *Nights* by Antoine Galland (2004), Edward William Lane (1838–40), Richard Francis Burton (1885–87), Joseph Charles Mardrus and Powys Mathers (Mardrus and Mathers 1956), and Husain Haddawy and Muhsin Mahdi (Haddawy and Mahdi 1990).

The importance of translation in the way the *Nights* have been transmitted is a central question to consider. Students can be encouraged to draw on their personal experiences and own observations in order to think about instances when one culture embraces aspects of other cultures in the form of stories, music, or even culinary traditions. How are languages and cultures transformed and enriched as a result of coming into contact with other cultures? In which ways is storytelling an important vector of cultural change? This would constitute the first stage in terms of thinking about the *Nights* as a hybrid and nomadic text whose meaning is unfixed and open for retelling, rewriting, and reinterpretation. Students might reflect on what it means to read the *Nights* in English or in a version that is transcribed, given that the stories were originally transmitted orally. These considerations can lead to an interesting classroom discussion about the processes that take place when a text appears in print and what alternative meanings are either gained or lost through the processes of transcribing and translating. One useful way of introducing the students to the complex intercultural context of the *Nights* is by comparing passages from different translations. In *Sheherazade through the Looking Glass: The Metamorphosis of the Thousand and One Nights*, Eva Sallis compares the different descriptions of Shahrazad produced in various European versions of the *Nights* in the eighteenth, nineteenth, and early twentieth centuries—namely, by Galland, Lane, Burton, and Mardrus (Sallis 1999, 85–107). Students can be invited to compare and contrast these different descriptions of Shahrazad and include the one in Haddawy's version.[4] By looking at juxtaposed descriptions, students will become aware that the use of language and style of each version is reflective of a particular perspective praising different aspects of Shahrazad's character, whether it is her beauty, knowledge, memory, virtue, eloquence, wisdom, wits, morality, or manners. This is the ideal time to introduce a number of key questions related to the *Nights* as a text that highlights the tensions between modes of perception as well as the hybrid and dialogical context of the *Nights*. Each translation of the *Nights* is in fact a re-creation in the sense that translators have added their own perspective to the stories (François 2008, 20). The way in which the stories have been transcribed, translated, and retranslated is a fascinating part of the text itself. This history needs to be treated not just as background information, but also as part of the way in which we, as present-day readers, engage with the text. This is why it is important for the students to read Haddawy's introduction to the Norton edition of the *Nights* that outlines the text's background and the complex history of its many translations in an informative and accessible style (Haddawy and Mahdi 1990, xi–xxxvi).

The history of the *Nights*, although uncertain, is always a source of fascination for readers. It is believed that the stories might have originated from Greece, Persia, and India. The first European version of the *Nights* is Galland's publication in French of a compilation of stories originating from different written and oral sources that are presented as "Arab tales." In fact, it is interesting to note that Galland's translation of the *Nights* into French predates the first Arabic publication of the text a century later in India, known as the "Calcutta I" publication. By drawing a connection between these elements of background and the variations in style observed in the excerpt, the instructor will be able to introduce the idea that the *Nights* is a text that lacks an "authority," which in turn gave its many translators the possibility of making the changes, omissions, and additions they wished to make (François 2008, 27). Considering the *Nights* as an unstable text with multiple origins will help the students to better appreciate the fact that the text is in fact situated at the intersection of Western and Arab cultural imaginations. It is also important to explore the meaning of the title (or many titles) of the *Nights*. The Arabic title (*Alf Layla wa-Layla*) translates into English as *"The Thousand Nights and One Night,"* which later became *"The Arabian Nights."* First, an interesting angle to consider is the sense of open-endedness implied in the title. As Jorge Luis Borges remarked, the title "One thousand and one night," by adding one night to the infinite number of nights, suggests a never-ending process of regeneration (Borges 2009, 45–46). This ad-infinitum number of nights is also reflective of the "embedded narrative" structure of the *Nights*, where stories are inserted into one another like Russian dolls (Todorov 2006, 230). As Evelyn Fishburn observes, "There is no canonical text of the *Nights*: the movement from orality to writing, the *Nights'* uncertain but widespread origins, and open ended and many-layered composition, receiving accretions, interpolations and imitations, make this an infinite text" (Fishburn 2005, 147).

After exploring the complex history and context of the *Nights*, the second important question to address is the role of the reader. A good starting point is Borges's recommendation in reading the *Nights* that "the reader should enrich what he is reading. He should misunderstand the text; he should change it into something else" (Borges quoted in Irwin 1994, 284). The initial session will need to prepare the students to reflect on their own reading of the story and on their role as generating meanings and interpretation. Borges's comment might seem disconcerting at first, as the idea of "misunderstanding" a text is not what students would normally be expected to do. This could be a way of starting a discussion about what it means to interpret a text or a culture. In other words, the questions students can consider: How can we make Shahrazad's story speak for us? What aspects of our own experience and expectations do we bring into a text? And what are these expectations when we are about to read and interpret a text with a title like *"The Arabian Nights"*? It is, however, important to keep it mind—and remind the students of—the distinction between the colonial appropriation of the *Nights* and the creative "misunderstandings" advocated by Borges. Some students might be aware of the political dimension inherent in the act of reading and reinterpreting a text from a culture that has historically been constructed in the West as "Other." For example, each European transla-tor in the past seems to have created his own version of an "Orient" often charged with stereotypical and voyeuristic representations of otherness. These are important responses to initiate before looking at the more spe-cific constructions of otherness in the text.

SHAHRAZAD AND THE WESTERN IMAGINATION

Looking at the translation of the *Nights* for Western audiences and the place the text occupies in the Western imagination is likely to generate comments about the relationships between Western and Eastern cultures. Questions that can be posed: Why would this particular text that is part of Arab/ Muslim literary heritage be of relevance to a Western audience? What was the motivation for introducing these stories to Western audiences in the eighteenth and nineteenth centuries? Why has Shahrazad become so well known? Students can be asked to note any reference in the frame story that relates to a specific cultural background, such as names, customs, food, places, customs, language, and religion. For example, Shahrayar and Shahrazad are name endings that suggest a Persian origin, while the title suggests an Arab context. This is a good time to point out to the class that the Arabic language and culture that underpin the text do not constitute the origins of the *Nights* but are the language and culture that have given the story a space to develop and evolve. As Bencheikh explains, "It is neither in India or in Persia that *The One Thousand and One Nights* was enriched by all the novels, narratives and tales that have progressively been added to one another, probably more as a result of their similarity of meanings than at random. It is Arab civilization and no other that allowed the stories to thrive, and it is its poets and narrators that magnified its content" (Bencheikh, Bremond, and Miquel 1991, 29; my translation). Inviting students to share what they know about the Middle East and what is commonly (and at times stereotypically) referred to as the "Muslim world," and how they situate the region both geographically and in their mind, is an important first stage for analyzing and extrapolating meaning from the *Nights*. This can lead to the following questions: Can the story of Shahrazad be read as a reflection of the society and culture within which it is set? And, if so, to what extent? To what extent can we consider a work of fantasy as the "true" reflection of a culture? What are the processes at work in such imaginings of the Middle East and Muslim/Arab culture in particular?

In order to explore the *Nights* as a dialog between East and West in more depth, the students need to be given some preliminary definitions of key concepts such as intertextuality, authorship, and dialogism with references to key theorists such as Julia Kristeva (1980), Roland Barthes (1977), Mikhail Bakhtin (2004) and Gérard Genette (1997). This could take the form of a handout with key elements of context, definitions, explanations, and examples from popular culture that can help them grasp the various processes of allusion, adoption, transformation, or irony that are involved in rewriting stories. A starting point for applying these concepts is to look at Edgar Allan Poe's satirical version of the story, "The One Thousand and Second Night." In Poe's story, on the one thousand and second night, the vizier's daughter tells the king parts of Sindbad's adventures in which the traveler talks about the latest scientific discoveries he had witnessed during his travels, such as train engines, the electro-telegraph, and the daguerreotype. The incredulous king accuses Shahrazad of lying and, driven by his anger, strangles her to death. Poe's Shahrazad accepts her fate "with good grace" (Poe 1998, 349). Fatema Mernissi's response to Poe's story in her book *Scheherazade Goes West: Different Cultures, Different Harems* can be used to generate a debate about Poe's dark and dramatic ending. Mernissi describes Shahrazad as "an avant-garde broadcaster informing Muslims about the West's scientific inventions [that] would have enhanced her husband's military power and allowed him to end the West's occupation of the Orient" (Mernissi 2001, 80).[5] The question that can be posed to the class is whether Poe devalues Shahrazad by having her killed by the king or whether she is shown as having more insights, wisdom, and knowledge than her husband. Poe's subtitle "Truth is Stranger than Fiction" is surely an interesting point of discussion that can be related to Shahrazad's power of the imagination as a gateway to scientific truth. At the same time, it is important for the group to consider Mernissi's objection to Shahrazad's "passive submission to her own death." As Mernissi explains, a Muslim woman in today's world cannot afford to be fatalist as "words are the only arms she has to fight the violence targeted against her" (Mernissi 2001 81). Students can be asked to look at Mernissi's objection to Poe's interpretation of Shahrazad in the light of women's struggle, not only in the Arab world, but in the world at large.

Another important aspect of Shahrazad's impact on the Western imagination relates to Orientalism, most of all in its gendered form. Looking at some critical perspectives such as the one provided by Edward Said's theory of Orientalism can solidify the idea of how the "Other" is constructed through processes of interpretation and perceptions. Said's ideas could be introduced at this point by distributing an extract from his introduction to *Orientalism* (Said 2003), where the author defines it as both a discourse and an invention about the Orient. Looking at nineteenth-century Orientalist paintings of odalisques can help initiate such discussions on how the West had often represented the Orient through images of stereotypically passive, helpless, and subservient women.[6] The idea of Orientalizing Arabs can also be introduced through some of the available documentaries showing the exoticization of Arab culture in contemporary Western contexts, such as Sut Jhally, Jeremy Earp, and Jack G. Shaheen's *Reel Bad Arab: How Hollywood Vilifies a People* (Jhally, Earp, and Shaheen 2006) based on Jack Shaheen's (2009) book *Reel Bad Arabs: How Hollywood Vilifies a People*. Hollywood representations can, in this respect, be useful to invite the students to reflect on the ways in which Shahrazad features in the collective imagination of the West as a symbol of the Orient. Students would generally be familiar with the story of *Aladdin and the Magic Lamp* that has been widely popularized by Disney, and its "Arabian Nights" song that has been the subject of controversies (*Aladdin* 1992).[7] To illustrate how pervasive these images are, the students can also view a clip from the Universal's 1942 film *Arabian Nights* that features "the harem ladies as dressed in nothing but flimsy, transparent bras and skirts" that, according to Mernissi, both trivializes Arab culture (in particular belly dance) and reduces Shahrazad to a sex object. As Mernissi states, "One could say that the West's understanding of Shahrazad and the harem world was skin-deep, cosmetic and superficial. The storyteller's yearning for a dialog between men and women found no echo in the West" (Mernissi 2001, 74). Students can be invited to discuss the implications of Mernissi's assertion and extend it to other forms of stereotyping attached to the image of the Muslim/Arab woman in the contemporary North American context.

Other visual materials such as ballet can be used to illustrate the idea of Shahrazad as a character embedded in the Western imaginings of the Orient. Students can view an extract from *Scheherazade* ballet choreographed by Michel Fokine with the music composed by Nikolai Rimsky-Korsakov and be invited to note what aspects of Shahrazad are emphasized in the performance, and how similar or different she is from the character portrayed in the story that they read. It is important to help students stretch their analysis beyond the simple condemnation of the Orientalist representation as inauthentic and examine what Said would call the "invention of the Orient." In other words, questions such as "What inventions of the Orient does the Orientalized Shahrazad embody, and what aspects of the

West's own repressed desires does she represent?" would be important to ask in order to explore her character as a perpetual reinvention. Students are generally aware of the negative stereotyping in the Western world, yet are often less aware of the complex ways in which otherness is created. It is tempting at this stage for students to interpret Western adaptations of the *Nights* as an erroneous representation of a "true" and "authentic" Orient, and it is worth reminding them of the uncertain origins of the "authentic text." Said's theory of Orientalism is more than a critique of cultural stereotyping in that it engages with the idea of the Orient as an invention. This nuance can challenge the students to think beyond the binary between authentic and inauthentic representations of the Other. By applying Said's idea of the Orient as an invention, students can start reading the character of Shahrazad as one that involves a dialogical cultural creation. It is essential to introduce the class to the fact that not only is the text available to us through translation but, most important, it is available to us through a series of colonial encounters. Acknowledgment of this foregrounding of the *Nights* as a liminal text situated between East and West is necessary in order to approach questions about cultural authenticity and hybridity. A relevant analogy could be made with the way in which multiculturalism in our contemporary society is sometimes constructed on the assumption that cultures can travel from one place to another while remaining whole, identifiable, and distinct. What the *Nights* tell us is that dominant systems of power shape how stories are read and interpreted. In this respect the text of the *Nights* is a prime example of what postcolonial critics have described as the cultural interdependence between the East and the West as terrains where both experiences are superimposed.

SHAHRAZAD, A FAIRY-TALE PRINCESS?

As Fatema Mernissi very aptly comments about the stories in the *Nights*, "The tales' cosmopolitan grace, their capacity to transcend cultural boundaries, does not extend to the relationship between the sexes. That is portrayed as an abysmal, unbridgeable frontier, a bloody war between men and women" (Mernissi 2001, 44). The frame story is likely to generate many interesting discussions about gender politics. The first aspect that deserves attention is the unconventional figure of Shahrazad—a resourceful, brave, and determined young heroine who does not hesitate to put her life at risk for others and who emerges as the antithesis of the conventional fairy-tale princess. She is described as an "intelligent, knowledgeable, wise, and refined" young woman who "had read the books of literature, philosophy and medicine" and "knew poetry by heart, had studied historical reports, and was acquainted with the sayings of men and the maxims of sages and kings" (Haddawy and Mahdi 1990, 14–15). As such, Shahrazad is closer to a Jane Eyre or one of Jane Austen's witty and resourceful heroines who is not afraid of confronting the rules made by men. As Alia Yunis puts it, "Shahrazad was a feminist centuries before the word became part of Western society. While she was hanging out in the Middle East and East, Cinderella, Sleeping Beauty, and Rapunzel were self-absorbedly waiting around to be rescued" (Yunis 2013, 398). Shahrazad as a "feminist hero-ine" counteracting the myth of the "maiden in distress" constitutes an ideal "entry point" into the gender subtext of the narrative. It offers students an opportunity to reflect on what might appear a contradiction in the *Nights* in the sense that while 'those' "female characters' roles are often confined to those of concubines, slave girls, servants or mothers, they are also often endowed with powerful personalities, including a powerful sexuality. Female sexuality is often acknowledged in the *Nights* as a significant part of wom-anhood, despite the fact that it is sometimes associated with the fantasy of women as dangerous and insatiable beings. This could lead to a discussion about how Shahrazad combines both intellect and sensuality and bridges the mind/body binary, attributes that have traditionally been set in opposi-tion to one another in Western culture, as Mernissi observes.

Even though her intelligence is an important aspect of her character, Shahrazad's intellect is not enough to change the course of history without her other talents as imaginative storyteller. As Mernissi puts it, "Knowledge alone does not enable a woman to influence men in power; witness the enor-mous number of highly educated women involved in social movements in the West today, who are nonetheless unable to keep modern Shahrayars in check. Hence the interest in analyzing Shahrazad's highly successful story" (Mernissi 2001, 47). Mernissi reads the tension between Shahrazad and King Shahrayar as a conflict between what she names "Truth" (the male claim of scientific and rational objectivity) and "Imagination" (the realm of the female inventive and subversive genius exemplified by Shahrazad). Whereas Truth is associated with masculine authority and the law of the male ruler, Imagination pertains to female resistance against authoritarian male rule through entertainment and pleasure. This tension could also be interpreted through the Freudian opposition between "reality principle" and "pleasure principle" (Mernissi 2001, 53).[8] Students can explore the idea of whether Shahrazad's imagination is what allows her to disobey the laws made by men. As Mernissi writes, "If Truth is so evident, why are imagina-tion and fiction not allowed to flourish?" (Mernissi 2001, 58). Students can be asked to apply this reading of Shahrazad to the world around them and note examples where the "male logo," in the name of "Truth," is used as a way of imposing one version of reality over others that can be imagined. Shahrazad's victory is to challenge the king's monolithic truth and to teach him that words and imagination are more powerful than force. At this stage, the class is ready to start reflecting on the value of Shahrazad's "feminism." Examples of how the character of Shahrazad has inspired contemporary feminist discourse are abundant. As Fedwa Malti-Douglas notes, "Were the Arabic Shahrazad to awaken, like some fairy tale princess, centuries after she first wove the stories of *The Thousand and One Nights*, she would undoubtedly be surprised by her numerous literary transformation" (Malti-Douglas 2006, 40). Malti-Douglas notes that gender has been central in the way her character has been used by both male and female writers. Looking at feminist renditions of Shahrazad, as Malti-Douglas does through her analysis of Ethel Johnston Phelps' short story "Sheherazade Retold," is a useful way of inviting students to consider the wealth of possibilities that feminist rewriting of fairy tales offers. In the same way Angela Carter (1979) rewrites Charles Perrault's tales in *The Bloody Chamber, and Other Stories,* Phelps in "Sheherazade Retold" depicts a resourceful female character that does not follow the conventions of the fairy-tale princess. Instead of falling in love with the king and both living happily ever after, Phelps' heroine follows a different path: "Using her earlier education provided by the best tutors, she of course wrote down for posterity a more polished version of her own thousand and one tales" (Phelps 1981, 173). The students can read Phelps's story in parallel to the text as a way of appreciating the possibilities for interpreting Shahrazad's feminism. This could also be the occasion for students to reflect on the origin of storytelling and the female tradition of anonymous stories, tales, and ballads passed from generations to generations by women. In fact, Jamel-Eddine Bencheikh argues that one of the reasons why Arab elites were reluctant to write down the tales is their subversive feminist power. He observes the irony of the tales when he writes, "The storyteller, whose duty it was to obtain grace of the cuckolded sovereign, put all her talent into creating tales that confirmed his distrustful feeling toward women" (Bencheikh, Bremond, and Miquel 1991, 57). This is why it might be important to encourage the students to read some of—if not all—the stories in the collection to get a sense of the world that Shahrazad creates.[9] Practical exercises are needed at this stage to reinforce the idea of "rewriting" stories as a process of critical understanding. This can be done through oral presentations (preferably in small groups to generate more ideas). The instructions would require that the students select a story from the collection; rewrite its plot, characters, setting, and other aspects (as necessary); and then comment on the ways in which their retelling of the story relates to the frame story, particularly in terms of recontextualizing issues pertaining to gender politics.

INTERROGATING SHAHRAZAD'S "FEMINISM"

Shahrazad has often been hailed as a feminist figure. Her character in particular has inspired many Arab women authors. Looking at the literature by women writers from the Arab world, more particularly the Maghreb, Christiane Chaulet-Achour (2014) sees her power as twofold. First, Shahrazad is able to use her voice in order to assert her being beyond the presence of her body. Second, by involving her sister, Dinarzad, who is lying under the conjugal bed and initiating the stories, Shahrazad establishes a line of transmission and solidarity between women. It is worth asking the students to comment on the relationship between the two sisters. An extract from Assia Djebar's (1987) novel *A Sister to Scheherazade* could be read in parallel to the story, as a way of illustrating the manner in which the narrative structure of the *Nights* lends itself to feminist rewriting of patriarchal discourse. While exploring the possibilities of reading Shahrazad's voice as questioning the patriarch status quo, it is also important to help the students consider the other side of the argument and the limitations of Shahrazad's "feminism." Playing the devil's advocate can be a useful strategy by asking, for example, questions such as "Is Shahrazad really a feminist?" or "Are there elements in the framing story that also suggest moralistic and patriarchal views of gender relationships?" The idea of women's superior ease with language might appear to be stereotypical, and so might Shahrazad's "emotional healing" of King Shahrayar (Sallis 1999, 95). Some Arab feminists have been critical of Shahrazad's model; Joumana Haddad, for instance, reads Shahrazad's strategy as "bribing the man's scheme" (Haddad 2010, 141). As she writes: "Correct me if I am wrong, but it seems obvious that this method puts the man in the omnipotent position, and the woman in the compromising, inferior one. It does not teach women resistance and rebellion, as is implied when the character of Scheherazade is discussed and analysed. It rather teaches them concession and negotiation over their basic RIGHTS" (Haddad 2010, 142).

Haddad's call for more radical methods for effecting gender change than Shahrazad's "huge imagination and good negotiation skills" is echoed by other authors (Haddad 2010, 143). Mernissi argues that Shahrazad is able to save her life because she has the privilege of being middle class and educated (Mernissi 1988, 15–17). Similarly, the Tunisian writer Fawzia Zouari urges women writers to free themselves from Shahrazad and, rather than patiently wait for their salvation, adopt a more proactive attitude in life (Zouari 1996, 11). All these different responses to Shahrazad can be offered to the students as examples of her character's adaptability and capacity to generate new, and at times contradictory, meanings and debates. It is important to help the students keep in mind the idea of the *Nights* as a text combining contradictory elements so that to become aware of their own role as readers able to create meanings through new—and at times conflicting—interpretations or, to use Borges's phrase, "misinterpretations."

A creative way of ending the study of Shahrazad would be to assign a project for assessment based on the multiplicity of ways in which her character can be represented. Sofia Samatar's online resource guide for teaching the *Nights* includes a final project that can serve as a model to devise a similar exercise. Students could choose to do a critical and analytical interpretation of Shahrazad's role in the *Nights* and/or other texts discussed in class or opt for an imaginative piece of work involving a creative rewriting of her character using a particular medium: art (painting, sculpture, drawing, etc.), music and drama (song, miniopera, play, etc.), creative writing (poetry, children's story, graphic novel, etc.), digital media (digital art, trailer, website, Wiki entry, blog, etc.). This would give the class a chance to apply and develop further some of the ideas explored in class about dialogism, reinterpretation, Orientalism, female agency, and voice.

CONCLUSION

As hybrid and dialogical, the *Nights* is an ideal text for students to challenge what has been popularized as the quintessential expression of "Arab culture." As such, it represents a rich and diverse resource for teachers seeking to explore the question of gender in the context of cultural interactions. As a text both familiar and unsettling, the *Nights* encourages intercultural dialog and urges its readers to reinterpret their assumptions. Engaging with the stories of the *Nights* in creative interpretative ways that stretch their significance can be an extremely rewarding and stimulating experience for students. More particularly, the character of Shahrazad can yield a multitude of meanings that have relevance in the context of today's reinterpretation of past colonial legacies and the need to generate new ways of understanding the relationships between East and West. Students can add to the process of rewriting the *Nights* in ways that open up possibilities for both creative and critical understanding of what it means to live in a culturally diverse world, a skill that has become indispensable in the humanities classroom today.

The study of Shahrazad and her many "children," to borrow the title from a collection edited by Philip Kennedy and Marina Warner, also offers a myriad perspectives on how to understand women's relationships with authority and their capacity to initiate social change (Kennedy and Warner 2013). In a globalized world where women are increasingly accessing domains that have traditionally been reserved for men but where they continue to face the brutal violence of authoritarian patriarchal regimes, Shahrazad's voice has never been so relevant. This unconventional fairy-tale princess, whether or not a feminist, will undoubtedly continue to inspire not only writers, painters, choreographers, cinematographers, and musicians, but also generations of teachers and students wanting to learn about how the human imagination can be used to understand and subvert relationships of power.

NOTES

1. In the rest of this chapter, I will refer to the *One Thousand and One Nights* as the *Nights*.

2. There are many variations of the heroine's name but I will use "Shahrazad" for consistency in this chapter, unless when quoting sources.

3. This translation based on the text of the fourteenth-century Syrian manuscript edited by Muhsin Mahdi is easily accessible and generally considered the most adapted to a contemporary readership (Haddawy and Mahdi 1990).

4. Samatar (2010), in her excellent resource guide for teaching the *Nights*, suggests a similar comparative exercise using a different passage from the framing story to compare the style of three translators: Lane, Burton, and Haddawy.

5. Mernissi also mentions Théophile Gautier's (1842) novella *La Mille et Deuxième Nuit*, where the heroine also dies, this time because she has no more inspiration (Gautier, Sand, and Puissant 1845).

6. For a discussion of odalisques in Orientalist constructions of female otherness, see Anissa Talahite (1998).

7. The film *Aladdin* (1992) opens with Aladdin describing his home as a place "where they cut off your ear / If they don't like your face," and concluding, "It's barbaric, but hey, it's home."

8. As Mernissi also points out, storytellers in medieval Baghdad were often seen as agitators and, as a result, censored and banned from public speaking (Mernissi 2001, 53).

9. Although there is no space here to discuss the stories told by Shahrazad, among the ones that address the question of gender in subversive ways is "The Story of the Porter and the Three Ladies."

REFERENCES

Aladdin. 1992. Directed by Ron Clements, John Musker, and Bill Perkins. Burbank, CA: Walt Disney Studios Home Entertainment.

Bakhtin, Mikhail. 2004. *The Dialogic Imagination: Four Essays.* Trans. Caryl Emerson and Michael Holquist. Austin: University of Texas Press.

Barthes, Roland. 1977. *Image-Music-Text.* Trans. Stephen Heath. London: Fontana.

Bencheikh, Jamel-Eddine, Claude Bremond, and André Miquel. 1991. *Mille et un contes de la nuit.* Paris: Gallimard.

Borges, Jorge Luis. 2009. *Seven Nights.* Trans. Eliot Weinberger. New York: New Directions.

Burton, Richard Francis. 1885–87. *The Book of the Thousand Nights and a Night, with Introduction, Explanatory Notes on the Manners and Customs of Moslem Men and a Terminal Essay upon the History of the Nights.* 16 vols. Benares: Kamashastra Society.

Carter, Angela. 1979. *The Bloody Chamber, and Other Adult Tales.* New York: Harper and Row.

Chaulet-Achour, Christiane. 2014. "Que faire de la sultane des *Nuits* pour une écrivaine au Maghreb aujourd'hui?" *Dalhousie French Studies Special Issue: Women from the Maghreb,* ed. Christa Jones and Anissa Talahite-Moodley, 103: 45–53.

Djebar, Assia. 1987. *A Sister to Scheherazade.* Trans. Dorothy S. Blair. London: Quartet.

Fishburn, Evelyn. 2005. "Traces of the One Thousand and One Nights in Borges." In *New Perspectives on Arabian Nights. Ideological Variations and Narrative Horizons,* ed. Wen-chin Ouyang and Geert Jan van Gelder, 81–90. London: Routledge.

François, Cyrille. 2008. "Préambule." In *Le Don de Shahrazad,* ed. Cyrille François, 7–40. Amiens: Encrage.

Galland, Antoine. 2004. *Les Mille et une nuits.* Paris: Flammarion.

Gautier, Théophile, George Sand, and Jules Puissant. 1845. *La mille et deuxième nuit.* Paris: Le pionnier.

Genette, Gérard. 1997. *Palimpsests.* Trans. Channa Newman and Claude Doubinsky. Lincoln: University of Nebraska Press.

Haddad, Joumana. 2010. *I Killed Scheherazade: Confessions of an Angry Arab Woman.* London: Saqi.

Haddawy, Husain, and Muhsin Mahdi. 1990. *The Arabian Nights.* New York: W. W. Norton.

Irwin, Robert. 1994. *The Arabian Nights: A Companion.* London: Allen Lane.

Jhally, Sut, Jeremy Earp, and Jack G. Shaheen. 2006. *Reel Bad Arabs: How Hollywood Vilifies a People.* Northampton: Media Education Foundation.

Kennedy, Philip, and Marina Warner, eds. 2013. *Scheherazade's Children.* New York: New York University Press.

Kristeva, Julia. 1980. *Desire in Language: A Semiotic Approach to Literature and Art.* Ed. Leon S. Roudiez. Trans. Thomas Gora, Alice Jardine, and Leon S. Roudiez. New York: Columbia University Press.

Lane, Edward William. 1838–40. *The Thousand and One Nights, Commonly Called, in England, the Arabian Nights' Entertainments: A New Translation from the Arabic, with Copious Notes.* 3 vols. London: Charles Knights.

Malti-Douglas, Fedwa. 2006. "Shahrazad Feminist." In *The Arabian Nights Reader,* ed. Ulrich Marzolph, 347–64. Detroit: Wayne State University Press.

Mardrus, Joseph Charles, and Powys Mathers. 1956. *The Book of the Thousand Nights and One Night.* London: Routledge and K. Paul.

Mernissi, Fatema. 1988. *Chahrazad n'est pas marocaine, autrement elle serait salariée.* Casablanca: Le Fennec.

Mernissi, Fatema. 2001. *Scheherazade Goes West: Different Cultures, Different Harems.* New York: Washington Square Press.

Naithani, Sadhana. 2006. *In Quest of Indian Folktales: Pandit Ram Gharib Chaube and William Crooke.* Bloomington: Indiana University Press.

Phelps, Ethel Johnston. 1981. "Sheherazade Retold." In *The Maid of the North: Feminist Folk Tales from around the World,* 167–73. New York: Henry Holt and Company.

Poe, Allan Edgar. 1998. *Tales of Mystery and Imagination.* London: Everyman's Library.

Said, Edward. 2003. *Orientalism*. New York: Vintage Books.

Sallis, Eva. 1999. *Sheherazade through the Looking Glass: The Metamorphosis of the Thousand and One Nights*. Richmond: Curzon.

Samatar, Sofia. 2010. *"Teaching the Arabian Nights in Wisconsin: A Resource Guide for Educators."* http://humanities.wisc.edu/assets/misc/Arabian_Nights_Guide_-_February_2015 .pdf.

Shaheen, Jack. 2009. *Reel Bad Arabs: How Hollywood Vilifies a People*. Northampton: Olive Branch Press.

Talahite, Anissa. 1998. "Odalisque et Pacotille: Identity and Representation in Leïla Sebbar's *Shérazade, 17 ans, brune, frisée, les yeux verts*." *Nottingham French Studies* 37 (2): 62–72. http://dx.doi.org/10.3366/nfs.1998-2.006.

Todorov, Tzvetan. 2006. "Narrative-Men." In *The Arabian Nights Reader*, ed. Ulrich Marzolph, 230–33. Detroit: Wayne State University Press.

Yunis, Alia. 2013. "My Arabian Superheroine." In *Scheherazade's Children*, ed. Philip Kennedy and Marina Warner, 395–400. New York: New York University Press.

Zouari, Fawzia. 1996. *Pour en finir avec Shahrazade*. Tunis: Cérès éditions, Enjeux.

Part III
Decoding Fairy-Tales Semantics
Analyses of Translation Issues, Linguistics, and Symbolisms

8

The Significance of Translation

Christine A. Jones

The meal was superb, and no one had ever enjoyed himself more than the King, whose witticisms were explained to Candide by Cacambo. No matter how translated, they still survived as bons mots. Of all the things that astonished Candide, this was certainly not the least.

—Voltaire (2005, trans. Burton Raffel), *Candide*, 65

In the opening pages of Voltaire's (2005) mid-eighteenth-century satire, *Candide*, a sheltered young man finds himself cast out of his comfortable German manor life and into a hostile world. On the only one of his many adventures that does not lead immediately to catastrophe, he and his South American guide, Cacambo, stumble upon the fabled land of Eldorado in Peru. There exist no currency, no courts, and no prisons. In their place the duo finds rivers of gold, a palace of sciences filled with marvels of mathematics and astronomy, and a welcoming royal palace where they are treated to hospitalities untold. When Candide hears Cacambo render the king's Peruvian witticisms in his native German, he finds in it just as much wonder as anything in this political utopia. Even in the land of magnificence and munificence, a great translation is still astonishing.

What Candide misses but the reader sees in the scene is that the king's bon mots did not really survive "no matter how translated"; they were either creatively invented by Cacambo or translated with creative verve. In either case, what Candide hears is the result of the clever Cacambo's poetic powers of "explanation," which ensure Candide's "astonishment" and positive response to the king. On a metanarrative level, too, the translator of Voltaire's book into English, Burton Raffel, embeds the craft of translation into the phrase by *not* translating the French words *bons mots* into *witticisms*.

DOI: 10.7330/9781607324812.c008

English allows that, but Raffel exploits the irony that to perfectly ensure that bons mots stay "bons" and do not change at all, is to not translate them and risk the reader's confusion.

Only once in the course of *Candide*, a travel narrative that sends the eponymous character all over the world, does the narrator tell an anecdote about translation. Because it occurs in Eldorado—a fabled land of marvel—the fact that Candide is German, Cacambo is Peruvian, and the king would logically speak a language that developed in complete isolation does not at all impede communication. The sheer unlikelihood of the scene coupled with Raffel's nod to the fact that Voltaire's text is in French puts the English reader at an extreme remove from what the king might have said. Comically, then, Raffel joins with Voltaire to illustrate how every translation is an act of interpretation that eclipses even as it presents the first-language text. Viewed in this light, the eighteenth-century French *Candide* was written by Voltaire, but the twenty-first-century English *Candide* was written—quite literally—by Raffel.

The marvel of rendering words wittily in a new tongue has been an integral part of the transmission, diffusion, and retelling that constitutes fairy-tale history. In North America, broad-based courses on the fairy tale have become standard features in folklore studies and English literature programs partially because of the rich trove of translated stories available for purchase in modern editions. Yet, modern editions such as the Penguin *Candide* (above) tend to collapse the hand of the translator and author, as though Voltaire wrote the English-language *Candide* as well, when in fact it is the handiwork of Raffel. This erasure can happen because the translator's name does not appear on the title page or because authors, editors, and reviewers privilege translations considered faithful or accurate. For the industry, the skill of translation consists in captivating the reader—or listener, in Candide's case—so well that she believes she has access to the original-language text. These commonplace habits in modern editorial practice render the translator's art invisible.

While the idea of reproducing the pleasure of one language in another proves desirable and has long been a tenet of translation practice, it lulls the reader into forgetting that languages do not have a one-to-one word correspondence and that translators are artful interpreters. A quick go at Google Translator suffices to remind us that translation is anything but direct! Gillian Lathey makes the argument that the history of children's literature erased the many people who rendered those stories in a second language and facilitated their dissemination. As she puts it, "Translators were more or less invisible agents in the process" of carrying ideas and plots from one language into another (Lathey 2010, 49). Her argument makes an excellent case, one I apply here pedagogically, for talking about translation in fairy-tale history. If we regard that history not as a pattern of originals and hopefully faithful translations, but as a reservoir full of many astonishing versions of stories, a world of opportunity opens up for using translation innovatively in the curriculum.

This chapter suggests thinking about English translation as more than a tool to transmit foreign-language tales, or a convenient way to teach them in a comparative or children's literature survey. When we consider translation a tool rather than a creative act, the early fairy-tale print tradition is reducible to a handful of authors: Giambattista Basile, Giovanni Francesco Straparola, Charles Perrault, Jacob and Wilhelm Grimm, and Hans Christian Andersen. All others who recrafted these stories in other languages are only agents of transmission. Yet, other-language versions of tales by translators have marked reception history with their strategic adaptations. That is to say, some choices made by translators have impacted how a story comes down through history just as much as choices made by the few people in the tradition we regard as authors. Restoring the creative act of translation, particularly English translation for our purposes, to the fairy-tale traditions we study and teach also rings more true to the nature of the form and how it moves through time. Andrew Teverson presents the fairy tale generally as

> a many-tongued genre, a cultural palimpsest; because even as it speaks of the time in which it is told, it carries the memory of other times in which it has circulated and flourished . . . The fairy tale may, as a result, seem timeless, but seems timeless not because it has no history, but because it has too many histories, because it is plural and many-voiced. (Teverson 2013, 5)

Some of those voices speak in tongues other than the one in which a text was first written. Fairy tales are not only polysemic, but they are also polyglot.

My case study for the exploration of fairy-tale multilingualism is the most frequently translated story collection in French history: Charles Perrault's (1697a) *Histoires ou Contes du temps passé* (*Stories or Tales of Times Past*). Few fairy-tale plots in any tradition have had as vibrant or as varied a print life as "Cendrillon" (Cinderella), "Le Petit Chaperon rouge" (Little Red Riding Hood), and "La Belle au bois dormant" (Sleeping Beauty); yet, perhaps because of their ubiquity, few seem as universal and as untouched by cultural specificity. Perrault's "Belle au bois dormant," for example, has offered something of her character to dozens of English-speaking Sleeping Beauties; they, in turn, affect how Perrault's character is read today. Although they are ascribed to Perrault, each also inhabits a language that speaks with its own historically and culturally specific ideology.

In the pages that follow, I will outline three ways of exploiting the intellectual value of English-language translation in courses on the fairy tale: (1) translation in the L2 classroom, (2) translation and character study, and (3) translation as fairy-tale history. Each section uses a French tale to illustrate a methodology applicable to any national tradition. Section 1 uses "Cendrillon" to illustrate how translation can give foreign-language learners a fresh view of the target-language text. Section 2 takes up two translations of "Le Petit Chaperon rouge" in the English-language classroom to perform a character study. Finally, through "La Belle au bois dormant," section 3 offers a lesson in how translation has impacted fairy-tale history.

ONE: TRANSLATION IN THE L2 CLASSROOM

As a scholar of the seventeenth and eighteenth centuries, I often teach Perrault's tales in French. Students tend to be immediately surprised by the plots of the stories, which violate expectations they have acquired through experience with North American cultural lore about the heroines, such as the animated films produced over the twentieth century by Walt Disney Studios. In addition, early-modern French poses certain challenges, not the least of which is its use of tenses, such as the subjunctive of the *passé simple* (the French literary tense) with which early language learners have almost no experience. Precisely because students think they know the stories so well and also struggle with the language, they often gloss over plot detail and flatten the semantic fullness of words to get through the reading. That is, they can miss the most idiosyncratic elements of the text in their attempts to comprehend the arc of the story and to align it with a plot they know. I have found that translation can be a highly effective way of illuminating for them the ambiguity of French grammar, syntax, and language. A story whose grammar they might have described as impenetrable can in this way become part of an intellectual repertoire they claim as their own.

When I teach "Cendrillon," students prepare by reading the story in advance, and then we focus in class on the famous scene when the heroine acquires her accoutrements for the ball. I choose this scene as a way to enter for three reasons. First, it is iconic—few students have not heard of the pumpkin becoming a carriage. Second, it provides an excellent lesson in flora and fauna, as some of the words (e.g., gray dappled mares) will not be familiar to even advanced students. Third, the French text of 1697 presents one of the first instances of a fairy with a magic wand, which makes

Cendrillon one of the first beneficiaries of such enchantment. Here, we focus on power: who has it, who does not.

Using the vocabulary list of things that transform, we look at each character's relationship to them and notice that nearly all the sentences in the scene are written in command mode: fairy commands, Cendrillon fetches, and fairy transforms. The fairy dictates all the action; Cendrillon is reactive. French forms of address confirm this power relation, as the fairy addresses Cendrillon with the informal *tu*, marking her authority over her. Students readily find in this scene that the fairy is all powerful and the heroine helpless, which conforms to what they have been told or remember from Disney. Heroines need fairies to succeed. This presupposition allows us to go back into the scene with new questions. To facilitate revisiting the power dynamic in mid- to upper-level classes, it can be useful to help students see it in a fresh way through translation.

My translation of choice dates from 1729, the very first English version of Perrault's collection, done by Robert Samber in London. I have students read aloud for indicators of power in Samber's translation:

> Her godmother, who saw her all in tears, asked her what was the matter?
> I wish I could—, I wish I could—; she could not speak the rest, the tears
> interrupting her. Her godmother, who was a Fairy, said to her, Thou wish-
> est thou could go to the ball, is it not so? Y—es, said Cinderilla [*sic*], with
> a great Sob. Well, said her godmother, be but a good girl, and I'll contrive
> thou shalt go. (Perrault 1729a, 162)

Students note Cinderella's stuttering and can contrast it readily to the heaviness of *thou*, a word they associate with biblical language. In its day, Samber's choice of *thou* for *you*, indeed adds a certain gravitas to the scene and embodies the fairy's authority over the girl.[1] This part of the scene is very consistent with the French.

By the middle of the transformation scene, however, the form of address changes:

> As she [the fairy] was at a loss for a coach-man, I'll go and see, says
> Cinderilla, if there be never a rat in the rat-trap, we'll make a coach-man
> out of him. You are in the right, said the godmother, go and see. (163)

When we dissect the scene, students find that the change in form of address directly follows an unexpected suspension of action: the fairy finds herself "at a loss." Without missing a beat, which Samber marks by giving her voice in the same sentence, Cinderilla steps into the breach: "I'll go." Then, the fairy validates this idea with "You are in the right." This time, the fairy shrewdly chooses the familiar singular form of address, introducing balance to their initially imbalanced power dynamic and elevating Cinderilla to the level of strategist in her own get-to-the-ball plan. Samber's fairy marks the shift linguistically, which helps students think about the way the fairy has manipulated the heroine: perhaps not because Cinderilla is incapable, but because she is ignorant and needs to learn.

This pronoun event in the English foregrounds relations of power and opens a conversation about form of address in creating those relationships. No such pronoun swap occurs in the 1697 French; again, the fairy uses "tu" throughout. So, how does power work in the French scene? In Perrault's text the fairy is more subtle, tucking the transfer of power into the French grammar: "Tu as raison . . . va voir" (you are right . . . go check). Here, the only shift—a formerly subtle and now glaring one—is that Cendrillon occupies the subject position of a full sentence, first in "I'll go" and then in "You are right." Before she could only whine half sentences in her own voice and respond to commands issued by the fairy. This linguistic moment, which marks a learning experience engineered by the fairy, is paramount for Cendrillon's character. But without the pronoun shift visible in Samber, students miss Cendrillon's move from object pronoun to subject pronoun. They benefit greatly from a discussion of Samber's choice to highlight the shift in form of address to follow how the object-to-subject move empowers the heroine in French.

If students can see that making Cendrillon the subject of the sentence and confirming her intelligence with "you are right" performs the same function semantically as the blunt substitution of *you* for *thou*, they will have learned something valuable about close reading. Then, even in French, the simpering would-be ballgoer does not look so passive now. Cendrillon learns from the fairy how to wield language to her advantage, something that is hard to see at first in the French, which empowers her to become an active participant in her own fate. She will increasingly take matters into her own hands in the course of the story. In fact, students then read Cendrillon's interaction with her sisters and at the ball with a new sense of her cleverness. Learning to see character development in the more difficult French grammar by reading in English first serves the larger pedagogical purpose of teaching careful L2 reading skills.

TWO: TRANSLATION AND CHARACTER STUDY

When we compare English translations to the 1697 French text, we discover quickly that translations perform radical adaptations of language,

word order, and so forth. Choices need to be made at every turn. Some of
them seem small, whereas others can alter the scene, the identity of character, and even the moral of the story. This comparative technique can
be fruitful and can include judgments about translation both for French
speakers and students who don't speak it. What could initially be con-
strued as the disadvantage of an English-only classroom—they do not
have access to the story's first language—can open students instead to
translation as a creative act that is not good or bad, but always ideologically motivated. Hunting for that ideology becomes possible when translations are juxtaposed, or rather when their semantic environments are read
against each other to illuminate interpretative possibilities that each one
permits and precludes. An English-English comparison could be full text
to full text or could concern a snippet of crucial text, such as a passage
that sketches out a heroine's core identity. One passage that works well on
its own is the beginning of "Little Red Riding Hood," which introduces
the reader to the girl and to the kinship ties that form her character before
she meets the wolf in the forest.

I choose two translations—one early British by Robert Samber and one
late American by A. E. Johnson—that are easy to contrast. My choices for
this exercise were deliberately separated by time, geography, and tenor, but
the same effect could come from juxtaposing any two translations from any
period. Students would have read both versions in advance and paid special
attention to the way they ground the heroine semantically in different sociocultural environments. Our discussion would begin with the opening lines
of the story, which identify the heroine and her life-world:

> There was once upon a time a little country girl, born in a village, the
> prettiest little creature that ever was seen. Her mother was beyond reason
> excessively fond of her; and her grandmother yet much more. This good
> woman caused to be made for her a little red Riding-Hood; which made
> her look so very pretty that everybody called her the little red Riding-
> Hood. (Perrault 1729b, 122)
>
> Once upon a time there was a little village girl, the prettiest that had ever
> been seen. Her mother doted on her. Her grandmother was even fonder,
> and made her a little red hood, which became her so well that everywhere
> she went by the name of Little Red Riding Hood. (Perrault 1962, 4)

Documenting the contrast in vocabulary, beginning with country/vil-
lage, helps students immediately see the girl in multiple lights. A child born
in a village but raised in the country would likely be isolated. A girl who
remained in the village would be known by everyone who lived there, and

so on. Then the conversation can move deeper into the personalities of the women who raised her.

In 1729, the emphasis falls first on the girl's age, pastoral environment, and relative anonymity: she is a country girl from a village. Students can discuss the implications of isolation, namely, her extreme dependence on the women in her life. This variant further psychologizes the girl by passing judgment on her mother's parenting skills: she was excessively fond of her daughter to the point of loving her "beyond reason." Her grandmother's doting, "yet much more," then loses all sense of propriety. Both women apparently lack good judgment and self-control, which puts a particular spin on "caused to be made for her a little red Riding-Hood." Perhaps the grandmother spends beyond her means. Certainly, she chooses a color for the hood that appears, against a total absence of tonal description elsewhere in the tale, loud and too remarkable for a vulnerable young person. Finally, students can think about the language of immoderation —everywhere in the first few lines—and why a little country girl needs a blazing hood made for riding, which we never see her do. What kind of personality emerges here? Certainly not a simple, dull one. All in all, the heroine of the 1729 "Little Red Riding-Hood" had a questionable upbringing and developed a bit of a sensual allure. Little about her seems innocent; on the contrary, she may well be the village charmer.

Comparison with Johnson's 1962 translation can begin with how his choice of phrasing controls the girl's environment with clearer parameters. This control can then be followed deeper into the domestic scene: "Her mother doted on her. Her grandmother was even fonder, and made her a little red hood." Students can think and talk about the fact that here no language of excess inflects how the matriarchs rear the girl. Without the judgment, what is the relationship of the grandmother to the girl? What about between the grandmother and the mother? Another sharp contrast occurs in the verbs governing the cape: in Samber, grandmother has the riding-hood made. Here, the grandmother makes the little red hood. A number of cultural contrasts between England circa 1729 and America circa 1962 could be teased out of these passages regarding affection for children and even the color red, whose valence seems to change too in the different contexts.[2]

More could be said about the differences between these passages, and students could go far with how they set up contrasting reader expectations for the story. For our purposes, suffice it to say that comparing two translations illuminates how words make meaning and every choice affects the tenor of the story. Juxtaposing an excessive British eighteenth-century country girl and an impressionable American twentieth-century village girl opens the door to discussions about what each writer/translator and each age needed her to be and why. It is worth noting here that such a conversation can easily take place without recourse to the question, "Which one is more like the French?" In fact, opting not to pose that question creates space for a lesson in translation as a form of cultural production: translators do not simply render another text; they create a new text with historical consequences, to which I will now turn.

THREE: TRANSLATION AS FAIRY-TALE HISTORY

A survey of how French and English texts have interacted over time reveals that no less than subsequent first-language editions in later periods, translations impact how Perrault's 1697 collection moved through time and across cultures. André Lefevere has argued that "only recently have literary histories begun to acknowledge the part played by translation in the evolution of a literature" (Lefevere 1992, 124). The *Histoires ou contes du temps passé* presents an ideal case study in translation as a form of transmission and history making. In anticipation of this lesson, an advanced one possible in French or English, students would have read most of Perrault's collection and understood the wide variety of its styles and themes. The lesson can then ultimately be about how traditions in interpretation develop. To set that up, I first share with students a curious event in its early print history when the order of the stories was changed. There are eight stories in Perrault's collection, most of which circulated widely in French and English.

This is the order in which they first appeared in 1697 and the names by which they are now known in English:

"La Belle au bois dormant" (Sleeping Beauty)
"Le Petit chaperon rouge" (Little Red Riding Hood)
"La Barbe bleue" (Bluebeard)
"Le Maître chat, ou le Chat botté" (Puss in Boots)
"Les Fées" (The Fairies)
"Cendrillon, ou la petite pantoufle de verre" (Cinderella)
"Riquet à la houppe" (Ricky with the Tuft)
"Le Petit Poucet" (Little Thumbling)

In French editions until about 1720 readers opened the volume to "La Belle au bois dormant," the longest tale at approximately fifteen pages; "Le Petit chaperon rouge" fills about three. This is a complex narrative with at least two movements. Beauty's prick of the finger and famous slumber happen around the middle, and a new story begins when she wakes: she has a secret liaison with the prince for months, marries him in a private ceremony against his mother's will, relocates with the children to her mother-in-law's home, and lives a quiet domestic life.

The tale of the sleeping princess also takes a violent turn: the Ogress stepmother orders that her grandchildren and the princess, whom she never liked, be killed and cooked for dinner. She savors their flesh when she thinks they have been served to her dressed in a Sauce Robert, a staple of the French culinary arts in 1700 and still today. (In point of fact, the butler has instead killed and served small animals to her highness.) Owing to the tale's great length, however, the plot has time to resolve the many problems it sets up, notably the Ogress, who becomes the main course for a vat of vipers and snakes. Death becomes the fairy tale, and it continues for two more stories. In the tale that follows this family drama, a young hooded heroine and an old woman are eaten alive in under three pages. Next comes Perrault's bloody tale of a serial killer: "Barbe bleue." The first three tales of the collection all have the heroine cross paths with a murderer.

This is an ugly lineup that offers no reprieve or comic relief until story number 4: "Maître chat." Students are surprised by this characterization, and it is useful here to pause and discuss how they expect a fairy tale to look. Typical answers include: short, moralizing, about children, and so forth. "La Belle au bois dormant" meets none of those expectations. Neither does "Barbe bleue" or "Maître chat." But their stereotype has an antecedent, I then show them, in a publishing choice circa 1720. Around 1721, a major French publisher in Amsterdam, the family Desbordes, changed the order of the texts. The frequent reprinting of this edition during about a twenty-five-year period had repercussions for French- and English-language editions in Amsterdam, Paris, and London. The Desbordes edition placed "Petit Chaperon rouge" first, followed by "Les Fées."[3] These are the shortest tales in the corpus, and they balance each other out beautifully with dystopian and utopian endings: young girl dies from talking to a wolf versus young girl lives by talking to a fairy. "La Belle au bois dormant," the longest story, was moved in position 4, which sandwiched it in the middle of the volume between nasty "Barbe bleue" and uplifting "Maître chat."

Other than rare exceptions in the eighteenth century, the 1721 Amsterdam table of contents prevailed in French-language editions. In fact, it served as the model for London-based Robert Samber when he produced the first English translation in 1729. Rather than using the 1697 edition, he used the most recent one. His choice stuck: subsequent British editions followed his lead, thus standardizing this order for the century's Anglophone readership.[4] At this point, students would discuss possible consequences of this change: How did the volume look now? What could have happened if Samber had used the 1697 order and "Sleeping Beauty" had been adopted as the viral model for fairy-tale plots rather than "Little Red Riding Hood"? Finally, how would the definition of a fairy tale change if we took "Sleeping Beauty" as the model instead of "Little Red Riding Hood"?

Part of what comes from this brief and pithy illustration is that fairy tales are quite varied, but our stereotypes of them are quite restrictive, owing partially to choices in translation made long ago. While this insight might be an appropriate goal of the lesson in how choices stick, it can also frame a close textual reading that helps students see translation, again, as instrumental in characterization and current stereotypes. To transition back into close reading, I choose Samber's 1729 "The Sleeping Beauty in the Wood," specifically the scene when the princess wakes. Like the others I have chosen in this chapter, this tale is highly iconic for students. Before they took the class, they would have expected a prince to charge into the room and over to the princess and wake her, perhaps with a kiss. Having read the 1729 English in anticipation of the lesson, they would know that Perrault's prince has only to enter the room and the spell breaks: overcome with emotion, he falls to his knees before he reaches the bed. In contradistinction to the withering prince, the princess is warm with desire once the spell breaks of its own accord and does not need to be kissed. She has the only direct speech in the scene: "Is it you my Prince, she said to him, you have waited a great while" (Perrault 1729c, 114).

This scene undoubtedly breaks with student expectation and can open up a discussion of fairy-tale history. What kind of identity did the prince and princess have in 1729? How does that challenge stereotypes North Americans bring to this story? With appropriate prompts regarding the tone of the scene and the power dynamic, the conversation will almost certainly turn to the subtle reprimand that comes through Samber's "waited a great while." It suggests that the princess's sleep was not so inert after all, and she has become impatient holding out for her trembling prince to show up. Students can try their hands at new versions of the line to flesh out the identities Samber's text hints at: if the prince is weak and the princess is terribly impatient, how would she sound? If she moved, what might she do? If the gender dynamic I am suggesting here that puts the princess— ironically—into the driver's seat of the scene proves subtle for students, it is usually because it flouts expectations: how could a princess in her sleep be dominant in a scene with her savior-prince?

Working back this far into the story's history sets the stage for a discussion of where the prince students expected to see, the one now known as

"Charming," came from. While there are many answers to this question, following one thread of the character suffices to make the point. French editors put words in the silent prince's mouth in a 1799 edition creating an enduring character never before associated in print with Sleeping Beauty or Perrault.[5] After the princess wakes and reprimands the prince, and the prince and princess have talked for hours (a dialog we do not see in any edition), the prince launches into a brand-new monologue. This speech entered the Anglophone market shortly thereafter, when the influential Benjamin Tabart, of Tabart and Company, London, published a version of the monologue in 1804. Tabart's celebrity for transforming older tales into children's literature helped create a robust niche market for fairy tales in English, and his choices impacted the subsequent appeal of the genre.

Significantly, students will not be unfamiliar with this style of prince, whom, for the sake of discussion, we will call Prince Charming:

> "What happiness, beautiful princess!" said the prince, looking at her with the greatest tenderness imaginable, "what happiness to be able to do you such a service, to see you smile so sweetly, and to be thus rewarded by your love! To think that the most powerful princess upon the earth could not have performed what I have done, in breaking the cruel enchantment that condemned you to sleep so long!" (Perrault 1804, 30)

Reading this monologue out loud and respecting its punctuation help make the point that this prince claims domination not only over the scene but over the princess. After two or three students read the monologue (dramatic abilities invariably improve with every reading as students feel safer and funnier in their delivery), the class would catalog the superlatives in this scene that gather about the prince and grant him a new identity. What powers does he have now that Samber did not give him? How does the language of the monologue create his role in this narrative? What does it do to the dynamic between the prince and princess or to the story as a whole to highlight the theme of conquest rather than delayed relief (as Samber did)?

As a final step in this lesson, one that would animate the discussion for a grand finale, I might have recourse to the scene in Walt Disney's *Sleeping Beauty* (1959), which could easily be shown in class. Interpreting this scene in terms of Samber's and then Tabart's prince would yield new insight into the all-powerful and all-important gesture that twenty-first-century Americans associate with Sleeping Beauty: the kiss. What comes out of this discussion is that fairy tales are not written, ossified, and then transported intact through time. They are made in layers with every subsequent version, especially those in English, adding nuance to what came before. Some of that nuance has had remarkable tenacity such that translation no longer looks like an addendum, but rather an integral part of how the meanings have gravitated around characters through the course of history.

Viewed as a maker of history, not simply of themes and characters but also of influential interpretations, translation studies can be a source of untapped pedagogical material for French- and English-language classrooms. Instead of worrying about how "good" or "bad" a translation looks against the first-language text, we can instead ask, How is this variation on the theme significant? What does the hero/heroine sound and look like? How might that depiction be related to its sociocultural home at the particular juncture of history in which it appears? By historicizing translations and acknowledging that they can also influence the reception/interpretation of the tale in its first language, we help contravene the presupposition among students that fairy tales are universal, that heroines always look the same, and that the older translations are, the simpler they are likely to sound. Sleeping Beauty exists no more concretely in history than Eldorado, but multiple sleeping beauties do, many of them English speaking, and scholarship has "waited a great while" to enter their rooms and admire them as subjects of pedagogical interest.

NOTES

1. Samuel Johnson's (2013) *Dictionary of the English Language* describes *thou* as "very familiar or very solemn language. When we speak to equals or superiors we say *you*; but in solemn language, and in addresses of worship, we say *thou*" (Johnson 2013, 2050).

2. For various reflections on the significance of the color, see Sandra Beckett (2008, 44–47).

3. Jaques Desbordes published editions of Perrault's *Histoires* in Amsterdam in 1697, 1700, 1708, and 1714, all marked "after the copy from Paris" (Perrault 1697b). After his death, his widow, "La Veuve Desbordes," took over the press and published a new edition under her name in 1721. While it also reads "after the copy from Paris," it was the La Veuve's 1721 edition that inaugurated the change in the order of the tales.

4. On this point, it is interesting to note that Maria Tatar (1999) includes neither Perrault's "Sleeping Beauty" nor its variants in her *Classic Fairy Tales*.

5. In point of fact, this chatty prince was not a late eighteenth-century invention. Two earlier versions of Perrault's (1799) "Belle au bois dormant" include the prince's swashbuckling speech, which was removed for the final 1697 printing. A 1695 illuminated manuscript of the collection contains it, and that version was printed in a 1696 issue of Paris's literary magazine, the *Mercure galant*. It appears that 1790s editors rediscovered and decided to reinsert the speech.

REFERENCES

Beckett, Sandra L. 2008. *Red Riding Hood for All Ages: A Fairy-Tale Icon in Cross-Cultural Context.* Detroit: Wayne State University Press.

Johnson, Samuel. 2013. "Thou." In *A Dictionary of the English Language: A Digital Edition of the 1755 Classic by Samuel Johnson*, ed. Brandi Besalke. Last modified December 5, 2013. http://johnsonsdictionaryonline.com/?p=12474.

Lathey, Gilian. 2010. *The Role of Translators in Children's Literature: Invisible Storytellers.* London: Taylor & Francis.

Lefevere, André. 1992. *Translating Literature: Practice and Theory in a Comparative Literary Context.* New York: Modern Language Association of America.

Perrault, Charles. 1697a. *Histoires ou Contes du temps passé.* Paris: Claude Bardin.

Perrault, Charles. 1697b. *Histoires ou Contes du tems [sic] passé. Avec des Moralitez. Par le fils de Monsieur Perrault. Suivant la copie, à Paris.* Amsterdam: Jaques Desbordes.

Perrault, Charles. 1729a. "Cinderella: or, The Little Glass Slipper." In *Histories or Tales of Past Times*, trans. Robert Samber. London: J. Pote and R. Montagu. Repr. in *The Classic Fairy Tales* [1974] 1980, ed. Iona and Peter Opie, 161–66. Oxford: Oxford University Press.

Perrault, Charles. 1729b. "The Little Red Riding-Hood." In *Histories or Tales of Past Times*, trans. Robert Samber. London: J. Pote and R. Montagu. Repr. in *The Classic Fairy Tales* [1974] 1980, ed. Iona and Peter Opie, 122–25. Oxford: Oxford University Press.

Perrault, Charles. 1729c. "Sleeping Beauty in the Wood." In *Histories or Tales of Past Times*, trans. Robert Samber. London: J. Pote and R. Montagu. Repr. in *The Classic Fairy Tales* [1974] 1980, ed. Iona and Peter Opie, 108–18. Oxford: Oxford University Press.

Perrault, Charles. An huitième. 1799. "La Belle au bois dormant." In *Contes des fées…par Charles Perrault, de l'Académie Française*, 31–55. Paris: Chez André.

Perrault, Charles. 1804. *The Sleeping Beauty in the Wood . . . A New Edition.* London: Tabart.

Perrault, Charles. 1962. "Little Red Riding Hood." In *Perrault's Complete Fairy Tales*, trans. A. E. Johnson. Harmonsworth, UK: Kestrel Books. Repr. in *Little Red Riding Hood: A Casebook* 1989, ed. Alan Dundes, 4–6. Madison: University of Wisconsin Press.

Sleeping Beauty. 1959. Directed by Clyde Geronimi. Burbank, CA: Walt Disney Productions.

Tatar, Maria. 1999. *Classic Fairy Tales.* New York: W.W. Norton.

Teverson, Andrew. 2013. *Fairy Tales. The New Critical Idiom Series.* New York: Routledge.

Voltaire. 2005. *Candide, or Optimism.* Trans. Burton Raffel. New Haven: Yale University Press.

9

Giambattista Basile's *The Tale of Tales* in the Hands of the Brothers Grimm

Armando Maggi

Rewriting is a fundamental aspect of the Western tradition of literary fairy tales. A literary fairy tale is a text composed by a writer in a particular cultural context. These tales are "literary" because they result from a specific author's poetics. Composing fairy tales in the twentieth and twenty-first centuries often means appropriating and retelling a handful of tales that have acquired the status of classics. Alert readers of this literary genre must be able to appreciate and dissect a given tale in the light of its models. The phenomenon of rewriting becomes particularly meaningful when it pertains to key texts of this tradition: Giambattista Basile's *The Tale of Tales* (published posthumously in 1634–36) and the Brothers Grimm's *Kinder- und Hausmärchen* (*Children's and Household Tales*; Grimm and Grimm 1822). Both collections are problematic examples of the interaction between oral transmission of folktales and literary creations. On the one hand, although Basile heavily relies on the oral tradition of Southern Italian folktales, his seminal collection is essentially literary. On the other, the Brothers Grimm, especially Wilhelm, deeply manipulated the oral tales they had collected to the point of turning them into literary products. Like Basile's (2007) *The Tale of Tales*, the Grimms' famous collection responds to its contemporary cultural environment, and thus its tales are not merely transcriptions of oral stories.

The title of my class is "Baroque Fairy Tales and Their Modern Rewritings." The course is taught in English and it is meant for an undergraduate audience. The main goal of this class is to teach the students how to approach folktales and fairy tales as artistic products that need to be examined with the same respect and critical attention we usually grant

DOI: 10.7330/9781607324812.c009

literary texts of national canons. Classes on folktales and fairy tales often use these texts as tools to investigate the cultural milieu in which they were either collected or created. In other words, we frequently focus on single motifs or themes in certain fairy tales to study, for example, the role of women or social tensions in Western society, but we fail to appreciate these tales, especially the oral ones, as artistic artifacts. My class places great emphasis on the complex interaction between oral and written texts through detailed close readings of selected fairy tales, starting with Basile's (2007) *The Tale of Tales*. Having in mind a ten-week course in a quarter system, I dedicate the first session to the crucial concept of "motif." I want my students to understand that folktales and fairy tales are inventive and dynamic conglomerations of motifs that travel through space and time, and I want them to appreciate the vitality of this genre as a form of storytelling that constantly re-creates itself. To make this point clearer, I bring to class Isha Lerner's (2002) *The Inner Child Cards: A Fairy-Tale Tarot*, which is a deck of tarot cards based on single fairy-tale motifs or characters. I invite a few students to pick a limited number of cards (according to the instructions that accompany the deck) and to "read their future" according to the "new" fairy tale that results from their selection. We dedicate the subsequent three sessions to an understanding of the structure of Basile's *The Tale of Tales* and to the analysis of his versions of major tales such as "Cinderella," "Sleeping Beauty," "Puss in Boots," and "Hansel and Gretel." For each of the three sessions, I assign five or six tales (including the frame tale) and have students choose a tale that they will be asked to analyze in class. I ask the students to identify the inner connections, the secret narrative echoes that sustain the tale in order to reveal its less obvious significance. In class I will choose a tale and will ask a few students to read their interpretations of the same tale. The students' active participation in class is essential. I tend to limit my lectures to introductory remarks and let the major concepts of a given session arise from the discussions. An essential goal of this class is to trigger the students' curiosity and ability to perform subtle close readings. My class is founded on close readings, but I also ask the students to become familiar with the secondary literature that will help them in this kind of approach. These are some of the readings for the first sessions of my class: Walter Benjamin's (1968) famous essay "The Storyteller"; chapters from Max Lüthi's (1984) *The Fairy Tale as Art Form*; and Neil Philip's (2003), "Creativity and Tradition in the Fairy Tale."

Basile's *The Tale of Tales* (*Lo cunto de li cunti* or *Pentamerone*) is the first collection of European fairy tales. Among the fifty tales of this seminal book, we find the first version of several classical tales such as "Cinderella" and

"Sleeping Beauty." Written in the seventeenth-century Neapolitan dialect, Basile's book was supposed to be "performed" during social gatherings at the local courts. *The Tale of Tales* has baffled generations of critics because of its paradoxical nature. It is a written text that however reads like the transcription of an oral one because it is composed in the contemporary Neapolitan dialect, which was primarily an oral idiom.

Did *The Tale of Tales* exert any influence on other subsequent European writers of fairy tales? The fact that it was written in the Neapolitan dialect did not work in its favor, because it made its transmission and understanding problematic (In recent years, however, more than one scholar has investigated the possible connections between the Italian book and the more famous French narrators of the late seventeenth century, including Charles Perrault.) A century later, however, important representatives of German Romanticism—such as Christoph Christian Wieland, Clemens Brentano, the Brothers Grimm, and Ludwig Tieck—openly recognized Basile's essential influence on their work. In an important essay, Suzanne Magnanini (2007) proves the existence of "a network of clients and correspondents reaching from Naples to Paris of one printer of *Lo cunto de li cunti*" and demonstrates that there was "no real impediment to the dissemination of Basile's fairy tales in France" (Magnanini 2007, 79). Magnanini explains that "Antonio Bulifon, a French expatriate working in Naples, utilized a number of marketing strategies to move far beyond the borders of his adopted homeland all of the books he printed, including dialect works such as *Lo cunto de li cunti*" (Magnanini 2007, 89).

The Brothers Grimm thought very highly of *The Tale of Tales*, which they saw as "the best and the richest" collection of folktales ever written in any European literature (Grimm and Grimm 1822, 277).[1] Moreover, they contended that the Italian book was almost "without inauthentic additions" (Tatar 2003, 258). This was also how the two German scholars wished their readers to perceive their collection. The Grimms insisted on the natural and spontaneous character of their *Children's and Household Tales*, as if their book had composed itself without their authorial intervention. It is thus evident that *The Tale of Tales* and *Children's and Household Tales* share some important traits, despite their significant cultural differences. Both books lie at the intersection between oral transmission and literary manipulation. A clear-cut distinction between the "literary" *Tale of Tales* and the "oral" *Children's and Household Tales* is in reality false and misleading.

In 1822 the Brothers Grimm published their "German adaptations" of all the stories included in Basile's *The Tale of Tales* as an appendix to the second edition of their *Children's and Household Tales* (1819). Jacob first wrote

thirty-eight of these adaptations. Wilhelm later edited his brother's summaries and worked on the remaining twelve Neapolitan tales (Rölleke 2004,
14). The Grimms removed their interpretations of the Italian tales from
all subsequent editions of their book because in 1846 the folklorist Felix
Liebrecht (1812–90) published the first complete German translation of
The Tale of Tales. The Grimms' adaptations of Basile's fifty tales had a fundamental goal. The two German scholars wished to prove that Basile, the
first and most important collector of folktales in their opinion, shared their
view on the essentially oral origin of folktales and fairy tales. The Grimms
acknowledged that significant cultural differences existed between seventeenth-century Southern Italian culture and nineteenth-century German
sensibility. First of all, Basile's tales at times used vulgar and sexual images
that were unsuitable for a German audience. More important, unlike the
Grimms, Basile did not believe in an intrinsically positive and benign providence that rules over the world. Typical of a baroque sensibility, Basile's
tales often depict a bleak and desperate reality devoid of all moral concern.
In the Grimms' view, however, this objective cultural distance could not
affect the overall meaning and structure of the fairy tale in general, because
in their opinion this artistic genre had a universal form. The Grimms' fifty
summaries, which take up a hundred pages, primarily tried to prove that
Basile's stories (their structure, their motifs, and their message) somehow
resembled their own German tales. Their synopses read like first rough
drafts and lack a stylistic consistency (some are just telegraphic plot summaries; others are extensive transcriptions; a few are unclear and rushed
abstracts). Although they intended to be as faithful as possible to the original Italian texts, the Grimms could not help but modify, to a various degree,
Basile's tales in order to bring them closer to their sensibility.

After the three sessions dedicated to a basic understanding of Basile's
book, we read some secondary literature on the making of the Brothers
Grimm's collection. For example, we study selections from Maria Tatar's
(2003) *The Hard Facts of the Grimms' Fairy Tales*. Then, we spend two sessions on the Grimms' rewritings of some classical tales already present in
Basile's book, such as "Cinderella" and "Puss in Boots." We spend an entire
class on the Grimms' reshaping of "Sleeping Beauty," through a comparison between Basile's, and Perrault's, and the Grimms' interpretation. It is
important to bear in mind, however, that the emphasis lies on the Basile-
Grimm dialog. To deepen our understanding of the Grimms' approach to
Basile, we read at least one of their adaptations of the Italian tales. For this
brief essay, I select "The Three Crowns" (Le tre corone), one of the most
compelling tales of the Italian collection. This tale presents a number of

thought-provoking themes, which usually trigger an intense discussion in class. This is my abridged version of Basile's "The Three Crowns":

THE THREE CROWNS

Once upon a time the king of Shaken Valley (valle scossa),[2] who could not have children, wherever and whenever said: "Oh heavens, send me an heir to my state, so that my house won't remain desolate!" (Basile 2007, 337). Once, while in a garden, he pronounced these words out loud and then heard a voice coming out of the bushes: "King, would you rather have a daughter who runs away from you or a son who destroys you?" After consulting with the wise men of his court, the king decides that, even though honor does not usually reside among women, a daughter would not be a danger for his life and his kingdom. That night, after having answered "woman, woman" (*femmena femmena*) to the voice in the bushes, the king slept with his wife and after nine months he had a little girl and locked her up in a sturdy palace in the attempt of avoiding his daughter's sad fate (Basile 1998, 755).[3] The king even arranged a marriage with the king of Lost Mind (*perditesta*), but when the princess came out of that palace to go to her fiancé, a strong wind arose and lifted her up, and no one saw her again. The air took her to the house of an ogress who lived in a dark forest. There the princess found an elderly lady, whom the ogress had left to guard her belongings. The lady at first warned the girl about the murderous ogress who only ate human flesh and then gave her the key to the house. The old lady suggested that the princess should clean the ogress's house very carefully and then hide. At this point, when the girl/princess takes the key and walks into the ogress's house, we learn that the girl's/princess's name is Marchetta. When the ogress came back and wanted to know who had cleaned the house so meticulously, the old lady told her that she had done it. But the ogress sensed that the old lady was lying. The ogress left again, and this time the old lady told Marchetta that when the ogress came back, she could reveal herself only if the ogress swore by her three crowns that she would not hurt the person who had worked so hard for her. Marchetta killed a duckling and made a good stew for the ogress. While she was eating that succulent meal, the ogress again asked who had been so kind to her. She said that she would give this person "the pupils of my eyes" and she would "keep him in my heart" (Basile 2007, 339). Finally, she gave in and said that if she knew who the nice housewife was, she swore by her three crowns that she would give her lots of caresses and broccoli. When Marchetta showed up, the grateful ogress promised her that she would treat her better than a daughter. She gave the girl the keys to the rooms but asked her not to open the last room, because that would make her furious. Finally the ogress assured Marchetta that she would give her a wealthy marriage. But when the ogress left, the girl could not resist her

curiosity and opened that forbidden door. She found three girls dressed
up in gold and sitting on three royal chairs. These girls seemed asleep.
They were the daughters of "the fairy" who had enchanted them because
they would run a great risk unless a princess came to wake them. Basile
does not specify who this mysterious fairy is. The fairy tried to protect her
daughters from their dangerous fate. Marchetta walked into the room and
her footsteps woke them up. The girls asked her for food, and Marchetta
cooked three eggs for them. After the meal, the three girls wanted to get
some fresh air. At that point the ogress came back and got so angry at
Marchetta that she slapped her in the face. Marchetta was so offended that
she asked the ogress to let her leave. Although the ogress tried to make
her change her mind by telling her that she was only joking, Marchetta
insisted on leaving. The ogress then gave her two gifts: first, a ring that
the girl should wear with the stone inside of her hand. She was supposed
to look at it only when in a moment of great danger she heard her name
repeated by the echo. The second gift was a male suit. Marchetta herself
had asked for it. Dressed as a man, Marchetta took off and soon entered a
forest, where she met a king who was hunting. The king was so impressed
with the good manners of this youth that he took him as his page. As soon
as she saw "him," the queen, his wife, fell in love with the page. Since the
page did not respond to her advances, the queen told her husband that
the page had tried to seduce her. The king had "him" arrested and con-
demned to capital punishment. After being dragged to the place of her
execution without knowing the reason, Marchetta cried out: "Oh Heavens,
what did I do to deserve the funeral of this poor neck before the burial
of this wretched body? . . . Oh poor me, and who is going to console me
in this last step? Who will free me from the gallows (*forca*)?" (Basile 1998,
767–69; Basile 2007, 342–43). "Orca" (ogress) the echo responded, and
Marchetta, remembering the ring she had received from the ogress, looked
at the stone for the first time. A voice was heard in the air three times:
"Let her go, she is a woman!" The king demanded that she tell the truth.
Forced by the circumstances, Marchetta recounted her entire life. The king
remembered a conversation he had had with the king of Shaken Valley,
Marchetta's father, compared it with what Marchetta was saying, and con-
cluded that she was being honest and that his wife had lied to him. He had
his wife thrown into the sea tied to a milling machine. The story ends with
a saying. Marchetta proved that "God finds a haven for a desperate ship."

My detailed summary, albeit faithful to the plot, cannot reproduce
Basile's baroque and deeply ironic style made of innumerable inventive metaphors and flourished descriptions. Basile's unique style, an essential part of
his storytelling, can only be appreciated by reading the complete text, which
is available in Nancy Canepa's excellent English translation (Basile 2007).
Before moving on to the Grimms' appropriation of "Three Crowns," we

discuss in class some fundamental themes and motifs present in this Italian tale, such the topic of curiosity, which finds in "Bluebeard" its most famous example, and the issue of cross-dressing, which plays such a central role in Basile's story. We emphasize that the princess needed to "become a man" in order to survive during her solitary journey away from the ogress's protective house. We also stress, however, that at the end of the tale the princess is saved thanks to her female identity and not to her male cross-dressing. The mysterious voice declares that the princess is innocent because in reality she is a woman and not a man. Being a woman, declaring her true identity is what saves the princess from the gallows. The king demands that the princess tell the truth, and her "truth" is that she is a woman. Basile's book abounds with clever and brave young female characters, who make use of all possible tricks (including passing themselves off as men) in order to survive and thrive in a hostile and bleak environment.

After a close reading of "The Three Crowns," we examine how the Grimms interpreted this tale. The Grimms' adaptations of Basile's stories focus on the plots but opt for a plain, unadorned syntax, which is closer to their own style. After reading the Grimms' synopsis of Basile's "Three Crowns," we shall see that the deletion of a few words at the beginning of the Neapolitan tale produces a chain reaction that affects the entire tale. This is my translation of the Grimms' summary (Grimm and Grimm 1822, 342–44):

THE THREE CROWNS

A king wishes for children and when once he expresses this wish aloud in a garden, a voice exclaims from a bush: "King, what do you want, a daughter or a son?" The king debates this matter with his counselors and finally chooses a daughter and replies his answer to the bush. After nine months his spouse brings a daughter into the world. She is locked up in a strong castle and carefully watched. When she has grown up, she is promised to a king. She must be taken to her spouse, and for this reason she leaves her residence for the first time. As soon as she steps out, the wind grabs her and takes her to a wood and drops her in front of the house of an ogress. There she finds an old woman who tells her: "Oh, unlucky you, it is over for you, when the ogress comes home and sees you! One thing I know, go inside the house and clean and tidy everything up, and then hide." When she comes home, the ogress rejoices at the unusual, beautiful order and tidiness, calls the old woman, and expresses her great admiration for everything. She goes away again, and the old woman says to Marchetta (this is the name of the king's daughter): "Now prepare something good,

but you can trust her only when she swears by the three crowns that she is
not going to do anything to you, only then can you let yourself be seen."
Marchetta kills a goose and prepares an excellent dish. The ogress comes
and asks: "Who cooked this?" "I did," says the old woman, "and don't
think too much of it." She eats and finds it so delicious that she swears by
many things that she will look with great favor on the person who cooked
it. Marchetta hears this from her hiding place but does not move. Finally
she exclaims: "I swear by my three crowns that out of love I will do anything for him." Then Marchetta jumps out and shows herself. The ogress
stays true to her word: "I will treat you like my daughter. I turn over to you
the keys to every room. You may open all of them, except the last one.
If you serve me well, I promise you by my three crowns that I will take
care of you generously." But as the ogress leaves, Marchetta is so tortured
by curiosity, that she opens the forbidden room. Three girls, all dressed
in gold, sit on three chairs and look asleep. Their mother had enchanted
them, because a great misfortune awaited them, unless a king's daughter
arrived and awoke them. Because of the noise she makes with her feet
when she walks in, they wake up and want something to eat. Marchetta
cooks three eggs apiece in some ashes. They step out of the door to catch
some fresh air, right when the ogress comes home and becomes so angry
with Marchetta that she slaps her. Marchetta takes offense and terminates
her service for the ogress and wishes to go into the vast world. She insists
on her decision, even though the ogress tells her so many kind words.
When she leaves, the ogress gives Marchetta a ring that she must wear
with the stone inside of her hand without paying attention to it, until in
a moment of great danger she hears the echo call her, the ogress's, name
(Orca). The ogress also gives her male clothes. In this outfit, Marchetta
meets a king who is hunting. Taking her for a beautiful lad, he hires her
as his page. The queen, however, falls madly in love with him and makes
advances to him.[4] Marchetta keeps her distance and, out of revenge, is
accused of making inappropriate advances to the queen. On her way to
death, she cries out: "Who will save me from the gallows?" The echo then
calls the ogress ("chi mme libera de sta forca?" "Orca").[5] Then Marchetta
remembers the ring and looks at the stone, and at once a mighty voice
resounds three times in the air: "Let her go, she is a girl!" The king has the
deceitful queen thrown into the sea, and Marchetta becomes his spouse.

For the Brothers Grimm, to summarize Basile's tales also means to make
them more coherent. This editing process mirrors the same cleansing to
which Wilhelm also submits the German tales, some of which undergo more
than one rewriting. This procedure is not to be seen as a form of falsification
or manipulation, but rather of clarification and purification, including the
elimination of sexual references and vulgar words. The rationale of Wilhelm's
editing is that behind each of Basile's "rough drafts" lies an original and pure

narrative form that waits to be retrieved, not re-created. As the Grimms state in the introduction to their summaries, Basile's ironic style responds to his "witty" and "facetious" Italian audience, and, judging by the tone of their German collection, irony and wit do not seem, in their view, to be a universal device of fairy-tale storytelling (Grimm and Grimm 1822, 278).

A fundamental "problem" of the Neapolitan tale is that it describes an active and resourceful young woman who faces and overcomes a number of obstacles. She even wakes up three princesses (and not only one) from the spell cast by their mother, even though we are not told who their mother ("the fairy") is. Instead of a handsome prince, a ballsy young woman rescues them. She dresses as a man and as a man faithfully serves a king. The Neapolitan girl does not need any providential prince; her character and determination guide her. When the ogress slaps her on the face, the girl is so offended that then and there she decides to leave. Basile's portrayal of the young Marchetta clashes with the Grimms' frequent depiction of a typical female character, who is usually successful insofar as she is pious and passive vis-à-vis the challenges of the world. A very rare exception is Gretel in the famous German tale.

Let us take a closer look at the Grimms' adaptation of "The Three Crowns." A problematic aspect of this tale is the mysterious voice at the beginning of the tale, which is not given an identity. Basile does not say who this voice is. Modern scholars of fairy tales are often uncomfortable with such gaps in Basile's narrations and strive to find a plausible solution at all costs (who is speaking? God? A fairy?). The Grimms are much more subtle in their interpretation of Basile's tale. By simply removing the two clauses from the mysterious voice's puzzling question to the king ("a daughter who runs away from you or a son who destroys you?"), the Grimms create a completely new disembodied character. Like Basile, the Grimms do not give an identity to this mysterious voice but instead of a defiant and enigmatic speaker in the German adaptation we encounter a subservient voice that simply asks the king to specify the gender of his desired successor, just to make sure the monarch's wish is fully satisfied. The voice in *The Tale of Tales* being an ominous oracle that forces the king to face an impossible riddle, the Neapolitan tale unfolds as the surprising fulfillment of that initial prophecy. What the German retelling omits is an essential point: in Basile, the heroine's destiny was determined before the beginning of the tale. In the Neapolitan version, the voice reveals that the tale will be coherent and meaningful, but in an obscure way.

The new national identity of the bodiless voice (from its almost mocking and all-powerful Neapolitan idiom to its curt and direct German counterpart) implies a new vision of what fate means. In the German retelling, the voice could be a reserved fairy hiding in the bushes. Unlike the fairies in *The Tale of Tales*, who often deride human beings and their suffering, the fairies in *Children's and Household Tales* tend to be agents of that benign fate that chastises evil and rewards good. A writer living in seventeenth-century Naples under the Spanish barbaric occupation could not share such a view, as *The Tale of Tales* shows in many tales. For Basile, even the belief in something like fate is questionable and even amusing, because in his view what we call fate is a series of brutal and unpredictable events.

The intrinsic goodness of creation is what guides the tales in *Children's and Household Tales*. The development of a hero's or a heroine's destiny seems linear and unpremeditated because, in the fairy tales according to the German authors, things cannot help but follow a natural and just order, the same order that regulates the birth and death of all beings. Editing out the two strange clauses from the mysterious voice's speech to the king, the Grimms move the Neapolitan tale closer to their narrative model. No unclear mystery lurks behind the beginning of the tale. In the German rewriting, the mysterious voice becomes the spokesperson of that benign providence that wishes to fulfill the king's justified desire. The new version of the story is about a princess who goes on a journey, overcomes some challenges thanks to her industrious and moral character, and finally is rewarded with a wealthy marriage.

When the Grimms delete the allusion to the ominous fate awaiting the princess, her imprisonment acquires a new meaning. This time, the king locks her up because this overprotective father wants to preserve his daughter for marriage, not because she may run away when he least expects it. And, in any case, the princess does not run away. This is another good reason for the Grimms to delete that "wrong" allusion from the voice's statement in the garden.

Marriage becomes the new leitmotif of "The Three Crowns." And, again, it makes sense, given that this is a tale about a princess on a quest for something, which can only turn out to be her marriage to a good king or prince, according to the ideology of the Brothers Grimm. The lengthy debate between the king and his wise men about the two possible options (a son who will destroy him or a daughter who will run away from him) becomes less important in the economy of the tale. The ministers' insistence on women's natural lack of honor, on their dishonesty, is of no narrative relevance, because in this German version the tale does not work as a wonderful contradiction of these noble men's misogynistic assumptions. Also, the role of the wind is now clearer. The wind comes down and takes the girl away because, in the fairy tales according to the Grimms, natural elements and animals collaborate with destiny. This gust of wind does not need an identity. It is not the messenger of a secret lover, as we find in Apuleius's tale of "Cupid and Psyche." In book 4 of Apuleius's *Metamorphoses* (the date of composition is uncertain), "the softly-blowing Zephyr" lifts up Psyche and leads her to Cupid's marvelous palace (Apuleius 1996, 251).

The wind leads Marchetta to the ogress's house because in that dark abode the girl will be able to show her "female skills" and positive nature. She cleans the house, cooks a nice meal, breaks a mysterious spell, and then leaves for her grand finale in her future husband's castle (Grimm and Grimm 1822, 343). The ogress makes no allusion to the wonderful marriage she may arrange for the good of Marchetta. She is willing to "take great care of" the girl, the Grimms have the ogress say, but no ogress is supposed to find a suitable spouse for a princess. In the Grimms' view, these cannibals can be nice and benign, but they still live outside the social norms of human society.

In the Grimms' adaptation, the good ogress gives Marchetta some male clothes, whereas in Basile the girl asks for them. The heroines of fairy tales à la Grimm are given magical gifts, because someone else knows better what these girls need. Nature (the wind) helps a good young woman; magical figures give her special gifts that will save her in future dangerous encounters. Things happen to her; she does not make them happen. The voice crying out, "She is a woman!" before Marchetta's execution sanctions her female identity according to the social standards this new Marchetta has shown to master perfectly (she knows how to cook and to keep a house clean). In Basile, the king demands the girl to tell "the truth," and we realize that her truth is her sexual gender. The truth that saves her is that she is a woman.[6] In the German version, as soon as the voice reveals that Marchetta is a woman, the manipulative queen is killed and Marchetta marries the king. For the king, to hear that his handsome page is in reality a lady is sufficient to determine the truth and have his wife executed. The king replaces a dishonest woman with a virtuous one. The monarch becomes the supreme agent of that natural order of things that demands that goodness eventually defeats all evil. At this point, it is easy for my students to understand that the removal of seemingly minor details has a significant impact on the overall meaning of the tale. One major point of contention between the baroque Basile and the Romantic Grimms becomes the role and meaning of womanhood. Whereas for the Grimms, a meek and often passive woman is a pillar of their conception of magic (the comatose young lady awaiting a prince's kiss) but also of their ideal society essentially ruled by male "natural" supremacy, Basile posits the image of an aggressive and feisty young lady as the cornerstone of his storytelling. Basile's "magic" does not rely on women's passivity.

This brief analysis of the Grimms' rewriting of Basile's "The Three Crowns" has shown how important minor details can be for the overall understanding of a tale. We have also seen how the deletion of two clauses from the mysterious voice at the beginning of the tale affects the rest of the narrative in its entirety. The new tale responds to a new ideology and a new vision of human destiny, human agency, and first of all female identity.

NOTES

1. Unless otherwise noted, all translations are mine.
2. Basile often gives peculiar and strange names to locations and characters.
3. The Italian words come from Michele Rak's Italian edition (Basile 1998), which has both the Neapolitan text and its Italian rendition. Canepa's translation is the most recent and most accurate English version (Basile 2007).
4. At this point, the German text uses the male pronoun for the princess.
5. These Neapolitan words in parentheses are in the German summary.
6. The term *woman* does not mean that the girl has lost her virginity.

REFERENCES

Apuleius. 1996. *Translated by J. Arthur Hanson.* Vol. 1: *Metamorphoses.* Cambridge: Harvard University Press.
Basile, Giambattista. 1998. *Lo cunto de li cunti.* Ed. Michele Rak. Milan: Garzanti.
Basile, Giambattista. 2007. *The Tale of Tales.* Trans. Nancy Canepa. Detroit: Wayne State University Press.
Benjamin, Walter. 1968. "The Storyteller." In *Illuminations*, ed. Hannah Arendt, trans. Harry Zohn, 83–109. New York: Schocken Books.
Grimm, Jacob, and Wilhelm Grimm. 1822. *Kinder- und Hausmärchen. Gesammelt durch die Brüder Grimm. Dritter Band.* Berlin: Reimer.
Lerner, Isha. 2002. *Inner Child Cards Workbook: Further Exercises and Mystical Teachings from the Fairy-Tale Tarot.* Rochester, VT: Inner Traditions / Bear & Company.
Lüthi, Max. [1975] 1984. *The Fairytale as Art Form and Portrait of Man.* Translated by Jon Erickson. Bloomington: Indiana University Press.
Magnanini, Suzanne. 2007. "Postulated Routes from Naples to Paris: The Printer Antonio Bulifon and Giambattista Basiles' Fairy Tales in Seventeenth-Century France." *Marvels and Tales* 21 (1): 78–92.
Philip, Neil. 2003. "Creativity and Tradition in the Fairy Tale." In *A Companion to the Fairy Tale*, ed. Hilda Ellis Davidson and Anna Chaudhri, 39–55. Cambridge, UK: Brewer.
Rölleke, Heinz. 2004. *Die Märchen der Brüder Grimm. Eine Einführung.* Stuttgart: Reclam.
Tatar, Maria. 2003. *The Hard Facts of the Grimms' Fairy Tales.* 2nd ed. Princeton: Princeton University Press.

10

Teaching Hans Christian Andersen's Tales
A Linguistic Approach

Cyrille François

As ONE OF THE MOST FAMOUS FAIRY-TALE WRITERS and one of the most translated authors in the world, Andersen should be given a prime place in a teaching unit on fairy tales. At the same time, as he was a Danish writer, both the language and the cultural context make it difficult for non-Danish-speaking instructors to grasp the many dimensions of his work. This chapter gives advice and suggests activities that can be used to work on Andersen's tales in an academic setting, focusing on a comparative analysis of translations to approach the particular language in which they were told. At the University of Lausanne, fairy tales are frequently taught in different programs (both at undergraduate and graduate level) in the English and French Departments, and in the Comparative Literature Center. Emphasis is placed both on the connection between the written collections of Charles Perrault, the Grimms, and Andersen, and on the differences between their specific texts. The tales of these authors have to a great extent become difficult to dissociate, and they are frequently found together in the same volume, such as *Tales of Grimm and Andersen* (1952); *My World of Fairy Tales: Stories from Grimm, Perrault, and Andersen* (1976); *101 Famous Tales for Children (Brothers Grimm, Andersen, Perrault)* (2013). The editors do not always stipulate who wrote which text, and one may think that the tales were written in the same language and era, and maybe even by the same author, since the translations tend to homogenize the style. It is thus important to contextualize the collections and to study them as literary works; one can then better understand why Andersen considered himself an author of tales while he saw the Grimms merely as collectors.

My approach is based on a close reading, and I try to show that fairy tales do not only differ when it comes to motifs, themes, or structures, but

DOI: 10.7330/9781607324812.c010

also in the way in which they are told. A linguistic approach allows for a better understanding of the texts and of the genre itself. I have used textual analysis to study fairy tales in comparative literature programs, but I am also using tales in the Department of French as a Foreign Language, in a course taught in French and entitled "A Linguistic Approach to Literary Texts." Covering a whole semester, this course for undergraduate students discusses the relationship between linguistics and literature through a textual linguistics approach based on Dominique Maingueneau (2010) and Jean-Michel Adam (2005). Tales prove to be effective educational materials since their conciseness usually allows for a close reading of the whole text. Furthermore, due to the dual audience of children and adults often sought in this genre, fairy tales frequently combine an apparent simplicity with more complex characteristics. In this regard, Andersen's tales raise questions that are interesting to study from a linguistic perspective, for example, concerning enunciation and syntax. With smaller adjustments depending on the program, the activities described here can therefore be used either in a course on fairy tales or in a linguistics course.

TEACHING ANDERSEN: DIFFERENT APPROACHES

Courses and research on Andersen's tales often emphasize the thematic dimension. The rich work of the Danish author undoubtedly calls for a reflection on themes such as death and life after death, friendship, social injustice, the figure of the artist, or objects and creatures around us. Another approach would consist in placing Andersen in the context of the fairy-tale genre, emphasizing his link to nineteenth-century Romanticism and especially to German literature. Comparisons can be made, for example, with texts of the Brothers Grimm, Johann Karl August Musäus, Friedrich de La Motte Fouqué, E. T. A. Hoffmann, Ludwig Tieck, and Adelbert von Chamisso, for the German connection, and Adam Oehlenschläger, Mathias Winther, Just Mathias Thiele, and the editions of Christian Molbech, for the Danish setting. A third approach, which is currently emerging after a long period of neglect, suggests studying Andersen's tales in the context of his entire work, thus recalling that he also wrote novels, plays, poetry, travel books, and autobiographies.

All these approaches to teaching Andersen are valid, and they offer good comprehension of his tales, especially if combined. This chapter aims to present a new approach to study Andersen's tales through a linguistics-oriented analysis, "a sadly neglected field of Andersen scholarship" (Hjørnager Pedersen 2004, 53).[1] For the purposes of this book, the guidelines offered here are based on translations, since instructors and students do not necessarily read Danish, but they can be adapted for students in a department of Nordic studies.

It could seem paradoxical to teach Andersen's tales with an emphasis on the language while working with translations. Translated texts are often questioned: "an unavoidable evil, which always betrays the original? in which there is always something missing?" (Chevrel 1989, 142). Nonetheless, if it were not for translations, we would not be able to read Andersen at all, and neither would we be able to read classics of our cultural heritage such as Homer, Aesop, Virgil, or the bible.[2] If literary works are to be taught in translation, however, it is important to discuss the process of translation. One should emphasize the otherness of the texts rather than pretend that they were originally written in English, to prevent students from "submit[ing] them to their own cultural norms" (Maier and Massardier-Kenney 2010, 1). In the case of Andersen, almost every English-speaking adult has known his tales since childhood and considers them part of English literature. One could almost see Andersen as "an English writer, read by millions of people who do not understand a word of Danish, and exerting more influence on English children's writing than any native Briton until Lewis Carroll" (Hjørnager Pedersen 2004, 16). The activities suggested here focus on Andersen's tales as translated texts and seek to access their linguistic characteristics, with the aim of deepening the students' understanding of these tales as literary texts.

CHOOSING A TRANSLATION

The goal of the present chapter is not to evaluate translations and point to the best one. On the contrary, in my teaching, I work with many translations, as will be explained later. The texts studied in class are given as handouts to the students. Nevertheless, it is also beneficial that students have a "reader," allowing them to discover Andersen's tales more extensively on their own. The choice is not easy since the only two complete English editions (Andersen 1974, 1949) have not been well received. Viggo Hjørnager Pedersen's (2004) and Sven Hakon Rossel's (1993) advice can be helpful in finding a good selection of tales, though they do not take into account the latest translations by Jeffrey and Diana Franks (Andersen 2003), Tiina Nunnally (Andersen 2004), Marte Hvam Hult (Andersen 2006), and Maria Tatar and Julie K. Allen (Andersen 2008). These are informed by the indispensable Danish critical edition (Andersen 1963–90) as well as by numerous scholarly works. When studying a translated text at college level, the translator's talent and mastering of both the source and the target languages are not sufficient selection criteria; he or she also needs to be up to date with the literature on the author. Sometimes, price and accessibility need to be taken into consideration. In this regard, the availability of Jean Hersholt's translation on the Internet is an advantage. As we work mainly with handouts and consequently do not need a common edition, I find it a good idea to present alternatives to students. This will emphasize that we cannot work with a reference edition of Andersen's tales and that we have a choice among many translations with different audiences, introductions, annotations, selections of tales, and translation choices. Consequently, students pay more attention to the books as material objects and compare the editions they find at home or in book sales.

The presentation of the translations can serve as an introduction to the otherness of Andersen's tales, given that they are Danish texts. We almost always read them in translations that have their own history, from the first nineteenth-century translations from the German, to contemporary versions. Comparing translations allows for a reflection on the language since some of them are rendered in a "sanitized" English, while others stay closer to the Danish original and hence sound stranger to an English-speaking audience. My students who work on French translations are often uneasy with Andersen's audacious style, and at first seem to prefer more "grammatically correct" translations. This activity allows them to "approach the literature of an unknown language in an 'active' fashion, to penetrate the logic of the translator, to seize the richness and the limits of their native tongue, to understand that a translation is never totally final, and that it can affect the interpretation of a work" (Chevrel 2007, 154; my translation).

INTRODUCING THE COURSE

This section will discuss a few activities that can be used in the first meetings. They can be abridged or developed to fit the needs of the specific program. Typically, in my linguistics course, I give a very concise biographical note and spend more time on the presentation of the books.

It is interesting to start with a discussion to find out which tales the students are familiar with and what they think of them. This usually leads to a list of characteristics of Andersen's tales as compared to other collections (the Grimms', Perrault's, etc.) and allows for a better understanding of what students consider to be a fairy tale. Here one could emphasize the length of the texts, which often exceeds the expectations of the genre ("The Snow Queen," for example, is thirty pages long).[3] Then it can be mentioned that only a few texts can be considered "typical" fairy tales with princes and princesses.[4] Andersen rather likes to tell stories about inanimate objects that behave and think like humans, such as "The Steadfast Tin Soldier" and "Little Ida's Flowers." Students also often bring up the melancholy nature of Andersen's tales, and some report having been upset by texts such as "The Little Match Girl" or "The Little Mermaid." These stories show Andersen's conception of the world and religious beliefs, according to which they are not as sad as they seem: indeed, both the mermaid and the little match girl will be able to find after death what they lacked on earth.

A biographical presentation of Andersen is a good opportunity to put the author in context and to talk about nineteenth-century Denmark. It is in fact also the best way to discuss some myths about Andersen and to prevent biographical *interpretations* of his tales, which are quite common and far too reductive, although biographical *details* can sometimes be relevant. All too often, readers tend to recognize the author in the ugly duckling or the little mermaid, but Andersen's fairy tales are much more than biographical. Andersen himself is partly to be blamed for such interpretations. His awkward physical looks and behavior created an image that he played with (see Briggs 2006, 183, on Andersen's travels to England). Furthermore, in his autobiographies, Andersen emphasized the misery in which he was brought up to finally succeed as one of the most famous Danish authors, and he compared his life to a fairy tale.

To get a better picture of Andersen's life, one could consult one of the biographies available in English, for example, that of Jens Andersen (2005) or Jackie Wullschlager (2000). Both underline two important facts. First, the author's initial love was for the stage: he enjoyed singing, dancing, and acting since his childhood in Odense. When he left his hometown for Copenhagen, it was to seek success on stage as a performer. He lived with this passion all his life, writing plays and visiting theaters across Europe. This passion explains why dialogues play such an important role in his work. Second, Andersen was not a novice when he published his first tales. Influenced by German Romantic authors (as mentioned earlier) and Walter Scott, among others, he had written plays, novels, and poetry—and quite successfully so in Germany—before he published the first collection of his tales in 1835. If Andersen is mainly known as an author for children in English today, he was first known as a poet in France and in Denmark he is still considered a "serious" author whose modern style revolutionized Danish literature.

One of the first meeting's important assignments is to study the publication of the books in which the tales were printed. In a course on fairy tales in general, I ask students to compare the paratexts of Andersen's and the Grimms' and Perrault's collections. In a program focusing on Andersen, they concentrate on his work and I add some information about Perrault and the Grimms. The main point to be made is that Perrault only published two collections of tales in three years, adding up to eleven texts (one of which was a novella). His production is thus limited in time and quantity. The Grimms published *Kinder- und Hausmärchen* in 1812 and reedited the book (with important changes) several times until 1857, to a total of 201 tales. Throughout their lifetime, they worked with tales, trying to improve one collection rather than creating different ones. Andersen also worked all his life with fairy tales, but in contrast to the Grimms, he published new texts every time a book came out. Here is an adapted version of the table I use, with the title of each collection:[5]

> Eventyr, fortalte for Børn (Tales, Told To Children, 1835–42)
> Nye Eventyr (New Tales, 1844–48)
> Eventyr (Tales, 1850)
> Historier (Stories, 1852–53)
> Historier [1855] (Stories, 1855)
> Nye Eventyr og Historier (New Tales and Stories, 1858–72)
> Eventyr og Historier (Tales and Stories, 1862–74)
> Femten Eventyr og Historier (Fifteen Tales and Stories, 1867)
> Tre nye Eventyr og Historier (Three New Tales and Stories, 1870)

Not only does this table help understand Andersen's tale output, it also allows for a discussion of the fairy-tale genre through the terms used by the author himself. Indeed, he used *eventyr* (tales) until 1850, then switched to *historier* (stories) before combining the two terms. The terms *eventyr* and *historier* are also used in the tales themselves. Arguably, Andersen's texts do not match the expectations of the genre that students have, and in-class discussions on the change of terms tend to lead students to reflect on the genre more generally. One might discuss the length of the texts, the lack of happy endings in a lot of stories, and the fact that many have been considered so immoral that they had to be adapted.[6] Reading the two first tales—"The Tinder-Box" and "Big Claus and Little Claus"—one can easily see that heroes are not necessarily rewarded for being good and that punished characters are not necessarily villains. Throughout this activity, students change their perspective from recognizing texts as tales, according to their preliminary conception of the genre, to reflecting on the fairy-tale genre as presented by the texts.

Andersen's tales appeared unconventional from the start within a genre that was heavily inspired by the Grimms.[7] The author made it clear that he was not a collector of folktales but a creator: "Grim[m] had never composed a tale, he was only a collector" (Andersen 1971–77, 10:93; my translation). Andersen wanted to be recognized as a great author; to him, tales were not a heritage to protect but texts to compose, as were poems and novels. In his foreword, he wrote that he wanted to tell tales "in [his] own way, authorizing [him]self every change [he] thought appropriate, letting the fantasy refresh the faded colors of the images" (Andersen 1963–90, 1:19–20; my translation).

THE LANGUAGE OF THE TALES

The way in which tales are told is an important dimension of the texts that instructors should address. Andersen is considered to have revolutionized the Danish language: his tales were written in a colloquial language that departed from the literary writings of that time.[8] His unique style was much criticized by his contemporaries, who often accused him of writing poorly. They did not see that it was the choice of an avant-garde author, who was also a pioneer of free indirect speech in Denmark and who went on to inspire numerous Danish writers (see Brøndum-Nielsen 1953). Not only did Andersen revolutionize the Danish language, but he also operated a revolution of the language of tales. Danish tales of the time, like those of Mathias Winther (1989), were inspired by the *Kinder- und Hausmärchen* and focused on the sequence of events in a paratactic style. Andersen added complexity to the tales with his unconventional syntax, the developments of new episodes, and the addition of descriptions and dialogues, among other characteristics. He tried to instill life into the tales rather than just telling a story. Students can get a feel for this special language by comparing Andersen's "The Wild Swans" with two similar texts by Winther and the Grimms (see François 2012). They tend to find the Grimms' style closer to their expectations of a tale.

This first comparison of three translated texts could be followed by a discussion on translation. Students should then read some articles on how to translate Andersen's tales. Apart from Viggo Hjørnager Pedersen's (2004) book, I recommend two articles by Diana Crone Frank and Jeffrey Frank (2006) and Sven Hakon Rossel (1993). Translations often feature a translator's note that is also worth reading in class. This activity is important to remind students that they are reading a translation and not a text written in English. They should also note that the numerous translations of Andersen's tales were all written in their own specific context. Julia Briggs's (2006) study on Andersen's early reception in England is insightful in this regard. Students will also see that the translators complain about the difficulties encountered in translating Andersen's tales. They point to specific issues such as alliteration, prepositions, and adverbs without equivalence in English; puns; and wordplay. In the end, translations all present flaws and qualities that usually result from translation choices.

Discussions based on the translations give a first impression of Andersen's peculiar language in the tales. The next step is to compare different translations of the same text. Instructors can choose a specific tale or numerous fragments.[9] The best way to compare them is to create a bilingual document: I usually put the Danish text in the first column and one or two translations in the others. Students are asked to find differences by themselves, and then we analyze the differences together in class and try to categorize them. Students sometimes fail to find the relevance of certain differences, but the explanations and the repetition of the exercise help them to organize their analyses.

Students can be intimidated by the Danish at first, but eventually manage better than we would have expected. The idea is not to ask students to read the texts in Danish directly, but to ask them to concentrate on certain features. Punctuation, for example, is accessible without knowing a word of Danish. Andersen's sentences can be rather long, sometimes with many semicolons. Translators tend to shorten them and insert periods. In the opening of "The Wild Swans," for example, Hersholt replaces the two semicolons with periods and divides a rather small sentence in two by suppressing a conjunction (*og*/"and"). In addition to punctuation, I also ask students to be attentive to the conjunction *og*, which Andersen uses a lot in a specific way and which translators tend to omit. The peculiar rhythm of the tales is often lost in favor of a syntax that is too respectful of English norms.

The subsequent teaching unit provides an in-depth analysis focusing on three main dimensions: one class meeting deals with enunciation, one with reported speech more specifically, and one with syntactical questions. In the meeting about enunciation, the emphasis is put on deixis. The narrator intervenes a lot in Andersen's tales and it is easy to spot the pronouns used to create interaction with the reader: *I, we, you*.[10] Used in conjunction with the present tense and sometimes with place deixis (*here, there, . . .*), like in the opening of "The Wild Swans," these pronouns refer to a situation of utterance in which the narrator and the reader are unified in a telling-tale-like scene. In a linguistics course, it is also interesting to work on Andersen's frequent use of the adverb *nu* (now) conjugated in the past tense. In "On Translating H. C. Andersen," the Franks explain how hard it is in English not to replace these by the more expected adverb, *then* (Frank and Frank 2006, 163–64).[11] Students of French as a foreign language are always amused to find "mistakes" that they have been taught to avoid in French translations of Andersen's tales; it illustrates the theoretical dimension of grammar.

The issue of deixis is important when studying tales; the comparison of texts by Perrault, Grimm, and Andersen is particularly valuable in this regard. In Perrault's tales, the first person and/or the address to the reader are relegated to the morals at the end of the text. These morals link the narrator and the reader in a comment on the tale, which often connects the story "of past times" (according to Perrault's title) to the present time. The tale itself is told almost without explicit narratological intervention. In the tales of the Grimms, there are few interventions of a narrator and there is generally speaking no identified narrator like in Andersen's tales. First person or apostrophes can be found mostly in the opening or the closing lines of a tale, in a ready-to-use formula, interchangeable from tale to tale, such as: "My tale is done" (Grimm and Grimm 2003, 58) or "I wish that you and I had been there too" (Grimm and Grimm 2003, 180). Studying deixis allows us to emphasize the Grimms' attempt at erasing signs of the situation of utterance, Perrault's dual mode in the tale and in the morals, and Andersen's aim to create telling-tale-like scenes where readers "should hear the storyteller in the style" (Andersen 1963–90, 6:4; my translation).

Reported speech is relevant to both linguistics and fairy-tale classes. It helps develop the reflection on enunciation through the distinction between "speaker" and "enunciator" and to practice identifying deictic terms. Students first focus on direct versus indirect speech. When the forms are recognized, we see how the narrator integrates reported speech in his tales. This allows for a connection between the linguistic analysis and a more general interpretation of the tales. Indeed, the use of reported speech is linked to the author's conception of the genre. The Grimms, for example, aim to present independent dialogues in direct speech that give an impression of reality. The narrator hardly intervenes at all, since the speaking turns follow one another. This is in line with the Grimms' conception of tales as nature's voice, rather than the work of a particular author. Andersen's tales also contain dialogues that almost seem theatrical, but there are moreover instances where direct speech is inserted directly into the narrative. A more overt narrator clearly shows that a selection of speeches is made to highlight certain elements; there is no wish to simulate a faithful dialogue. The tales even contain personifications, with the narrator inventing speeches: "it was as if the sea seemed to say, I can look threatening too" ("The Wild

Swans" in Andersen 1949, 120). Giving the floor to characters or organizing their speech are thus strategies related to the type of narrator.

Andersen's tales permit a further reflection on reported speech as the narrator tends to erase the distinction between his own words and those of the characters through the omission of quotation marks or the use of free indirect speech. This feature can be used ironically to underline some characters' twisted logic or wickedness, but it is mainly used in an empathic way: while he tells the story, the narrator worries about his characters or rejoices with them.

At least one meeting should center on syntax, even though the subject has partly been discussed earlier. Andersen's use of the Danish language is disconcerting: "Seen from a school-master's point of view, Andersen's style is alarming! Interjections, incoherence in tense, etc.—aspects any teacher would try to correct, but which, seen from an aesthetic point of view, [are] indispensable since it is these that make Andersen's telling significant" (Hansen and Lundholt 2005, 15). As mentioned above, the length of the sentences and the use of the conjunction *og* are important. We try to develop this point here to see how sentences are built. They often aggregate different elements paratactically, mixing narrative, descriptions, and dialogue; the sequence of events is frequently interrupted. To summarize, I use a pastiche by Edvard Collin, a close friend of Andersen's. It underlines the built orality of Andersen's language, the precision of the description which aims to show rather than to tell the readers things, and the use of images and onomatopoeia to give life to the narrative: "He brought life to even the driest sentence. He wouldn't say: 'The children got into the carriage and drove off.' Rather: 'Then they got into the carriage, goodbye Father, goodbye Mother, the whip cracked, snip, snap, and off they went, yee-ha, get moving!'" (J. Andersen 2005, 220).

Teaching Andersen is inevitable in a course on fairy tales, but instructors may encounter problems if they do not read Danish. Problematizing the use of translation allows us to put the texts in context and to tackle the question of their "otherness" as Danish works. By comparing translated texts, it is also possible to analyze Andersen's style more carefully, and understand how and why his tales can be distinguished through the special way in which they are told, and this arguably to a further extent than through differences with regard to motifs or plots. The study of fairy tales has undergone significant developments in the past decades, but the linguistic level still needs to receive the attention it deserves. Telling tales involves speech: it all goes back to language. Students are very receptive of such an approach to Andersen's tales. It gives them a better understanding of the

Danish author's work, but it also provides them with a broader conception of the fairy-tale genre and analytical skills for comparing and reflecting on translations, as well as textual analysis skills that they can use in their wider college curriculum.

NOTES

1. Interested readers can nonetheless find some studies in English, such as Viggo Hjørnager Pedersen's (2004) and a useful edited volume in narratology: Hansen and Lundholt (2005). About Andersen's tales more generally, interested readers can find numerous studies in English (de Mylius, Jørgensen, and Hjørnager Pedersen 1993, 1999, 2008; Immel, Haase, and Duggan 2006; Rossel 1996; Sondrup 2004; among others).

2. On the subject of Nordic literature taught in the United states, see Niels Ingwersen and Susan Brantly (2010).

3. To work on the length of the tales more specifically, one can compare three thematically similar stories, with that of Andersen's being much longer: the Grimms' "The Six Swans," Winther's "The Eleven Swans," and Andersen's "The Wild Swans."

4. This is in part also valid for the Grimms' collection, which contains numerous religious tales and animal tales, less familiar to students.

5. I translate *eventyr* as "tales" rather than "fairy tales," since the generic term corresponds better to Andersen's texts.

6. Briggs quotes insightful examples, such as Clara de Chatelain explaining how she renders "The Red Shoes" closer to Andersen's spirit than does Andersen himself (Briggs 2006).

7. Cay Dollerup's book on the translation and reception of *Kinder- und Hausmärchen* in Denmark provides a good background on the fairy-tale genre of that time (Dollerup 1999). Comparisons with Mathias Winther's (1989) "folktales" and Christian Molbech's tale-collections are also useful (see e.g., Molbech 1843).

8. See, for example, Johan de Mylius (1988), who also speaks of a second revolution of the language of the tales, around the 1850s. Anker Jensen (1929), Peter Skautrup (1953), and Paul Rubow (1943) discuss the language of the tales in Danish studies. In English, the best information can be found in Viggo Hjørnager Pedersen (2004).

9. To help with selection, Viggo Hjørnager Pedersen (2004) offers numerous appendices comparing different translations, either through a whole segment of a text or with specific sentences focusing on specific features.

10. Comparing translations helps to think about these pronouns. The Franks, for example, point to some transformations made by Hersholt (Frank and Frank 2006, 162).

11. One could also work on the distinction between the formal *De* (you) and the informal *du* (thou) in "The shadow" (Ingwersen and Brantly 2010, 157–59).

REFERENCES

Adam, Jean-Michel. 2005. *La linguistique textuelle: Introduction à l'analyse textuelle des discours.* Paris: Nathan.

Andersen, Hans Christian. 1949. *The Complete Andersen.* 6 vols. Trans. Jean Hersholt. New York: Limited Editions Club. http://andersen.sdu.dk/vaerk/hersholt/index_e.html.

Andersen, Hans Christian. 1963–1990. In *Eventyr.* 7 vols. ed. Erik Dal. Copenhagen: DSL / Hans Reitzel.

Andersen, Hans Christian. 1971–1977. In *H. C. Andersens Dagbøger 1825–1875*, ed. Kåre Olsen and Helge Topsøe-Jensen. Copenhagen: G. E. C. Gad.

Andersen, Hans Christian. 1974. *The Complete Fairy Tales and Stories.* Trans. Erik Christian Haugaard. Garden City: Doubleday.

Andersen, Hans Christian. 2003. *The Stories of Hans Christian Andersen.* Trans. Jeffrey Frank and Diana Crone Frank. Boston: Houghton Mifflin.

Andersen, Hans Christian. 2004. *Fairy Tales.* Trans. Tiina Nunnally. London: Penguin.

Andersen, Hans Christian. 2006. *Fairy Tales.* Trans. Marte Hvam Hult. New York: Barnes and Noble.

Andersen, Hans Christian. 2008. *The Annotated Hans Christian Andersen.* Trans. Maria Tatar and Julie K. Allen. New York: Norton.

Andersen, Jens. 2005. *Hans Christian Andersen: A New Life.* Trans. Tina Nunnally. New York: Overlook Duckworth.

Briggs, Julia. 2006. "A Liberating Imagination: Andersen in England." *Marvels & Tales* 20 (2): 179–92. http://dx.doi.org/10.1353/mat.2007.0001.

Brøndum-Nielsen, Johannes. 1953. *Dækning: Oratio tecta i dansk litteratur før 1870.* Copenhagen: Festskrift udgivet af Københavns universitet.

Chevrel, Yves. 1989. "Foreword: Is there a Future for the Study of Translated Literature?" *Revue de Littérature Comparée* 63 (2): 141–5.

Chevrel, Yves, ed. 2007. *Enseigner les œuvres littéraires en traduction, Actes de la Dgesco.* CRDP: Académie de Versailles.

de Mylius, Johan. 1988. "Andersens anden revolution." In *Litteraturbilleder: Æstetiske udflugter i litteraturen fra Søren Kierkegaard til Karen Blixen*, 37–60. Odense: Odense Universitetsforlag.

de Mylius, Johan, Aage Jørgensen, and Viggo Hjørnager Pedersen, eds. 1993. *Andersen and the World: Andersen og Verden.* Odense: Odense Universitetsforlag.

de Mylius, Johan, Aage Jørgensen, and Viggo Hjørnager Pedersen, eds. 1999. *Hans Christian Andersen: A Poet in Time.* Odense: Odense Universitetsforlag.

de Mylius, Johan, Aage Jørgensen, and Viggo Hjørnager Pedersen, eds. 2008. *Hans Christian Andersen: Between Children's Literature and Adult Literature.* Odense: Universitetsforlag.

Dollerup, Cay. 1999. *Tales and Translation: The Grimm Tales from Pan-Germanic Narratives to Shared International Fairytales.* Amsterdam: John Benjamins Publishing Company. http://dx.doi.org/10.1075/btl.30.

François, Cyrille. 2012. "'C'est la plume qui fait le conte: 'Die sechs Schwäne' des frères Grimm et 'De vilde Svaner' de Hans Christian Andersen." *Fééries: Études sur le conte merveilleux (XVIIe–XIXe siècle)* 9: 55–84.

Frank, Diana Crone, and Jeffrey Frank. 2006. "On Translating H. C. Andersen." *Marvels & Tales* 20 (2): 155–65. http://dx.doi.org/10.1353/mat.2007.0005.

Grimm, Jacob, and Wilhelm Grimm. 2003. *The Complete Fairy Tales of the Brothers Grimm.* Trans. Jack Zipes. New York: Bantam Books.

Hansen, Per Krogh, and Marianne Wolff Lundholt, eds. 2005. *When We Get to the End . . . Towards a Narratology of the Fairy Tales of Hans Christian Andersen.* Odense: Writings from the Center for Narratological Studies 1, Universitetsforlag.

Hjørnager Pedersen, Viggo. 2004. *Ugly ducklings? Studies in the English Translations of Hans Christian Andersen's Tales and Stories.* Odense: Universitetsforlag.

Immel, Andrea, Donald Haase, and Anne Duggan, eds. 2006. "'Hidden, but Not Forgotten': Hans Christian Andersen's Legacy in the Twentieth Century." *Marvels & Tales* 20 (2).

Ingwersen, Niels, and Susan C. Brantly. 2010. "Nordic Exposure: Teaching Scandinavian Literature in Translation." In *Literature in Translation: Teaching Issues and Reading Practices, Translation Studies*, ed. Carol Maier and Françoise Massardier-Kenney, 148–66. Kent: Kent State University Press.

Jensen, Anker. 1929. *Studier over H. C. Andersens Sprog.* Haderslev: C. Nielsen.

Maier, Carol, and Françoise Massardier-Kenney, eds. 2010. *Literature in Translation: Teaching Issues and Reading Practices, Translation Studies.* Kent: Kent State University Press.

Maingueneau, Dominique. 2010. *Manuel de linguistique pour les textes littéraires.* Paris: Armand Colin.

Molbech, Christian. 1843. *Udvalgte Eventyr og Fortællinger: En Læsebog for Folket of for den barnlige Verden.* Copenhagen: C. A. Reitzel.

Rossel, Sven Hakon. 1993. "Hans Christian Andersen Research in the United States." In *Andersen and the World—Andersen og Verden*, ed. Johan de Mylius, Aage Jørgensen, and Viggo Hjørnager Pedersen, 517–30. Odense: Odense Universitetsforlag.

Rossel, Sven Hakon, ed. 1996. *Hans Christian Andersen: Danish Writer and Citizen of the World.* Amsterdam: Rodopi.

Rubow, Paul V. 1943. *H. C. Andersens Eventyr. Forhistorien—idé og form, sprog og stil.* Copenhagen: Gyldendal.

Skautrup, Peter. 1953. "Fortællersprog." In *Det danske sprogs historie*, ed. Peter Skautrup, 230–45. Copenhagen: Gyldendal.

Sondrup, Steven P., ed. 2004. *H. C. Andersen: Old Problems and New Readings.* Odense: Universitetsforlag.

Winther, Mathias. 1989. *Danish Folk Tales.* Trans. T. Sands and J. Massengale. Madison: Wisconsin Introductions to Scandinavia.

Wullschlager, Jackie. 2000. *Hans Christian Andersen: The Life of a Storyteller.* London: Penguin.

11

Teaching Symbolism in "Little Red Riding Hood"

Francisco Vaz da Silva

I OFTEN TEACH AN OPTIONAL COURSE ON FAIRY TALES to undergraduate social-anthropology students. This is usually the first contact they have with fairy tales in an academic setting, and I mean to make it memorable. Many of my students find themselves fascinated by the topic of symbolism in fairy tales but cannot quite fathom why. This course aims to develop the students' intuitive grasp of fairy-tale meanings into a level of explicit comprehension. It shows how to make sense of (apparent) nonsense in traditional narratives. This chapter describes the basic contents of four preliminary sessions, spanning two weeks, in which we experiment with addressing fairy tales in terms of creative variations. The aim of these sessions is to explain why, and how, intertextual readings are required to understand fairy tales. Using a hands-on approach, we explore the well-known theme of "Little Red Riding Hood" by means of three texts: "Le Petit Chaperon rouge" by Charles Perrault, "Rotkäppchen" by the Brothers Grimm, and a French orally collected variant called "Histoire de la mère-grand" ("Tale of Grandmother"). In order to make sure that no linguistic misapprehensions get in the way, I provide the students with annotated translations of the texts.

A FLIP OF THE MIND

We start with *why* intertextual readings are necessary to understand a given tale. In the first week, I propose the notion that understanding fairy tales entails something akin to a flip of the mind. In a nutshell, the illusion of

DOI: 10.7330/9781607324812.c011

urtexts has to go. I point out that fairy tales have developed in oral settings, and traditional creativity differs markedly from literary authorship. Traditional themes come in multiple variants, and it would be arbitrary to presume that any one variant is more authentic than another. The very notion of "authentic" assumes that once upon a time there was an original, authorial text that oral transmission then attempted to replicate by rote—but the presumption of an authorial, authentic text is itself a literary assumption. In oral traditions you find no original, fixed texts—just myriad variants endlessly echoing one another—and, in fact, oral tale-telling is all about creatively retelling old stories in new ways (see Vaz da Silva 2012).

In order to get these points across, I ask the students to read two classical studies on the transmission of folk stories. First, we discuss a paper by Frederic Bartlett (1920), which examines how individual memory addresses new stories. In a nutshell, Bartlett shows that when people are asked to memorize and then recall an alien story, they tend to transpose its unfamiliar elements into familiar terms and to omit whatever data remain meaningless. In other words, recollection processes depend on meaningful associations. Then we discuss a paper by Roman Jakobson and Petr Bogatyrev, which examines the transmission of familiar, traditional stories (Jakobson and Bogatyrev 1982). These authors argue that since stories in oral settings are not preserved in a durable medium (unless a folklorist happens to be around), the innovations of individual tale-tellers will endure only insofar as they are accepted and retold. In other words, individual creations are transmitted by word of mouth only insofar as they are recognized as valid permutations on accepted lore. But, since audiences are selective regarding what they actually accept and retell, stories are relentlessly shaped according to the successive tale-tellers' values and tastes. By dint of this cumulative mechanism of selective appropriations, materials in the traditional chain will tend to comply with the shared cultural norms and values. The crucial point, then, is that folklore is an adaptive process.

In accordance with Jakobson and Bogatyrev's discussion I reserve the word *tale* for the traditional themes that are retold in myriad ways, and use the term *variants* for the concrete retellings of each tale. The crucial implication is that a traditional tale exists in all its variants, and no single variant ever represents a tale. It may appear strange that folktales are stable entities despite the fact that no two variants are ever alike. But think of it: two or more variants convey the same tale as long as they use equivalent motifs (otherwise those variants would impart different tales). So we could say that a tale is a stable pattern variously retold in symbolically equivalent variants; or we might say that variants transform one another in accordance with the stable pattern of the tale. Either way, the point is that traditional storytelling is about creatively using symbolic equivalences to spin new variants of the tale, rather than about listless memorization. In essence, this is why tales are stable although no two variants are ever alike.

Once it is clear that the transmission of tales involves symbolic reckoning, the students are ready to discuss Alan Dundes's ideas on the symbolic equivalence of allomotifs. Dundes (2007) argues that if a number of different motifs can fill the same slot in a tale, then those allomotifs are symbolically equivalent, and a comparison should clarify what the conceptual basis for that equivalence is. Comparing allomotifs, in other words, is the way to gain access to implicit formulations of symbolic equivalences. Once the students wrap their minds around this idea, we are ready to proceed to the next phase.

"LE PETIT CHAPERON ROUGE": A LAYERED TEXT

After the first week of discussions has shown that the transmission of traditional stories hinges on the creative use of symbolic equivalences rather than on replication by rote, we are ready to inquire on *how* to undertake intertextual readings in order to understand a given tale. Now starts the second introductory week of this course, the aim of which is to help the students get a grip on the task of seeking the stable notions underlying different variants of the tale. There is usually a palpable feeling in the class that now the fun begins.

Most students know the tale of "Little Red Riding Hood" through the literary texts by Charles Perrault (1697), "Le Petit Chaperon rouge," and Grimm (1812), "Rotkäppchen." But, as folklorist Paul Delarue (1951b) showed, there used to be a French oral tradition quite independent from the literary variants. There are obvious differences between the two literary texts and the oral variants, and those differences are a good foundation for seeking the shared conceptual underpinnings of "Little Red Riding Hood."

First, I ask the students to compare the oral variant, "Tale of Grandmother," with Perrault's "Le Petit Chaperon rouge" and bring out the main differences.[1] A giddy session usually follows, as some dissimilarities are quite remarkable. In the oral variant, the familiar wolf turns out to be a *bzou* (a werewolf); the unnamed paths to grandmother's house are named after needles and pins; there is a cannibal meal, for the girl partakes of grandmother's flesh and blood before joining the werewolf in bed; and there is a happy end: when the girl realizes that she is in bed with the wolf, she pretends she has to go relieve herself outside and then runs away. So now the students realize that "Little Red Riding Hood" is more complex than meets the eye. They also realize that the traditional traits in the oral variant shed a new light on Perrault's text. In particular, the "morality" appended at the end of the story by Perrault now stands out because it presents the wolf as a man-wolf:

> One sees here that young children,
> Especially young ladies,
> Pretty, shapely, and well bred
> Are very ill advised to listen to all sorts of people,
> And it is hardly strange
> That so many get eaten by the wolf.
> I say the wolf, for all wolves
> Are not of the same kind.
> Some of them are charming,
> Not loud, nor bitter, or angry,
> Who, being intimate, easygoing, and sweet,
> Follow the young ladies
> Right into their homes, right into their alcoves [*ruelles*];[2]
> But, alas! It is well known that these mellifluous wolves
> Are the most dangerous of all wolves.[3]

This morality, clearly not meant for children, explains that the wolf is of the anthropomorphic kind. Thus, Perrault warns his grown-up readers that the tale can be read on more than one level at once. This is actually a point he makes in the dedicatory letter of his manuscript, which declares that tales contain "a very sensible morality that listeners can apprehend more or less fully according to the degree of their penetration" (Barchilon 1956, 113).[4] The morality appended to "Le Petit Chaperon rouge" implements this view. It adds to the plain, literal message of the text—children should be careful lest a wolf eat them—a metaphoric level of understanding: the wolf is a human predator. On reading it, grown-ups realize (or they may confirm a nagging suspicion) that the act of pouncing on a young woman to eat her *in a bed* amounts to a sexual violation. In short, Perrault provides a layered text where the wolf-man eats a girl in both the literal sense (as a wolf will) and in a metaphoric sense (as a sexual predator will).

Arguably, Perrault's wolf-man carries an extra layer of meaning that refers to popular traditions. The double dimension of the creature's transgression, alimentary and sexual, conspicuously meets the folk reputation of werewolves. For example, a sixteenth-century German werewolf was

famously convicted for both raping a woman and eating her flesh, which
he "esteemed both sweet and dainty in taste." Similarly, in the folklore of
the Isle of Guernsey, a great eater is proverbially said to eat like a *varou*,
and the expression *aller en varouverie* entails "debauchery" (Summers 1933,
204, 257). The point is, werewolves are supposedly ravenous creatures in
both the alimentary and the sexual senses (in both the literal and the figu-
rative senses of the verb *manger*, "to eat"), and Perrault plays on precisely
this duality regarding an anthropomorphic wolf that eats a young woman
in bed. Therefore, it is arguable that "Le Petit Chaperon rouge" works on
at least three levels according to the degree of its readers' "penetration."
Innocent readers will take it as a scary warning tale, whereas Perrault hints
a tale of rape, and readers conversant with folklore are bound to recognize
a werewolf theme.

I often take the time to let the students know that werewolves are a
feature of the French oral tradition across a number of tale types. (The
term *tale types* refers to the standard classification of folktales in the Aarne-
Thompson-Uther international index [henceforth, ATU]; see Uther 2004.
Thus, "Little Red Riding Hood" is ATU 333.) To take an example, folklorist Geneviève Massignon collected a variant of "The Maiden Who Seeks
Her Brothers" (ATU 451) in which the ogre haunting the forest cabin
is called a *malbrou*. To elucidate this term, Massignon remarks that *malbrou* is akin to the term *brou* that designates the forest ogre in variants of
"The Children and the Ogre" (ATU 327) from the Poitou region. And
she notes that in variants of "Little Red Riding Hood" from the Nivernais
region, the ogre haunting the forest hut is a *loup-brou* (Massignon 2006,
225–26). Indeed, "Tale of Grandmother" describes the ogre as a *brou*,
which, the tale-teller explains, is "like the *brou* or the *garou*; in Nivernais we
also say *loup-brou* or *loup-garou*" (Delarue 1985, 373n2). In sum, the *bzou* in
this variant is like the proverbial tip of the iceberg—a clue to werewolves
lurking in oral tales.

PERRAULT AND TRADITION

Although the werewolf theme is usually popular with students, in this
context I use it basically to discuss the vexed question of the relationship
between Perrault's text and the oral tradition. Here is an outline of the argument I lay out for discussion with the students.

Since the extant traditional variants were collected in the nineteenth and
twentieth centuries, any suggestion that Perrault's seventeenth-century text
derives from these modern texts would be anachronistic. Chronologically

speaking, Perrault's text is the oldest extant example of "Little Red Riding Hood." But then, you should not put too much faith in chronology when dealing with oral traditions. Only rarely are oral variants captured in writ (and so dated variants are scarce); moreover, since oral variants usually transform other variants, you cannot really date a given theme after the fortuitous date when a text featuring it was collected. Usually, oral variants use themes that have long been around in various guises. Bearing this caveat in mind, we turn to Delarue's study of the oral tradition of "Little Red Riding Hood." Delarue showed that over half of the modern French oral variants bear no motifs resembling the well-known contents of Perrault's text (e.g., the red hood, flower picking along the way); he also showed that almost all the collected oral variants feature a stable string of motifs (e.g., the paths of needles and pins, the cannibalistic meal) not apparent in "Le Petit Chaperon rouge." These facts, considered together, reveal a strain of variants owing nothing to Perrault's text—in other words, an independent oral tradition (Delarue 1951b; cf. Tenèze 1973, 45–48).[5]

The continuity of this oral tradition over time is not in doubt. In fact, barely one century or so elapsed between Perrault's manuscript (1695, see Barchilon 1956) and the days when the instructors of the oldest tellers of independent collected oral variants walked the earth. (For instance, Nannette Lévesque, an illiterate tale-teller certifiably born in 1803, must have drawn on eighteenth-century lore for her independent variant; see Tenèze and Delarue 2000, 4, 12–13, 99–103.) It is hard to conceive that in this short time span Perrault's text could have yielded a full-fledged oral tradition, and it is mind-boggling that Perrault's story might have spawned a tradition that lacks precisely Perrault's motifs while displaying other motifs not featured in Perrault's text. (Think about this for a moment.) However, everything falls nicely into place if we imagine that Perrault drew on oral variants of his own time, presumably bearing a close family resemblance to those variants collected at a later date, to spin his own variation on the traditional theme.

The werewolf motif provides an example of how Perrault may have transposed some rough folk motifs into images that were relevant to his aristocratic milieu. Folklorist Victor Smith was told, in a region where he collected a few independent oral variants of "Little Red Riding Hood" in the 1870s, that there "everybody or almost everybody believes in the werewolf" (Tenèze and Delarue 2000, 79). We do not have to take this anecdote literally to acknowledge the pervasiveness of hoary werewolf traditions (see Summers 1933; Vaz da Silva 2008). And here is my point. Whereas it would be absurd to suggest that the ancient werewolf belief derives from Perrault's wolf-man, Perrault's wolf-man is readily explainable as a clever euphemism for the werewolf. By means of playful understatement, Perrault turned the werewolf of immemorial folklore into the sophisticated pedo-phile who preys on well-born girls. As he transposed a werewolf theme into an attenuated form fit for aristocratic consumption, Perrault obtained a symbolically layered masterpiece yielding readings at various levels of "pen-etration," as intended. (This point applies to other aspects of Perrault's text, too, as will be seen.)

I often find it useful to point out that Perrault's double-entendre had a mixed reception in literary circles. On the one hand, Angela Carter—who translated Perrault's *contes*, and rewrote some of them—transposed his notion of (as she translates it) "smooth-tongued, smoothed-pelted wolves [that] are the most dangerous beasts of all" (Carter 2008, 3) into her own statement that "the worst wolves are hairy on the inside" (Carter 1995, 117; Carter 1997, 64, see 66, 194, 203). Carter, who was keenly attuned to sym-bolic equivalences, recognized in Perrault's most dangerous of all wolves an allusion to the fabled werewolf. Hence, she put her own spin on the received notion that werewolves in human shape are the worst wolves of all. On a distinctly different track, Delarue represented the positivistic stance of many folklorists as he flatly declared that the wolf in "Little Red Riding Hood" is just a real, flesh-and-blood wolf (Delarue 1951b, 290). This stance got him into a memorable fix because it fails to acknowledge the testimony of "The Story of Grandmother," which Delarue himself took as an example of the French oral tradition of tale type 333 (Delarue 1985, 373–74), while also ignoring Perrault's statement on the issue. And, as Yvonne Verdier (1995, 175–76) noted, Delarue's positivistic stance is at variance with the fact that Delarue classified "Little Red Riding Hood" in the French folktale catalog among tale types 300–399, which are "*wonder* tales" dealing with "*supernatu-ral* adversaries" (Delarue 1985, 393–94; my emphasis).

It is instructive to realize that a folklorist's refusal to heed a symbolic element in his materials puts him at odds with his oldest source ("Le Petit Chaperon rouge"), with his own chosen example of oral independent variants ("Tale of Grandmother"), and with the classificatory criteria he retained in his folktale catalog. Whereas Carter's grasp of symbolism proves illuminating, the consequences of a folklorist's disregard for meanings can be pathetic—a lesson to keep in mind.

SYMBOLIC EQUIVALENCES IN "ROTKÄPPCHEN"

Bearing this lesson in mind, we venture one step ahead in the semantic field of "Little Red Riding Hood" as we consider the Grimm variant. Ever since

H. V. Velten (1930) suggested that "Rotkäppchen" does not stray far from "Le Petit Chaperon rouge," this is the predominant view on the subject (see Zipes 1993a, 32–33). The available evidence for the idea that Perrault's text looms large in the genealogy of "Rotkäppchen" stands on three facts: First, this text was provided to the Grimms by Jeanette Hassenpflug, an educated young woman hailing from a French-speaking Huguenot family acquainted with French tales and culture. Second, a number of phrases in Grimms' text look like loose translations—or, at times, verbose developments—of sentences in Perrault's variant. And third, as Delarue (1951a, 200; 1951b, 254–55) decisively notes, all the oral motifs missing in Perrault's variant are also absent in the Grimm text.

All this evidence is undeniable. Still, both Velten and Delarue acknowledge a chain of oral retellings between Perrault's text and the Grimm variant. Since tales in oral settings are transmitted by means of symbolic equivalences, rather than through rote replication, a number of symbolic translations may be expected. With this in mind, I ask the students to carefully reread the Grimm variant. We take good note of the fact that in this variant (unlike in Perrault's text) there is a particular emphasis on the metaphoric dimension of "straightness." The girl on her way to her grandmother's house is supposed to look straight ahead and not stray from the path lest she break her bottle. In this metaphorical line, keeping to the straight path denotes virtue—and straying from it amounts to moral perdition. Indeed, the young woman leaves the path in response to the wolf's plea to stop behaving seriously, as if going to school, when it is so much fun being in the woods. Even so, the metaphor of female perdition in the Grimm text echoes the metaphor of lupine lust in Perrault's morality. The two literary arrangements convey the same moral message—careless young women who give in to the lupine seducer will likely be eaten—but they do so by different means. Whereas Perrault writes a clever morality to bring out the metaphoric (sexual) dimension of the wolf's meal, the Brothers Grimm deliver a metaphor of female straying and perdition. The point here is that the Grimm text creatively builds on (rather than merely replicates) its predecessor.

The second point I wish to make is that, beyond Perrault, the Grimm text also interacts with oral traditions humming in the background. "Rotkäppchen" includes, in fact, two oral variants. After the main text, offered by Jeanette Hassenpflug, there is the short abstract of another variant presumably provided by Marie Hassenpflug, if not by "the Marie from the Wild household," as stated in Bolte and Polívka 1913, 284 (see Rölleke 1991; Bluhm 2000). Both variants stray from Perrault's plot in ways that bear traces of oral traditions. Marie's story develops in a way reminiscent of ATU 124, "Blowing the House In" (recall "The Three Little Pigs"), in which the wolf may die by burning or drowning as he tries to enter the house; and Jeanette's variant develops in a way reminiscent of ATU 123, "The Wolf and the Kids," as it features the release of the grandmother and the girl from the wolf's belly followed by the beast's death. The Grimms may also have drawn a couple of details from Ludwig Tieck's *Leben und Tod des Kleinen Rotkäppchens* (see Zipes 1993a, 35). In any event, it is clear that the Grimm text is hardly a mere paraphrase of its literary predecessor.

Delarue, to sustain the notion that Jeanette's contribution is mostly a paraphrase of Perrault's text, dismisses its peculiar ending as a "contamination" by a theme popular in German tradition (Delarue 1951b, 284–85). However, the contamination metaphor hardly explains anything at all. Just like in epidemiology there are biological reasons why some organisms will spread to colonize other organisms, so in narratives there are semantic reasons why some motifs may appear in different stories. The bottom line is, one must engage with symbolic equivalences in order to fathom those semantic reasons. In other words, appraising the meaning of the rescue from the wolf's belly requires looking at other comparable motifs in the "Little Red Riding Hood" tradition.

At this point I ask the students to again turn to "The Story of Grandmother," which presents a happy ending that pervades a number of oral variants in France and in some areas of Italy (Tyrol and Abruzzo). After the girl realizes she is in bed with the wolf, she resorts to a desperate ruse:

> "Oh, grandmother, how hungry I am to go outside [*que j'ai faim d'aller dehors*]!"
> "Do it in bed, my child!"
> "Oh, no, grandmother, I want to go outside."
> "All right, but only for a short time."
> The *bzou* tied a woolen thread to her foot and let her go. When the little girl was outside she attached the end of the thread to a plum tree in the courtyard. The *bzou* was getting impatient and saying: "Are you making ropes? Are you making ropes?" [*Tu fous donc des cordes? Tu fous donc des cordes?*]
> When he realized that nobody answered him, he jumped out of bed and saw that the little girl had escaped. He chased her, but arrived at her house just at the moment she entered. (Delarue 1985, 374)

Keep in mind that this particular ending coexists with a variety of other legitimate endings. For instance, in a group of oral variants collected in the French Alps in the 1950s, the wolf sometimes eats the girl (like in Perrault) and at other times it is killed—on occasion by a hunter (as in Grimm), and at other times by drowning in a river whereas the girl gets across safely (Joisten 1971, 286–97). In some illuminating instances, the young woman goes across the stream with the help of laundresses, who then make sure the wolf drowns in the water (Tenèze 1973, 61–66; Verdier 1995, 194, 206). Helpfully, Verdier points out that the role of those laundresses in the tale matches the job of laundresses in the social reality of yore: the job of washing newborns and corpses, that is, of helping in childbirth and in death. Verdier also notes that in some oral variants "the trip to the grandmother's little house . . . presents all the characteristics of an initiatory visit . . . entry [feet first] lived as death, exit [cutting a thread like the umbilical cord of a newborn] as birth" (Verdier 1997, 116–17).

In light of this tradition, it is clear that the Grimm variant draws a metonymic link between the forest cabin and the forest demon. The girl enters the wolf's body (she enters the cabin in oral variants), drawing a parallel with dying; then she exits the wolf (she exits the cabin in oral variants), drawing a parallel with birth by caesarian section. The examination of allomotifs shows that "Rotkäppchen" matches a strain of oral variants that correlate the young woman's rebirth with the wolf's death. More exactly, the Grimm variant transforms both Perrault's morality and an initiatory strain in the oral tradition. And so the students realize that getting acquainted with an oral variant actually helps them understand the familiar literary texts by Perrault and Grimm. This is because the literary texts use the same symbolic language as the folk variants. Both Perrault and Grimm have built on traditional metaphoric idioms, which is why bringing out those idioms in the oral tradition helps illuminate the literary texts.

In order to clarify this proposition, I ask the students to focus on an intriguing image in the Grimm text. When the mother warns the girl not to stray from the path, she specifies, "otherwise you'll fall and break the glass, and your grandmother will get nothing" (Grimm and Grimm 2014, 85). The bottle-breaking image is (as far as I know) unique to the Grimm variant. But it is not hard to show that it matches other allomotifs.

Recall that the mother's injunction is a metaphorical depiction of moral perdition. It refers to succumbing to temptation (lured by a wolf) and leaving the righteous path. Within this metaphoric thread, breaking the glass (or the bottle—*das Glas*) likely connotes the shattering of the girl's integrity. Recall Sigmund Freud's general remark that female genitals are often symbolized by "vessels and bottles" and other containers, the opening of which signifies lost virginity (Freud 1989, 192, 199). In European traditional societies, where drawing water at the fountain was part and parcel of young women's chores, the symbolic connection between the intact maidens and their vessels was unmistakable.[6] Hence, the breaking of a young woman's pitcher used to be a metaphor for the loss of her virginity (e.g., Portuguese slang expressions for breaking a maiden's pitcher, such as *romper o cabaço* and *quebrar a bilha*, connote defloration). The same idea crops up in fairy tales. "The Three Oranges" (ATU 408), for instance, features a shady character who breaks her own pitcher at the fountain before usurping the rightful bride's place in marriage (Goldberg 1997, 74–83). In precisely the same strain, the mother's warning to Rotkäppchen about a broken wine bottle bespeaks the concern that the girl might compromise her virginity.

The defloration image is particularly compelling in "Rotkäppchen" because, of course, a shattered wine bottle involves a red flow. However, the Brothers are careful to contain the implications of this bold metaphor. At the end of the story the bottle is still intact, and the girl vows obedience to her mother—a happy end that agrees with the Brothers' well-attested zeal for expunging sexual scenes (see Tatar 1987, 7–11). But, of course, the very display of an intact bottle to deny a sexual scene confirms the metaphoric value of the glass. Displaying an intact bottle for a prim ending is but a special use (a negative instance) of the broken-bottle metaphor. Thus, the Brothers manage to preserve the sexual symbolism *and* to present an educational warning tale (much as, we recall, Perrault achieves a tale of rape that can be told to mixed audiences). This is a prime example of how folktales keep going through variation—of how tale-tellers adapt a traditional scheme to their own particular tastes and agendas while transmitting the tale one more step into the future.

At this point, one or more students are bound to notice that the equivalence between wine and blood in the (un)broken-bottle metaphor echoes another form of the same equivalence in oral variants. You may recall that in "Tale of Grandmother" the girl drinks her grandmother's blood as "wine." Here is the relevant episode:

> The little girl enjoyed herself picking up needles. Meanwhile the *bzou* arrived at her grandmother's, killed her, put some of her flesh in the crate [*arche*] and a bottle of her blood on the sink [*bassie*]. The girl arrived and knocked at the door.
>
> "Push the door," said the *bzou*, "it's latched with a wet straw."
>
> "Hello, granny, I'm bringing you a hot loaf and a bottle of milk."
>
> "Put them in the crate. You take the meat that's in it and a bottle of wine that is on the sink."
>
> As she ate, there was a little cat that said: "Phooey! The slut! Eating the flesh, drinking the blood of her granny!" (Delarue 1985, 373)

The symbolic link between wine and blood is both ancient and pervasive. It underlies the Eucharist, of course, and also comes across in a host
of proverbial sayings such as, "wine makes blood" (see Albert 1991, 82;
Cardini 1991, 101). This is presumably why the wine Rotkäppchen takes
to her grandmother is supposed to strengthen the old woman; and yet,
oral variants show that the girl strengthens herself as she drinks her grandmother's blood in the guise of wine. While no single variant brings the two
wine-as-blood iterations together (which is an example of why no single
variant ever expresses a tale all by itself), the comparison of variants unveils
a blood link between the older woman and the girl.

Note that while oral variants acknowledge that the girl ingests her
grandmother's blood, Perrault and Grimm (as usual) choose to tread lightly
on a delicate subject. I submit for discussion in class that Perrault may have
replaced the vampiric motif of the old woman's blood passed on to the girl
with the transmission of something else that is red (but avoids shocking
delicate sensitivities). The fact of the matter is that the two literary texts that
lack the motif of transmitted blood also feature the motif of a red garment
transmitted between the older and the younger women. Thus, the notion
that something red is passed on among women still lingers in the literary
texts. Usually, this suggestion triggers a moment of thrill in the classroom
as the familiar red cap starts making sense. It helps that Angela Carter, in
her own rewriting of the story, pronounces the transmitted garment "quite
a bloody red. Quite bloody" (Carter 1997, 61).

By now the students realize that the motif of the wine bottle in Grimm
is not an isolated motif at all; rather, it resonates with a pervasive blood
theme in the tale. In order to establish that the wine bottle matches a set
of blood motifs in the story, I ask the students to again consider the "Story
of Grandmother." The girl on her way to her grandmother's house amuses
herself collecting needles, which fits the fact that most oral variants name
the two paths to the forest house after needles and pins. Other names for
the paths include nettles, pebbles, briars, and roses.[7] Perceptively, Verdier
remarks that all those pins, needles, thorns, brambles, and rocks "scratch,
prick, cut," and so elicit blood (Verdier 1997, 105–7). Overall, these allomotifs share the implication that the girl oozes blood on her way to her
grandmother's house. With hindsight it becomes clear that Grimms' bearer
of a wine bottle partakes of this image of a pubescent virgin brimming with
blood on her way to the forest cabin.

And now I ask the students to reread the corresponding scene in
Perrault's text. Here the girl carries a cake and a pot of butter for granny,
and she amuses herself gathering hazelnuts, chasing butterflies, and picking

flowers along the way. Perrault does not retain the paths' traditional names
and so elides the pricking details. Even so, he conveys the underlying meaning in an elegant way. Basically, Perrault says it with flowers. In accordance
with the French expression *jeunes filles en fleurs* ("maidens in bloom"), which
designates menarcheal girls, Perrault depicts a flower-bearing girl heading to
her defloration.[8] Now the students realize that Perrault conveys with flowers what other folk variations portray as a "pricking" path leading into the
woods. And the fact that the Grimm text depicts an actual path of flowers
into the woods also fits the pattern of a menarcheal girl walking the walk to
meet her destiny in the forest hut. Here is the Grimms' final arrangement
of this scene (in the 1857 edition):

> She caught sight of the beautiful flowers all around and thought: "If you
> bring Grandmother a fresh bouquet, she'll be delighted. It's still early
> enough that I'm sure to get there in plenty of time."
>   Little Red Riding Hood left the path and ran off into the woods look-
> ing for flowers. As soon as she picked one, she spotted an even more beau-
> tiful one somewhere else and went after it. And so she went even deeper
> into the woods . . . When she had gathered so many that she couldn't hold
> any more in her arms, she suddenly remembered Grandmother and got
> back on the path leading to her house. (Tatar 2012, 151)

Quite interestingly, the notion that the girl follows a path of flowers
meant for her grandmother agrees with the mother's warning not to spill
the wine meant for her grandmother. The fact that both the flowers and the
wine are meant for her suggests the equivalence of the two motifs. Indeed,
by now the basis of this equivalence is clear. Breaking the bottle is code
for shattering the girl's integrity; and, of course, losing one's flowers is the
literal meaning of defloration. This is why the metaphor of the wine bottle
says the same thing as the metaphor of maidens in bloom. A straying young
woman will break her "glass" or lose her "flowers," depending on the metaphor you use—she will, in a word, bleed in the forest.

We saw that while the Brothers Grimm deny that the girl breaks the
bottle, they do highlight the broken-bottle metaphor. This is not an isolated
case. In "The Twelve Brothers" (KHM 9), for example, a "blood-red" flag
displayed at the birth of a girl sends her brothers into exile in the forest.
The brothers promise they will shed the "red blood" of any girl they meet
(Tatar 2012, 38), and they become hunters, which means they begin shed-
ding the blood of their prey in the forest. The first edition actually specifies
that "whenever they encountered a maiden, she . . . lost her life" (Grimm
and Grimm 2014, 29), but this passage was elided later. Anyway, the sister

who was announced by a red flag—she who impersonates the red blood the brothers swore to spill—eventually joins her brothers in the forest. According to the first edition, on arrival she is met with a stark injunction: "Kneel down! Your red blood will flow this very second!" (30). Which was later to be replaced by the softer announcement of the brothers' vow to "kill any girl who crossed our threshold" (Tatar 2012, 40). Overall, the clear implication is that the sister is bound to bleed—indeed, oral variants feature her bleeding in the forest cabin (Vaz da Silva 2014)—but the Brothers Grimm blur this entailment as they say the brothers forgive their sister. Like in "Rotkäppchen," the Grimms make use of traditional symbolic codes, but then soften the entailments of those codes. Thus, they manage to preserve traditional symbolism while making sure that morality prevails. While each of their *Kunstmärchen* appears anodyne (if perhaps disquieting) in itself, intertextual readings bring out the rich symbolic contents of these texts.

CONCLUSION

In this short discussion, I have reported the contents of the first two weeks in my fairy-tale course. These introductory sessions make the point that dealing with fairy tales involves a flip of the mind. This mental conversion comes from realizing that traditional storytelling is about the creative retelling of tales by means of symbolic equivalences, which implies that the reckoning of meanings (either consciously or otherwise) is at the core of storytelling. Consequently, the study of traditional tales must deal with symbolism. But this is not the same thing as imposing your own preset interpretive key (of whatever persuasion) on tales; rather, it is about identifying the constant ideas underlying variations in a given tradition.

The heuristic process of seeking out meanings through textual comparison usually proves illuminating to the participants in this course. By the end of this two-week preliminary introduction to symbolic analysis, the students are usually eager to explore extensively the symbolic field of a fairy tale and then to experimentally cast their nets wider so as to incorporate other symbolic fields. As they eventually realize that the same approach applies to other aspects of folklore and popular culture, some students will look out for meaningful patterns whenever stable themes come in countless variations (as in films, ads, tweets, Internet chats, etc.). One lesson from this course is that old themes often linger in the modern popular culture, and no single text ever provides the key to a traditional theme. In principle, *all* the variants of a given theme are relevant to the search for meanings. The two-week introduction I have described, using but three variants, is a mere appetizer.

NOTES

1. English translations of "The Tale of Grandmother" are readily available (see Delarue 1980, 230–32; 1989, 15–16; Zipes 1993a, 21–23). Delarue (1980, 373–74) used this variant as an example of French oral texts that are quite independent from Perrault's "Le Petit Chaperon rouge." Sometimes scholars speak about "The Tale of Grandmother" as though it was *the* authoritative text representative of the French oral tradition. It is not, of course, for in oral settings no variant is more "authentic" (and, therefore, authoritative) than any other. Still, it is a good comparative counterpoint to Perrault's text, and I use it as such.

2. According to *Le Nouveau Petit Robert*, the word *ruelle* designates the space between beds, or between a bed and the wall; and, by extension, an alcove or sleeping room.

3. I translate from Perrault (1989, 256), partly following Zipes (1993b, 93). Unless otherwise stated, all translations are mine.

4. This dedication was signed by Perrault's son Pierre, then seventeen years old. Whatever Pierre's role may have been in this project, almost no one has seriously doubted that the clever allusions and the moralities in the reworked tales are Charles Perrault's work (see useful discussions and data in Barchilon 1956, 19–28; Delarue 1954; Soriano 1977, 21–70).

5. For a summary of Delarue's conclusions, see Delarue (1985, 381–83). An English version of this summary is available in Delarue (1980, 380–83; 1989, 16–20).

6. This is a widespread analogy. The first woman in Greek mythology, Pandora, was molded with earth and filled with various things, like an earthenware jar (Vernant 2006, 43, 266). The symbolic link between women and earthenware jars is just as clear in the modern American Southwest (Babcock 1994).

7. The English version translates Verdier's reference to *épines ou roses*, "briars or roses" (Verdier 1995, 177), as "roots or stones" (Verdier 1997, 105), which is nonsensical.

8. Here I have to leave aside a number of threads cropping up in Perrault's text. For instance, the hazelnuts the girl picks on her way to her grandmother in Perrault match the hazel hedge around the old woman's cabin in Grimm. This shared association of hazel with the forest cabin should be interpreted in light of the supernatural connotation of hazel trees (and nuts, and wood) in folklore. Also, the butter the girl carries in Perrault's variant matches the milk jar she carries in "The Tale of Grandmother." The notion that the girl carries dairy products to her grandmother correlates with the cannibalistic meal in which she eats the old woman's breasts (Verdier 1997, 109–10), just as the wine-carrying motif correlates with drinking the old woman's blood as wine. But, again, these symbolic explorations cannot be pursued here.

REFERENCES

Albert, Jean-Pierre. 1991. "Le vin sans ivresse: Remarques sur la liturgie eucharistique." In *Le ferment divin*, ed. Dominique Fournier and Salvatore D'Onofrio, 77–91. Paris: Editions de la Maison des sciences de l'homme. http://dx.doi.org/10.4000/books.editionsmsh.2408.

Babcock, Barbara A. 1994. "Pueblo Cultural Bodies." *Journal of American Folklore* 107 (423): 40–54. http://dx.doi.org/10.2307/541072 http://www.jstor.org/stable/541072.

Barchilon, Jacques. 1956. *Perrault's Tales of Mother Goose: The Dedication Manuscript of 1695 Reproduced in Collotype Facsimile with Introduction and Critical Text*. Vol. 1. New York: Pierpont Morgan Library.

Bartlett, Frederic C. 1920. "Some Experiments on the Reproduction of Folk-Stories." *Folklore* 31 (1): 30–47. http://dx.doi.org/10.1080/0015587X.1920.9719123.

Bluhm, Lothar. 2000. "A New Debate about 'Old Marie'? Critical Observations on the Attempt to Remythologize Grimms' Fairy Tales from a Sociohistorical Perspective." Trans. Deborah Lokai Bischof. *Marvels & Tales* 14 (2): 287–311.

Bolte, Johannes, and Georg Polívka. 1913. *Anmerkungen zu den Kinder- u. Hausmärchen der Brüder Grimm*. Vol. 1. Leipzig: Dieterich'sche Verlagsbuchhandlung.

Cardini, Franco. 1991. "*Hoc est sanguis meus:* Le vin dans l'Occident médiéval." In *Le ferment divin*, ed. Dominique Fournier and Salvatore D'Onofrio, 101–7. Paris: Editions de la Maison des sciences de l'homme. http://dx.doi.org/10.4000/books.editionsmsh .2412.

Carter, Angela. 1995. *The Bloody Chamber*. London: Vintage.

Carter, Angela. 1997. *The Curious Room: Collected Dramatic Works*. Ed. Mark Bell. London: Vintage and Random House.

Carter, Angela. 2008. *Little Red Riding Hood, Cinderella, and Other Classic Fairy Tales of Charles Perrault*. New York: Penguin Classics.

Delarue, Paul. 1951a. "Les contes merveilleux de Perrault et la tradition populaire: Introduction." *Bulletin folklorique d'Ile-de-France* 13 (1): 195–201.

Delarue, Paul. 1951b. "Les contes merveilleux de Perrault et la tradition populaire: Le Petit Chaperon rouge." *Bulletin folklorique d'Ile-de-France* 13 (2–4): 221–28, 251–60, 283–91.

Delarue, Paul. 1954. "Les contes merveilleux de Perrault: Faits et rapprochements nouveaux." *Arts et Traditions populaires* 2 (1): 1–22.

Delarue, Paul, ed. [1956] 1980 . *The Borzoi Book of French Folk Tales*. Trans. Austin E. Fife. New York: Knopf. Repr., New York: Arno Press.

Delarue, Paul. 1985. *Le conte populaire français: Catalogue raisonné des versions de France et des pays de langue française d'outre-mer*. 2nd ed. Vol. 1. Paris: Maisonneuve et Larose.

Delarue, Paul. 1989. "The Story of Grandmother." In *Little Red Riding Hood: A Casebook*, ed. Alan Dundes, trans. Austin E. Fife., 13–20. Madison: University of Wisconsin Press.

Dundes, Alan. 2007. "The Symbolic Equivalence of Allomotifs: Towards a Method of Analyzing Folktales." In *The Meaning of Folklore: The Analytical Essays of Alan Dundes*, ed. Simon J. Bronner, 319–24. Logan: Utah State University Press.

Freud, Sigmund. 1989. *Introductory Lectures on Psycho-Analysis*. Trans. James Strachey. New York: Norton.

Goldberg, Christine. 1997. *The Tale of the Three Oranges*. Helsinki: Academia Scientiarum Fennica.

Grimm, Jacob, and Wilhelm Grimm. 1812. *Kinder- und Haus-Märchen. Gesammelt durch die Brüder Grimm*. Vol 1. Berlin: Realschulbuchhandlung. https://de.wikisource.org/wiki /Kinder-_und_Haus-Märchen_Band_1_(1812).

Grimm, Jacob, and Wilhelm Grimm. 2014. *The Original Folk and Fairy Tales of the Brothers Grimm: The Complete First Edition*. Ed. and trans. Jack Zipes. Princeton: Princeton University Press.

Jakobson, Roman, and Petr Bogatyrev. 1982. "Folklore as a Special Form of Creativity." In *The Prague School: Selected Writings, 1929–1946*, ed. Peter Steiner and trans. Manfred Jacobson, 32–46. Austin: University of Texas Press.

Joisten, Charles. 1971. *Contes populaires du Dauphiné*. Vol. 1. Grenoble: Publications du Musée dauphinois.

Massignon, Geneviève. 2006. *De bouche à oreille: Anthologie de contes populaires français*. Paris: Corti.

Perrault, Charles. 1697. *Histoires ou Contes du Temps Passé Avec des Moralitez*. Paris: Claude Barbin.

Perrault, Charles. 1989. *Contes*. Ed. Marc Soriano. Paris: Flammarion.

Rölleke, Heinz. 1991. "New Results of Research on Grimms' Fairy Tales." In *The Brothers Grimm and Folktale*, ed. James M. McGlathery, 101–11. Urbana: University of Illinois Press.

Soriano, Marc. 1977. *Les contes de Perrault: Culture savante et traditions populaires*. Rev. ed. Paris: Gallimard.

Summers, Montague. 1933. *The Werewolf*. London: Kegan Paul.

Tatar, Maria. 1987. The *Hard Facts of the Grimms' Fairy Tales*. Princeton: Princeton University Press.

Tatar, Maria. 2012. *The Annotated Brothers Grimm*. The Bicentennial ed. New York: Norton.

Tenèze, Marie-Louise. 1973. "Motifs stylistiques de contes et aires culturelles: Aubrac et France du Centre." In *Mélanges de folklore et d'ethnographie dédiés à la mémoire d'Elisée Legros*, 45–83. Liège: Musée walon.

Tenèze, Marie-Louise, and Georges Delarue, eds. 2000. *Nannette Lévesque, conteuse et chanteuse du pays des sources de la Loire*. Paris: Gallimard.

Uther, Hans-Jörg. 2004. *The Types of International Folktales: A Classification and Bibliography, Based on the System of Antti Aarne and Stith Thompson*. 3 vols. Helsinki: Academia Scientiarum Fennica.

Vaz da Silva, Francisco. 2008. "Werewolf, Wolf, Wolves." In *The Greenwood Encyclopedia of Folktales & Fairy Tales*, ed. Donald Haase, vol. 3, 1025–27. Westport: Greenwood Press. doi: 10.1336/0313334412.

Vaz da Silva, Francisco. 2012. "Tradition without End." In *A Companion to Folklore*, ed. Regina F. Bendix and Galit Hasan-Rokem, 40–54. Chichester: Wiley-Blackwell. doi: http://dx.doi.org/10.1002/9781118379936.ch2.

Vaz da Silva, Francisco. 2014. "Fairy-Tale Symbolism." In *The Cambridge Companion to Fairy Tales*, ed. Maria Tatar, 97–116. Cambridge: Cambridge University Press. http://dx .doi.org/10.1017/CCO9781139381062.007.

Velten, H. V. 1930. "The Influence of Charles Perrault's *Contes de ma Mere l'Oie* on German Folklore." *Germanic Review* 5 (1): 4–18.

Verdier, Yvonne. 1995. "Le Petit Chaperon rouge dans la tradition orale." In *Coutume et destin: Thomas Hardy et autres essais*, ed. Yvonne Verdier, Claudine Vassas, and Daniel Fabre, 171–206. Paris: Gallimard.

Verdier, Yvonne. 1997. "Little Red Riding Hood in Oral Tradition." Trans. Joseph Gaughan. *Marvels & Tales* 11 (1–2): 101–23.

Vernant, Jean-Pierre. 2006. *Myth and Thought among the Greeks*. Trans. Janet Lloyd and Jeff Fort. New York: Zone Books.

Zipes, Jack. 1993a. "The Trials and Tribulations of Little Red Riding Hood." In *The Trials and Tribulations of Little Red Riding Hood*, 2nd ed., ed. Jack Zipes, 17–88. New York, London: Routledge.

Zipes, Jack, ed. 1993b. *The Trials and Tribulations of Little Red Riding Hood*. 2nd ed. New York, London: Routledge.

Part IV
Classical Tales through the Gendered Lens
Cinematic Adaptations in the Traditional Classroom and Online

12

Binary Outlaws
Queering the Classical Tale in François Ozon's Criminal Lovers *and Catherine Breillat's* The Sleeping Beauty

Anne E. Duggan

WITHIN THE DOMAIN OF FAIRY-TALE STUDIES, QUEER THEORY has yet to receive the critical attention that it deserves, particularly given the centrality of sexuality in fairy tales.[1] This situation increasingly is changing, evident in the work of Kay Turner and Pauline Greenhill, among others.[2] Approaching fairy-tale texts and films from the perspective of queer theory can help students understand the ways in which fairy-tale plots can subvert what is often—and problematically—taken for granted in classical tales: the heteronormative plot, upheld by a specific configuration of gender roles. As Turner has argued, "Even if many tales hurtle headlong toward normative reunion, marriage, and stability, often the route navigates a topsy-turvy space filled with marvels, magic, and weird encounters that don't simply contradict the 'normal' but offer, or at least hint at, alternative possibilities for fulfilling desires that might alter individual destinies" (Turner 2012, 248). French fairy-tale films provide a compelling area of study with respect to queer theory because of the existence of a genealogy of French queer directors—including Jean Cocteau, Jacques Demy, and François Ozon—who have drawn from the fairy-tale genre to represent nonnormative forms of sexuality.[3] Although Catherine Breillat is not considered a queer director, her cinematic work can fit broadly within the notion of queer in its subversion of normative forms of heterosexuality, as will become evident below. Rather than focus on the kinds of subtle camping or queering of the fairy-tale characteristic of the films of Cocteau and Demy, here I will turn to the fairy-tale films of Ozon and Breillat, who very explicitly alter classical plots to create queer versions of classical tales.

DOI: 10.7330/9781607324812.c012

In order to approach Ozon's *Les Amants criminels* (1999, Eng. *Criminal Lovers*, 2001) and Breillat's *La Belle endormie* (*The Sleeping Beauty*, 2010) from a queer perspective, it is important to provide some basic theoretical parameters for queer approaches to the fairy tale that would be accessible to undergraduate students, graduate students, or both, depending on the level of the course. I have successfully drawn upon the material I am presenting here in both undergraduate and graduate settings. In the case of undergraduate students, I always provide them with a choice of topics; they only need to work with queer readings if they feel comfortable doing so. Whether they choose to use queer theory in their analysis or not, they are able to grasp the general concepts and understand how one might carry out such a reading in relation to fairy-tale film, evident in class discussions. In presenting queer theory to both undergraduate and graduate students, I have found the work of Alexander Doty and Steven Angelides particularly accessible. Students can then move on to a comparative analysis of the classical tale from which each director draws ("Hansel and Gretel" in *Criminal Lovers*; "Sleeping Beauty" in *The Sleeping Beauty*). Against the backdrop of queer theory, such comparative analysis allows students to consider the importance of the changes made to the classical tale that make the cinematic adaptation a queer one, at the same time that it encourages students to probe the sites where the classical tale might give way to or open up queer possibilities.

Before proceeding any further, it is necessary to add that both films, and especially *Criminal Lovers*, contain explicit sexual material that could be challenging for some students; instructors should thus alert students to the sexually explicit nature of the films and perhaps provide the option of alternative films when discussing sexually explicit adaptations of fairy tales. For general education undergraduate courses at Wayne State University, I have not had any issues thus far in assigning films that contain sexually explicit material, and I believe it is precisely because of my frank discussions with the students beforehand about the nature of the films, my efforts to explain the context for such representations, and the fact that I provide them with alternative films they can focus on if the subject makes them uncomfortable, even if the class as a whole discusses the films. Also, I make films available through streaming, which reduces the discomfort of watching more sexually explicit material together as a class and puts less pressure on students who wish to work with an alternative film. When approaching fairy-tale film from a queer perspective, instructors may also consider using Cocteau's *La Belle et la Bête* (1946, *Beauty and the Beast*) and Demy's *Peau d'âne* (1970, *Donkey Skin*), which furnish less sexually explicit material from which to draw.[4]

QUEER THEORY

In order to understand the ways in which queer theory can be used to analyze the fairy-tale films of Ozon and Breillat, it is useful to begin with a
definition of "heteronormativity," which queer theory works to problema-
tize, denaturalize, and subvert. Lauren Berlant and Michael Warner provide
a succinct definition of "heteronormativity" that carefully distinguishes it
from "heterosexuality": "By heteronormativity we mean the institutions,
structures of understanding, and practical orientations that make heterosexuality seem not only coherent—that is, organized as a sexuality—but
also privileged" (Berlant and Warner 1998, 548n2). Part of what makes normative heterosexuality seem coherent is a particular configuration of gender relations supported by such binaries as masculinity/femininity, active/
passive, subject/object, which organize the identities of what comes to be
perceived of as the clearly demarcated categories of "man" and "woman."
By detaching "heteronormativity" from "heterosexuality," one can foreground the constructedness and regulation of heterosexuality—including
the constructedness and regulation of gender norms that support heteronormativity—as well as open up heterosexuality to its queer possibilities,
thus blurring the boundaries between heterosexuality and homosexuality.

Both Doty and Angelides insist on the impossibility of separating sexuality from gender, which mutually support each other. They suggest that
queer comes to signify, in Doty's words, "binary outlaw" (Doty 1993, xvi) in
its refusal to uphold binary distinctions such as queer and straight or male
and female. He states: "I ultimately use it [*queer*] to question the cultural
demarcations between the queer and the straight (made by both queer and
straights) by pointing out the queerness of and in straights and straight
cultures, as well as that of individuals and groups who have been told they
inhabit the boundaries between the binaries of gender and sexuality: transsexuals, bisexuals, transvestites, and other binary outlaws" (Doty 1993, xv–
xvi). The binary outlaw, then, does not respect the logic of either/or that
upholds heteronormativity. Angelides explains:

> In order for something to be only one or the other, it is therefore neces-
> sary to prohibit a term being both one *and* the other. Anything that is both
> one and the other contradicts the logic of either/or and must be repressed,
> disavowed, or excluded. As we have seen, in the hetero/homosexual struc-
> ture the position of both/and is occupied by bisexuality; hence its contra-
> dictory presence must be erased. (Angelides 2001, 188)

While Angelides focuses on bisexuality, the same logic applies to gender: in order to uphold categories of "male" and "female" and consequently

"heteronormativity," it is necessary to prohibit subjects from being *both* masculine and feminine. Within such a logic, expressions of sexuality that include female ejaculation and heterosexual sodomy, and figures like the tomboy or the cross-dresser, all put into question normative gender and sexuality precisely by rejecting the binaries that maintain heteronormativity.[5]

Moreover, queer theory questions the very possibility of "pure" heterosexuality that would be supported by ideal incarnations of femininity and masculinity. In many respects, queer theory works to expose heteronormativity as a purely utopic—or dystopic—construction that pushes subjects toward an ideal that can never be attained—not even in fairy tales, as queer readings of classical tales would suggest.[6] Angelides insists that "instead of reifying sexuality identity categories, queer theory takes as its project the task of exposing the operations of *heteronormativity* in order to work the hetero / homosexual opposition to the point of critical collapse" (Angelides 2001, 168). Queer carries out this work, in Ellis Hanson's words, by challenging "the familiar distinctions between normal and pathological, straight and gay, masculine men and feminine women" (Hanson 1993, 138).

In order to make these concepts concrete for students, instructors can generate a table drawn from the critical overview they provide to foreground the binaries that uphold heteronormativity, shown in Table 12.1.

Importantly, distinctions between man and woman, masculine and feminine, are essential in upholding the distinction between heterosexuality and homosexuality, straight and queer. The minute we introduce the notion of a feminine man or a masculine woman, a passive man or an active woman, the binary structure supporting heteronormativity begins to collapse into queerness. Queer can thus come to signify homosexuality as well as forms of heterosexuality that are not heteronormative, all of which is inseparable from gender identities and sexualities that do not fit neatly into the binary structure, including transsexuals, transgenders, bisexuals, tomboys, and transvestites. In this vein, Hanson eloquently describes queer as "that no-man's land beyond the heterosexual norm, that categorical domain virtually synonymous with homosexuality and yet wonderfully suggestive of a whole range of sexual possibilities" (Hanson 1993, 138).

These notions of queer are useful in approaching the fairy-tale films of Ozon and Breillat for several reasons. First, both films destabilize normative gender roles, either emphasizing the implicit complexity or challenging the normative representation of gender in the source tale. Second, just as characters move between masculinity and femininity, so they drift between (nonnormative and normative) heterosexual and homosexual relations, which challenges any clear delineation between gay and straight. Third,

Table 12.1

Man	*Woman*
Masculine	Feminine
(Masculine) Men	(Feminine) Women
(Male) Subject	(Female) Object
Active (Male)	Passive (Female)
Heterosexuality	Homosexuality

through the staging of the main character's sexual initiation, both films suggest that the "climax" of the heteronormative fairy-tale plot may not, in the end, be all that it is cut out to be. By getting students to compare and contrast the filmic adaptation with the source tale, the strategies of queering the classical tale can be brought to the fore.

OZON'S CRIMINAL LOVERS

Considered by some to be "France's first mainstream queer *auteur* (Hayward 2008, 113), Ozon blends film noir with fairy tale to create *Criminal Lovers.* The first part of the action—to which we return throughout the film in several flashbacks—revolves around the high school student Alice, who wishes to kill her classmate, the French North African Saïd; and her boyfriend Luc, who cannot manage to have an erection with her. Alice's impulse to murder Saïd is fueled both by her desire for the North African, a taboo object of desire in mainstream French society, and by her anger at Saïd for desiring her. In order to push Luc into killing Saïd, Alice lies to Luc, telling him that Saïd was involved in her gang rape, which never happened. Alice seduces Saïd in the shower of the gymnasium in order to allow Luc to stab him with Saïd's switchblade. They drag the body to their car, and drive off to the woods, robbing a jewelry store along the way. It is when they arrive at the forest "that the narrative turns into a queer variation of a Hansel and Gretel-like fairy tale" (Schilt 2011, 51).[7]

In this second narrative strand, Alice and Luc drag Saïd's body through the forest to bury him but realize that they lost their trail, and they begin to wander. Eventually Luc finds the cabin of the "ogre," a large foreign-accented man whom Luc voyeuristically watches bathe.[8] Later, when the man appears to be away, Luc returns with Alice, they enter the cabin, and, hungry, they start devouring bread. Suddenly, the ogre returns and throws Alice and Luc in the cellar, where, to the children's astonishment, they find Saïd's dead body. Later, the ogre takes Luc out of the cellar, feeds him, and has the boy assist him with domestic chores, including bathing him. On two occasions the ogre brings Luc to orgasm. In the meantime, a starving and powerless Alice remains in the cellar, and Luc secretly feeds her. Finally, Luc manages to free Alice and they flee the ogre's cabin. They start making love before a waterfall in an idyllic and explicitly Disney-like scene, surrounded by cute little woodland creatures, but are interrupted with the arrival of the police. The police kill Alice, while Luc and the ogre are taken into custody, with Luc yelling to the police to leave the ogre alone.

The film presents many interesting overlaps and contrasts with the Grimms' "Hansel and Gretel" (Grimm and Grimm 2003) summarized in Table 12.2. The table could be adapted for classroom use to help students generate connections between the tale and the film based on common plot elements such as the initial crime, the question of lack and Otherness, and the shifting of passive and active roles between male and female characters. This can be done in small groups, after which the class as a whole can come together and fill in the table on the board.

Drawing on Table 12.2, we gain several insights into the filmic adaptation of the tale. In some respects, Alice's character recalls that of the bad stepmother in the Grimm tale: it is her impulse to kill that sets the action in motion, and like the bad stepmother, she is purged from the story at its conclusion. Whereas in the Grimm tale, Hansel is the active character in the first part of the story and Gretel the active character in the second, in Ozon's film, this is reversed and it is Alice who dominates in the first part of the film and Luc in the second. That Luc is feminized is evident in his implicit identification with Gretel (given the structure of the story), as well as in his inability to perform his male role sexually with Alice. Significantly, when Alice prepares to seduce Saïd before the pair kills him, it is Luc who expertly applies her makeup, and even looks into the mirror with Alice as the two faces seem to blend together (Figure 12.1). For her part, Alice often plays a masculine role in her sexual and psychological domination of Luc. She cunningly takes the lead in devising the plan to kill Saïd, the racial Other whom both characters desire, a taboo desire they need to repress or "kill."[9] Luc and Alice, then, are *both* masculine and feminine, passive and active, predator and prey. Interestingly, this is also true for the Grimm tale: Hansel is active then passive; Gretel is passive then active; the siblings are the witch's prey, then the witch becomes the prey of Gretel. Gender and subject positions are mutable, mobile, and unstable, in both the tale and the film.

Hunger and food are important themes in the tale and the adaptation, taking on sexual dimensions in Ozon's film. When Luc and Alice arrive at

Table 12.2

	"Hansel and Gretel"	Criminal Lovers
Crime	Stepmother desires to "kill" children with the help of her husband	Alice desires to kill Saïd with the help of Luc
Killing the Other	Gretel kills the witch, the social Other	Luc, spurred on by Alice, kills Saïd, the racial Other, the forbidden object of desire
Lack	Lack of food	Luc cannot have sex (lack of satisfaction); later, lack of food
Forest as Transi- tional Space	Children move from real- istic cottage bordering the woods to losing themselves in the forest before finding the witch's cottage	Children move from real- istic bourgeois home and school to losing themselves in the forest before finding the ogre's cabin
The Other's Abode	Children arrive hungry and eat the cottage made of cake and bread	Children arrive hungry and eat bread
Feeding and Eating	Witch wants to fatten Han- sel to devour him; witch starves Gretel	Ogre wants to fatten Luc to sexually devour him; ogre starves Alice
Escape	Gretel frees Hansel	Luc frees Alice
Conclusion	Witch dies; we learn step- mother dies; family reunited	Alice dies; Luc and ogre go to prison

the ogre's cabin, they are famished. Later, the ogre has Luc eat rabbit as well as, the film suggests, part of Saïd's leg. Saïd's connection to the rabbit is made earlier when Luc hits a rabbit on the road leading to the forest where they will bury Saïd; Alice insists that they bury the rabbit before burying Saïd, thus creating a metonymic and metaphoric connection between the two murdered creatures. Interestingly, when the ogre takes Luc out of the cellar to play a domestic role in his home, he refers to Luc as *mon lapin* ("my little rabbit"), a term of endearment that can have sexual connotations.[10] In this way, Luc becomes, in Andrew Asibong's words, "the 'foreign body' we always thought of as somebody—or something—else" (Asibong 2005, 206), moving from predator to prey, from Same to Other, within the film. Now it is the ogre who will devour, here *sexually*, the "little rabbit" Luc. (It should be noted that one could view the killing of Saïd as a sexual act or

Figure 12.1. Luc (Jérémie Renier) gazes into the mirror with Alice (Natacha Régnier) in François Ozon's *Criminal Lovers* (2001).

rape: before the murder, Luc and Alice caress Saïd's switchblade—or phallus—that Luc stole from him; they use the same switchblade to "penetrate" and kill him.)

But Luc is not simply a victim of the ogre; the ogre releases Luc to his own queer desires. It is only through sexual relations with the ogre that Luc can fully access his own sexuality, orgasm, and finally—at least begin to—make love to Alice. Indeed, the film pushes us to ask ourselves: What happens if Hansel falls in love with the ogre (or Gretel with the witch)? As such, the film demonstrates the point of Turner's piece "Playing with Fire," a queer reading of "Frau Trude" in which Turner argues that the girl whose curiosity impels her to visit the marginalized witch in fact desires the older woman, the forbidden object of desire (Turner 2012). What Turner teases out of the Grimm tale becomes explicit in the filmic tale of Ozon: the boy very clearly desires the ogre, evident the first time Luc gazes upon the ogre while the latter bathes. Although *Criminal Lovers* does not conclude with the happy ending of "Hansel and Gretel"—that is, with the reestablishment of the (patriarchal, heteronormative) home—there is a sort of union between the ogre and Luc, both of whom will find themselves, not within the space of the home, but within the diametrically opposite space of the prison. One wonders what Ozon is trying to say here about queer desire and its place in French society in the late 1990s.

Ozon's characters can be considered "binary outlaws" in several respects. First, Luc and Alice constantly move between conventionally masculine and feminine roles: Alice is the sexual aggressor, while Luc is passive and later carries out domestic work; Alice is victimized by the ogre, while Luc plays the traditional hero and saves her. The comparison with "Hansel and Gretel" emphasizes the gender fluidity of the source tale, on which Ozon capitalizes for his film. Second, Luc moves between heterosexuality and homosexuality. In order to gain access to heterosexuality, Luc must pass through a homosexual initiation that frees up his desire. Luc's inability (this time, due to the arrival of the police) to complete the heterosexual act, however, and his longing gaze at the ogre as both are taken into custody at the end of the film, would suggest that Luc's desire for a man is privileged over any desire he might have for Alice. For her part, Alice plays the dominant (traditionally masculine) role in heterosexual relations with Luc and even with Saïd, whose murder could be read as a rape-murder she oversees in the way that it plays out, an ironic turn of events given her earlier accusation of Saïd.[11] Her performance of heterosexuality challenges normative representations of heterosexual sex typical of either mainstream fairy tales such as "Cinderella" or "Snow White" (specifically in the tradition of Charles Perrault and Disney) or Hollywood film, where the female lead plays the passive role, either waiting for a prince or falling victim to male sexual aggression.

BREILLAT'S THE SLEEPING BEAUTY

Breillat's filmic adaptation of Charles Perrault's "Sleeping Beauty" (Perrault 1981) presents interesting connections and contrasts with both the source tale and Ozon's *Criminal Lovers*. Like Ozon's film, Breillat's characters move between masculine and feminine, homosexual and heterosexual, active and passive. Her version of "Sleeping Beauty" interpolates Hans Christian Andersen's "The Snow Queen" in such a way as to foreground the chiasmatic relation between the two tales: in "Sleeping Beauty," the heroine passively sleeps, and it is the prince who seeks her; in "The Snow Queen," the hero figuratively sleeps, and it is the heroine who seeks him (Andersen 2012). By weaving these tales together, Breillat challenges normative gender and sexual constructions, and like Ozon, privileges homosexual sex as the site for the main character's sexual awakening.

Like Perrault's tale, the action of Breillat's film is initiated by an old and spiteful fairy, who curses the newborn princess to die at sixteen, when she pierces (*transpercer*) her hand, which a good fairy is able to modify to a one-hundred-year sleep. Drawing on an opening in Perrault's tale in which the narrator informs us the princess had the pleasure of "agreeable dreams" during her long slumber, the good fairy insists that the young princess, Anastasia, will have "life in a dream" during hers. Then the film moves to a six-year-old Anastasia, who pretends to be the knight Vladimir and hates dresses. While reading her favorite book, the dictionary, she significantly comes across the definition of *hermaphrodite*. Reluctantly and rather ridiculously dressed for a ballet performance as a Japanese geisha, an idealized form of femininity, Anastasia accidentally pierces her hand with a hairpin and then is sent off on a dream-journey that becomes a quest for her true love, Peter (Figure 12.2).

One of the first stops in her journey is a humble home near the woods, where a mother and her son Peter seem to be waiting for her arrival. For lack of female clothing, Anastasia's adoptive mother dresses her as a boy. Anastasia and her adoptive brother become very close, until one night Peter sees the Snow Queen and feels as though a sword of ice pierces (*transpercer*) his heart. As in Andersen's tale, the boy gets a splinter (snowflake) in his eye and only sees the negative around him, until one night he disappears with the Snow Queen. Anastasia then begins her quest to find Peter and comes across a young albino royal couple, Romany robbers, and an old Lapland woman, all of whom assist her in her quest. It is when the six-year-old Anastasia is about to find Peter that a sixteen-year-old Anastasia awakes from her long slumber to find Johan, the grandson of Peter, in her bedroom. But it is the Romany girl, now a woman, whom Anastasia had met in her slumbers, who initiates Anastasia's sexual awakening, preparing the princess for her less-than-ideal sexual experience with a fickle Johan. The film concludes with Anastasia's entry into the "real" world, pregnant with a son she will name Vladimir, and a disappointing and tentative reunion with Johan.

By interpolating "The Snow Queen" into the narrative of "Sleeping Beauty," Breillat can highlight the parallels between the two tales and play with shifting gender positions in her film, evident in Table 12.3. Again,

Figure 12.2. Anastasia (Carla Besnaïnou) begins her quest dressed rather awkwardly as a ballet geisha girl in Catherine Breillat's *Sleeping Beauty* (2010).

students can be put into small groups to generate a list of parallels between the two narratives. Then the instructor can move from group to group and put their answers on the board, getting students to see the ways in which the interpolation of "The Snow Queen" subverts the problematically gendered narrative of "The Sleeping Beauty."

Unlike Perrault's "Sleeping Beauty," the narrative focuses on the princess's quest for Peter (or the "prince") and not the prince's (Johan's) quest for the princess, thanks to the interpolation of "The Snow Queen." Making her *The Sleeping Beauty* into a female quest story, Breillat transforms the princess's slumber into a "rite of passage" from childhood to womanhood, which is "often reserved, in literature and cinema, for boys" (Garcia 2011, 32). The notion that somehow Anastasia *is* the knight Vladimir is suggested

Table 12.3

Sleeping Beauty Narrative	*Snow Queen Narrative*
Anastasia pierces (*transpercer*) her hand	Ice pierces (*transpercer*) Peter's heart
Anastasia sleeps	Peter "sleeps" (seduced into numbness by Snow Queen)
Implicitly, prince (Johan) seeks Anastasia	Explicitly, Anastasia seeks Peter
Passive heroine and active hero	Passive hero and active heroine

precisely by this questlike structure of the film. That Anastasia is both knight and (sleeping) princess is foregrounded in the child's fascination with the term *hermaphrodite*, and ends up materializing in the pregnant Anastasia, who carries the boy Vladimir within her physical body. While the film follows Anastasia's challenging journey, it is not even clear how Johan found the palace where the passive Anastasia sleeps, thus short-circuiting the male quest of classical versions of "Sleeping Beauty."

In her analysis of Breillat's earlier films, Lisa Coulthard discusses Breillat's "interrogation of faux-masculine chivalry" (Coulthard 2010, 61), a concept applicable as well to Breillat's *The Sleeping Beauty*. Drawing from the work of Slavoj Žižek, Coulthard argues that within the scheme of heteronormative forms of courtly love, desire can only be sustained by distance; proximity to the "Real" of the lady "leads to brutal revulsion and rejection" (Coulthard 2010, 62). In effect, explicit sex disrupts "an idealized rhetoric of distanced desire through an emphasis on actual, desiring female bodies" (Coulthard 2010, 65). That is, within heteronormativity, male desire is maintained through a sort of concealment, repression, or distancing of female desire and actual sex. It is notable in Breillat's film that Johan refuses to take Anastasia out of her sleepy, fairy-tale world and bring her into his "real" world, a gesture that would take away Anastasia's allusive appeal to him. He insists on the strength of his (idealized) love for her, all the while engaged in sexual relations with another woman in the "real" world. When a pregnant Anastasia escapes out into the real world and encounters Johan again, she clearly has become disenchanted with her so-called prince charming.

But there is an opening in the film to a form of desire that satisfies in ways the heteronormative relation with Johan does not: Anastasia's relation with the Romany woman. Earlier in the dream sequence, Anastasia and the Romany girl share a closeness that recalls Anastasia's relation to Peter; however, the Romany girl does not abandon her. When Anastasia wakes, it is the Romany woman who sexually fulfills Anastasia. Drawing from Garcia, we might view the homosexual initiation into sexuality as another means of questioning the heteronormative romance plot. For Garcia, "Breillat sets out to overturn the male fantasy that forms the subtext of nearly all the romantic fairy tales upon which young girls are weaned—that men awaken the virgin to her sexuality and, by extension, to her identity" (Garcia 2011, 33). Although Johan is present when Anastasia wakes up, it is the Romany woman who truly awakens Anastasia to her own sexuality. Breillat's film thus circumvents, again, the traditional plot of the source tale in which agency—including that of defining the heroine's place in society (i.e., through sexuality or marriage)—resides with the hero.

To return to the concept of "binary outlaws," Breillat's film, like Ozon's, creates fluid gender and sexual identities that challenge heteronormativity. By blending Perrault's "Sleeping Beauty" with Andersen's "Snow Queen," Breillat is able to destabilize gender oppositions underpinning Perrault's heteronormative tale. Anastasia is "hermaphrodite" in the sense that she constantly shifts between roles associated with femininity and masculinity (including passivity and activity), just as the character of the "prince" (Peter/Johan) similarly moves between active and passive, masculine and feminine positions. Anastasia is both male and female, both active and passive, both heterosexual and homosexual. And as in Ozon's *Criminal Lovers*, in Breillat's *The Sleeping Beauty* sexual initiation happens through a same-sex encounter that leads to an unsatisfactory heterosexual encounter, putting the fairy tale of heteronormativity into question.

Although these two films can be challenging for students, together they serve as productive sites for approaching the queer possibilities of the fairy-tale genre. With a brief background in queer theory, students can carry out comparative analyses of the films and their source tales in ways that foreground the queering operations of the films, as well as the queer possibilities of the source tales and more generally of the classical fairy-tale tradition. Ozon's film capitalizes on the gender instability of the Grimms' "Hansel and Gretel" to create a queer fairy tale, while Breillat's film produces an interplay between Perrault's "Sleeping Beauty" and Andersen's "Snow Queen" that destabilizes the heteronormative gender and sexual structures constitutive of Perrault's tale and that points to the nonheteronormative fissures in Andersen's tale. Luc and Anastasia become emblematic of the binary outlaw as they move between masculine and feminine, heterosexual and homosexual, active and passive. As such, both films simultaneously challenge the classical heteronormative tale and generate new, queer fairy-tale forms.

NOTES

1. Sexuality plays a central role, for instance, in tales by the French fairy-tale writers of the 1690s, who experimented with cross-dressing in ways that resulted in sexual experimentation; the contemporary tales of Emma Donoghue are explicitly queer classical fairy tales.

2. See for instance Turner and Greenhill's (2012) *Transgressive Tales* as well as my *Queer Enchantments* (Duggan 2013). See also a special issue of *Marvels & Tales*, with guest editor Lewis Seifert (2015), on "Queer(ing) Fairy Tales."

3. On the historical connection between fairy tales and queer directors in French cinema, see Alain Brassart (2007) and Nick Rees-Roberts (2008, 31). For queer readings of Cocteau, see Irène Eynat-Confino (2008) and Susan Hayward (1996); for queer readings of Demy, see Anne Duggan (2013).

4. Again, Eynat-Confino (2008) and Hayward (1996) are good sources for queer readings of Cocteau; also see chap. 2 of my *Queer Enchantments* (Duggan 2013).

5. On heterosexual sodomy and female ejaculation as queer forms of sexuality, see Straayer 1996, 240–44; on the tomboy, see Halberstam 1998, 60.

6. On queer openings in Grimm tales, see essays by Cristina Bacchilega, Andrew J. Friedenthal, and Kay Turner in *Transgressive Tales* (Turner and Greenhill 2012); see also my own reading of Demy's queering of "Donkey Skin" in *Queer Enchantments* (Duggan 2013).

7. Associations can also be made with Lewis Carroll's *Alice in Wonderland*, as Thibaut Schilt has noted, given Alice's inability "to distinguish fully between reality and make believe" (Schilt 2011, 54), and the importance of the figure of the rabbit that weaves its way through the film.

8. We discover later in the film that the foreign-accented man is cannibalistic, like the cannibalistic witch of "Hansel and Gretel," a variant of ATU 327, "The Children and the Ogre." Thus folklorists have long viewed the witch of "Hansel and Gretel" as an ogrelike creature due to her desire to consume children and to the parallels it shares with similar tales in which the function of the witch is carried out by an ogre.

9. Mark Hain explains: "Alice's hatred of her own desire, in this case, desire for the racial Other, is displaced onto the object of desire. The film thus evokes the fear of desiring the Other (another race) as much as desiring the same (homosexuality), as it's clear that both Alice and Luc are attracted to Saïd and dangerously conflicted at how this complicates their conception of normative desire" (Hain 2007, 286).

10. *Lapin* can also refer to a "lusty" or "red-blooded fellow"; *un chaud lapin* (literally "a hot rabbit") refers to "a man concerned with sexual pleasures." See the French dictionary *Le Petit Robert*. I would like to thank Christa Jones for pointing out the explicitly sexual connotations to me.

11. I do not mean to suggest that women raping men is acceptable. Alice's actions cannot be separated from the fact that Saïd is of North African origin and could be viewed as a racially motivated rape-murder.

REFERENCES

Andersen, Hans Christian. 2012. *The Snow Queen and Other Tales*. Ed. Max Bollinger. London: Sovereign.

Angelides, Steven. 2001. *A History of Bisexuality*. Chicago: University of Chicago Press.

Asibong, Andrew. 2005. "Meat, Murder, Metamorphosis: The Transformational Ethics of François Ozon." *French Studies* 59 (2): 203–15. http://dx.doi.org/10.1093/fs/kni139.

La Belle et la Bête. 1946. Directed by Jean Cocteau and René Clément. France.

Berlant, Lauren, and Michael Warner. 1998. "Sex in Public." *Critical Inquiry* 24 (2): 547–66. http://dx.doi.org/10.1086/448884.

Brassart, Alain. 2007. *L'homosexualité dans le cinéma français.* Paris: Nouveau Monde.

Coulthard, Lisa. 2010. "Desublimating Desire: Courtly Love and Catherine Breillat." *Journal for Cultural Research* 14 (1): 57–69. http://dx.doi.org/10.1080/14797580903363090.

Criminal Lovers (Les Amants criminels). 2001 (1999). Directed by François Ozon. United States: Strand Releasing.

Doty, Alexander. 1993. *Making Things Perfectly Queer: Interpreting Mass Culture.* Minneapolis: University of Minnesota Press.

Duggan, Anne E. 2013. *Queer Enchantments: Gender, Sexuality, and Class in the Fairy-Tale Cinema of Jacques Demy.* Detroit: Wayne State University Press.

Eynat-Confino, Irène. 2008. *On the Uses of the Fantastic in Modern Theatre: Cocteau, Oedipus, and the Monster.* New York: Palgrave. http://dx.doi.org/10.1057/9780230616967.

Garcia, Maria. 2011. "Rewriting Fairy Tales, Revising Female Identity. An Interview with Catherine Breillat." *Cinéaste (New York, N.Y.)* 36 (3): 32–35.

Grimm, Jacob, and Wilhelm Grimm. 2003. *The Complete Fairy Tales of the Brothers Grimm.* Trans. and introduced by Jack Zipes. New York: Bantam.

Hain, Mark. 2007. "Explicit Ambiguity: Sexual Identity, Hitchcockian Criticism, and the Films of François Ozon." *Quarterly Review of Film Studies* 24 (3): 277–88. http://dx.doi.org/10.1080/10509200500486387.

Halberstam, Judith. 1998. *Female Masculinity.* Durham: Duke University Press.

Hanson, Ellis. 1993. "Technology, Paranoia and the Queer Voice." *Screen* 34 (2): 137–61. http://dx.doi.org/10.1093/screen/34.2.137.

Hayward, Susan. 1996. "La Belle et la Bête." *History Today* 46 (7): 43–48.

Hayward, Susan. 2008. "François Ozon's Cinema of Desire." In *Five Directors: Auteurism from Assayas to Ozon,* ed. Kate Ince, 112–34. Manchester: Manchester University Press.

Peau d'âne. 1970. Directed by Jacques Demy. France.

Perrault, Charles. 1981. *Contes.* Ed. Jean-Pierre Collinet. Paris: Gallimard.

Rees-Roberts, Nick. 2008. *French Queer Cinema.* Edinburgh: Edinburgh University Press. http://dx.doi.org/10.3366/edinburgh/9780748634187.001.0001.

Seifert, Lewis C. 2015. "Introduction: Queer(ing) Fairy Tales." *Marvels & Tales* 29 (1). http://digitalcommons.wayne.edu/marvels/vol29/iss1/1.

Schilt, Thibaut. 2011. *François Ozon.* Urbana: University of Illinois Press.

The Sleeping Beauty (La Belle endormie). 2010. Directed by Catherine Breillat. United States: Strand Releasing.

Straayer, Chris. 1996. *Deviant Eyes, Deviant Bodies: Sexual Re-orientations in Film and Video.* New York: Columbia University Press.

Turner, Kay. 2012. "Playing with Fire: Transgression as Truth in Grimms' 'Frau Trude.'" In *Transgressive Tales: Queering the Grimms,* ed. Kay Turner and Pauline Greenhill, 245–74. Detroit: Wayne State University Press.

Turner, Kay, and Pauline Greenhill, eds. 2012. *Transgressive Tales: Queering the Grimms.* Detroit: Wayne State University Press.

13

Teaching "Gender in Fairy-Tale Film and Cinematic Folklore" Online
Negotiating between Needs and Wants

Pauline Greenhill and Jennifer Orme

Teaching fully online a third-year undergraduate University of Winnipeg Women's and Gender Studies (WGS) course called "Gender in Fairy-Tale Film and Cinematic Folklore" (GFFCF) offered significant challenges, but also considerable rewards. Though the course's final form was strongly influenced by the particular demands of Internet delivery, like any other course, live or online, GFFCF reflected a compromise between pedagogical goals, available materials, and approaches to the content (see, e.g., Garrison 2011; Simpson 2012). Our chapter explores how we worked to balance the latter three issues, particularly in terms of the online medium's usually positive influence on our teaching. We detail our strategies in creating and delivering the course and evaluate our success in meeting our objective to find appropriate forms of adaptation from live delivery to online. We compare Pauline's experience of teaching the same course live with Jennifer's as the inaugural professor for the online version, examine student participation and feedback, and discuss our insights about how to improve the course.[1]

PAULINE: AN ORIGIN STORY

I first prepared and taught distance courses when teaching Canadian Studies at the University of Waterloo, Ontario, in 1989. The system then involved sending a single package of audio lectures on cassette tapes, readings, and supplementary material through the mail; and receiving written

DOI: 10.7330/9781607324812.c013

assignments, and returning them with feedback and grades also by post. Because the turnaround was so slow and long-distance telephone costly, I needed to anticipate problems and provide full explanations in advance. Doing so improved my live teaching; I relied less on student questions for clarification, seeking to provide maximum background from the outset.

I first used fairy-tale films in a second-year University of Winnipeg (UW) course called "Gender and Folklore: A Survey" in winter 2006.[2] I was chatting about my plans with my then departmental colleague Sidneyeve Matrix; she suggested I try showing fictional films based on traditional culture. I chose Nietzchka Keene's *The Juniper Tree* (1990) and asked students to compare it with the Grimm version (ATU 720).[3] The result was an excellent discussion. Having successfully dipped my toe in the waters, on the course's next outing in 2008, I also showed *Snow White: A Tale of Terror* (1997, Michael Cohn) and the Jean Cocteau classic *La belle et la bête* (1946, *Beauty and the Beast*). That year I had several students majoring in Theatre and Film, and they suggested that I develop a course entirely on fairy-tale films. Matrix had by that time joined the Film Department at Queen's University, Kingston, Ontario, and was teaching a fairy-tale film course with great success. We commiserated over the lack of suitable readings, ultimately resulting in our edited collection, *Fairy Tale Films: Visions of Ambiguity* (Greenhill and Matrix 2010).

I offered GFFCF live in winter 2011. I based it around Matrix's and my book, but also used a feminist film theory text (Kaplan 2000).[4] Despite the requirement at the time that I obtain performance rights for the films I showed in class, I had a larger range of legal choices than we would later have when teaching online, with so much material available on VHS and DVD. I wanted to start by destabilizing the Disneyfied reputation of fairy-tale films as anodyne children's fare (see Zipes 2005), so I showed David Kaplan's brilliant short *Little Red Riding Hood* (1997) (see Orme 2015) in the first class. In the second, I showed Micheline Lanctôt's (English-subtitled) *Le piège d'Issoudun* (2003, *The Issoudun Exit/Trap*, English title *The Juniper Tree*). Riffing on "The Juniper Tree" (ATU 720), this story of a woman who kills her children is set in present-day Montreal, Canada. In retrospect, the latter's topic—maternal filicide—was quite challenging for so early in the course, as was the film's unrelentingly depressing neorealism.[5] Later in the course, however, a particular class favorite, *The Wolves of Kromer* (1998, Will Gould), offered a lighthearted but serious consideration of homophobia. Depicting a fictional British town where the human wolves are gay men, it uses "Little Red Riding Hood" (ATU 333) to focus a reflection on sexualities and prejudice. By happy coincidence, I had three French exchange graduate students, who assured their astounded Canadian colleagues that Jacques Demy's (English-subtitled) *Peau d'âne* (1970, *Donkey Skin*)—a variant of the familiar "Cinderella" (ATU 510A)—truly was a children's film in France, despite its evocation of father-daughter incest. Films of fairy tales are not the only course topic, and I wanted to integrate Canadian content, so in addition to Lanctôt's *Le piège* I showed Zacharias Kunuk's *Atanarjuat: The Fast Runner* (2001), an exploration of murder and retribution in historical Inuit culture. I showed *Capturing the Friedmans* (2003, Andrew Jarecki), which employs home movies and a vernacular video diary to present the multiple, competing accounts related to a child sexual abuse case; it generated lively engaged critique from the class.[6]

I also included television productions. *Mutzmag* (1993, Tom Davenport), adapting a less well-known tale type (ATU 327B, "The Brothers and the Ogre"), features a spunky heroine who defeats a witch and a giant, and the story does not end heteronormatively in marriage. "Gingerbread" (1999) from *Buffy the Vampire Slayer* (Joss Whedon, season 3, episode 11) uses "Hansel and Gretel" (ATU 327A) to explore moral panics (also a theme in *Capturing*). These works allowed for reflection on similarities and differences between versions of ATU 327A and ATU 327B, including divergent views of witches—as human helpers in *Buffy* and as evil cannibals in *Mutzmag*.

PEDAGOGICAL GOALS

"Gender in Fairy-Tale Film and Cinematic Folklore" was WGS's first foray into distance courses. In some ways it may not have been an ideal initial offering, given that none of the prerequisites was available online. But with the contemporary vogue for fairy tales, including the appearance of a number of American movies and television series riffing on fairy tales and fairy-tale themes beginning around 2011, we felt this course could attract student interest. And the topic itself, concerning mediated culture, seemed well suited to online delivery. We were also swayed by the fact that offering this course fully online significantly increased the pool of faculty with expertise in the area to teach it, since they did not need to be located in Winnipeg.

Making sure all materials—including lectures, readings, and films—were available online also means that the course is accessible to students outside Winnipeg, including those in rural communities and First Nations.[7] In practical terms, too, the course does not suffer the frequent drawback of Winnipeg winter-term classes; weather issues sometimes make attendance sporadic at best. In order to take full advantage of the temporal flexibility online learning can afford, we chose an asynchronic model for the course so that neither the students nor the instructor need to be online at any one specific time or day of the week. With all materials continuously available, only electrical failures and computer problems limit students' accessibility. However, because online class content is available twenty-four hours a day, seven days a week, brief technical disruptions are not permitted as excuses for lateness. The asynchronic model also means that students have at minimum a full week to complete their assignments. Information sheets explicitly state that work should be submitted well before deadlines to avoid last-minute problems. All materials are available to students from the first day of the course; students thus have the option of working a faster pace and at whatever time of day/night they choose, making online learning attractive to students seeking to finish their degrees quickly, working full time, and/or running households.[8]

On the other hand, this asynchronic model means that because students and instructor are not logging on together at specific times, immediate feedback from the professor and between students only happens if they chance to be online at the same time. However, under the Western Canadian Deans Agreement, to which seventeen universities in British Columbia, Alberta, Saskatchewan, and Manitoba are signatories, senior undergraduate and graduate students at any member institution may take courses at any of the others.[9] This means that students in GFFCF may be in three different time zones (Pacific, Mountain, and Central), while the professor is in a fourth (Eastern). Though the course may be available elsewhere in Canada and internationally, we have had no such registrations.

Discussions require different handling from those in classroom-based courses. Whereas in the latter setting, nonverbal cues can clarify or expand what is said, all communication in an online course is written. Students may not see an instructor's clarifications, corrections, or questions for a week or more, or indeed not at all, as they move from one week to the next. And just as the instructor lacks nonverbal feedback from students, students cannot read her expression and tone of voice. Thus, she must explicitly and carefully word feedback that is often communicated with a smile, a nod, or a raised eyebrow in the classroom.

Rather than emulating a MOOC (Massive Online Open Course) as our model for online delivery, we worked to replicate the UW live course experience.[10] Online learning has the distinct benefit of allowing for self-directed learning, resulting in a more personalized learning experience. Further, we worked to replicate as much as possible the live course's advantages. University of Winnipeg uses the online platform Desire2Learn as its learning management system, which we found adequate to our needs. We developed content that took advantage of its flexibility, but still offered the extensive contact and quality feedback we associate with live courses. At our primarily undergraduate university, students can expect to be taught by, and to have significant portions of their work graded by, tenured and tenure-track faculty, though some courses are taught on contract by area experts. But there is no default assumption, as in larger institutions, that graduate students will deliver and grade the majority of undergraduate course content. Even at the introductory level, WGS courses are almost always taught by faculty holding doctoral degrees.

"Gender in Fairy-Tale Film and Cinematic Folklore" was created with a planned lifespan of five years with the knowledge that although Pauline authored the course, she would not teach the individual sections. Women's and Gender Studies does not have another resident faculty member with expertise in all the disciplines covered in this interdisciplinary course. Jennifer, whose doctorate is in English Literature, has been teaching online since 2009, and her own research and teaching in fairy-tale studies, gender and queer theory, and film dovetailed nicely with the course content and our goals. With online delivery, the fact that she is based in Toronto, Ontario, rather than Winnipeg, is a nonissue.

Any third-year undergraduate WGS course at UW involves a great deal of critical, reflective, and expository writing. Teaching cultural criticism and communication skills are essential elements of our departmental pedagogical philosophy. Requiring that students write a lot leads to the expectation of prompt and detailed feedback and responses to that work, so that students may develop their critical, analytical, and writing skills. Further, WGS students rarely find themselves in third-year classes with more than fifty students; twenty to thirty is a more common class size at that level. This means that students not only get to know each other, but also that they frequently collaborate (with the faculty's wholehearted encouragement and blessing) on improving each other's work. We sought to provide a similar experience in the online offering of GFFCF. Thus, we negotiated a class cap of forty-five students; the actual number registered was around twenty.

COURSE CONTENT

Readings and films needed to be legally available online for the course's full five year lifetime. Further, we wanted the costs for texts and additional materials to be approximately the same, or less than, most comparable live courses. Having Greenhill and Matrix's (2010) text available free of charge on Digital Commons is a great advantage, but copyright somewhat restricted our use of other books and articles. In late fall 2012, considerable extension of fair dealing in copyright (users' rights, more or less the Canadian equivalent of US copyright's "fair use") for educational contexts led to greater availability of written materials, and a liberalization of UW copyright policy.[11] If we prepare the course again in 2017, we may offer students access to PDF files of some book chapters. But, erring on the safe side, the current version only uses journal articles available on databases to which UW's library subscribes, or selections from ebooks the UW library holds.

Since Amazon Instant Video is unavailable in Canada, iTunes and/or Canadian Netflix were the film sources for the first year; we now add the Cineplex Store. Given that the written materials are available free of charge on Digital Commons or at the UW Library, via the course website, the eight dollar per month cost for Netflix (to which most students already subscribed) and the relatively low cost for renting or purchasing films on iTunes or Cineplex (usually between one and ten dollars), put this course expense far below the usual for UW Arts courses (around US$125). As importantly, we needed to ensure that students could legally access the films they needed online, and that those we used would be available for the course's full five-year lifetime. Our solution is to base the discussions on films of well-known fairy tales and give students the opportunity to make their own specific movie choices. We provide a list of possibilities for weekly viewing in the later half of the course, and for final essay projects.

The main lectures are delivered as audio only.[12] We provide outlines on which students can make their own notes—a technique Pauline also uses in live course delivery—rather than using more exclusively presentational modes like PowerPoint slides. Pedagogically, having students interact with outlines while listening to a lecture increases their involvement and thus their learning. Each class includes not only the lectures, outlines, and readings, but also links to illustrative online material referred to in the lectures, including supplementary web-resources like SurLaLune and D.L. Ashliman's Folktexts; films legally available online (via Folkstreams, for example); and Internet Movie Database entries for films mentioned.[13] In addition, a collection of handouts includes documents providing basic writing instruction, as well as detailed grading criteria rubrics, which Jennifer has developed over many years as an online instructor.

Because this course deals with cinematic folklore, we include quite a wide range of filmic subjects, reflecting Pauline's background in folkloristics. Though the focus is on films "incorporating traditional culture as part of a fictional narrative," including fairy-tale film adaptations, we also look at documentary films "produced [by professionals and/or academics] as ethnographic records to describe and/or represent a culture or tradition in a realistic mode" (Greenhill 2012, 484). We include discussion of vernacular films, mostly "home movies, produced by amateurs to record significant events in the lives of their families and communities" (Greenhill 2012, 484). But we also examine "fictional films produced [with significant involvement] by Indigenous individuals and communities, about their traditional and popular culture, often aimed simultaneously at their own groups and at outsiders, usually with implicit political intention to recast and/or correct settlers' and outsiders' too often simplistic and/or stereotypical views of their societies"[14] (Greenhill 2012, 484).

Offering the course at a third-year level, we have several alternatives as prerequisites: the first-year "Introduction to WGS," the WGS second-year "Gender and Folklore," or the English department's second-year "Fairy Tales and Culture." With these diverse options, we consider the need to get the WGS students prepared for folklore and/or fairy tales and the English students prepared for WGS and/or folklore. Thus, we structure the course in two sections (see Appendix 13.A). In the first half, weeks 1–4 lay the groundwork for analytical approaches to cinematic folklore and film theory. In it, students are assigned brief summary-and-response essays for each of the three articles read per week and one comparison essay for the guest video lectures in week 5.

The second half of the course concentrates on film analysis. From week 6 to 11, students post discussion responses demonstrating the connections they make from that week's critical readings to one film. They also create an online conversation by replying to the posts of at least two other students. One disadvantage Jennifer found in organizing the course in this way is lack of interaction between students in the first half of the course. The Reading Response (RR) assignments encourage students to complete all of the readings, demonstrate their ability to synthesize the material, and engage with the concepts within them through their commentaries. However, because these assignments are submitted only to the instructor for grading, rather than in a more collaborative setting such as the discussion boards, the learning community we hope to create in the course is delayed until discussion begins in week 6. Students do not take advantage of discussion forums offered, such as "Q&A" and "Interesting Stuff," in which they are encouraged to ask questions of each other and the instructor and post links to blogs, videos, and events relevant to the course, presumably because these forums are neither required nor graded. In future iterations of the course, we will plan earlier community building; one possible solution is to split the RR into two parts: a summary submitted to the instructor for grading, and discussion postings for student responses and questions.

The course culminates in a final conference-presentation length essay on the student's choice of one film. In total, 12 classes follow the weeks of the regular term, and we seek to replicate on average two and a half hours class time for each week, including lectures, film viewings (by each student on her/his own), and assigned web discussions. One distinct advantage of the online format was that lectures follow the needs of the subject matter rather than being shaped by how much could be covered in individual class sessions. Thus the earlier lectures are over an hour and a half long, and some later ones not much more than fifteen minutes.

We begin with an introduction that welcomes students, walks them through the course scaffolding, and asks them to introduce themselves on the discussion boards by telling who they are and why they chose to take the course. The next two class sections address foundational concepts and theories. One on the basics of fairy-tale films, cinematic folklore, and gender (Greenhill 2012), and another on feminist and queer film theory, ensure that all students, no matter what their prerequisites and background, have the necessary fundamentals. The fourth class is on home movies and documentary films. Although no specific films are assigned, the link to Folkstreams online means that students can view documentaries by folklorists as streaming video. We may in the next offering assign at least one film, since the first group of students did not demonstrate that they chose to watch any.

The fifth class uses three video guest lectures, available only through this course, by experts Cristina Bacchilega, Sidneyeve Matrix, and Jack Zipes, recorded during a meeting of Pauline's research team in 2011.[15] Students' comparison assignment asks them to engage with each lecture's arguments and place them in relation to each other. This midpoint class moves students from foundational critical and theoretical arguments about gender and cinematic folklore to providing examples of research and arguments by major figures in fairy-tale (film) studies today. The video lectures, including embedded PowerPoint presentations and other illustrations, demonstrate different methodological approaches and diverse but complementary arguments. Matrix's lecture proposes a perspective on science fiction films that comingle with folktale and fairy-tale motifs via her concept of "cybercinematic folklore" (popular filmic texts, motifs, and ideas about computers and the Internet). Bacchilega discusses the role of storytelling as a performative act within *Pan's Labyrinth* (2006, Guillermo Del Toro), *Enchanted* (2007, Kevin Lima), and *La barbe bleue* (2009, *Bluebeard*, Catherine Breillat).

Zipes's "Hyping the Grimms' Fairy Tales" looks at the long history of fairy tales' placement in consumer culture all the way back to the Grimms' own selling of their famous collection of *Kinder- und Hausmärchen* (*Children's and Household Tales*, e.g., Grimm and Grimm 1812–1815).

Having watched these scholars in action, students move to the four classes most directly related to fairy-tale films and begin their own analytic and interpretive work collaboratively on the class discussion boards (discussed below). As we have said, film assignments were constrained by legal online availability. Although this created a somewhat conventionalized view of fairy-tale films as addressing primarily well-known narratives, we were confident it offered a fairly wide range. Further, in conjunction with the critical readings aligned with them, these films allowed us to address gender issues saliently.[16] We ultimately chose as our fairy-tale foci four well-known stories that spawned multiple cinematic adaptations: "The Little Mermaid" (Hans Christian Andersen), "Cinderella" (ATU 510A), "Little Red Riding Hood" (ATU 333), and "Snow White" (ATU 709).

Pauline created and audio-recorded the majority of the lectures. In addition to the fifth week's guest lectures on video, the sixth class lecture, "The Little Mermaid, Transbiology, and Memetics," is audio-recorded by Pauline's M.A. teaching assistant, Marie Raynard, as guest lecturer, and draws on her expertise in transbiology theory to encourage students to think about the transformations of women into beasts. The following module, "Cinderella and Cinderfella: (Trans)Gendering Fairy Tales and Their Characters," explores films using sex/gender reversal to offer a different perspective on fairy tales. Then, "'Little Red Riding Hood': Feminism and Crime" addresses Pauline's interest in fairy-tale crime films (see e.g., Greenhill and Kohm 2013). And the class "'Snow White': Fairy-Tale Horror and Mothering" deals with the significant roles of female subjects.

We also include a module on "Fabulations and Composites," drawing on Kevin Paul Smith's eight possible ways for fairy-tale intertexts to work in literature: authorized (explicit in the title), writerly (implicit in the title), incorporation (explicit in text), allusion (implicit in text), revision (giving an old tale a new spin), fabulation (creating a new tale), metafiction (discussing fairy tales), and architextual/chronotopic (in setting/environment) (Smith 2007, 10). Thus original fairy-tale films such as *Pan's Labyrinth* (see Orme 2010) or *The Fall* (2006, Tarsem Singh) are also part of the course. The penultimate module, "Cultures Telling Their Own Stories," encourages students to look at films developed within and/or with the collaboration of Indigenous cultures, such as *Atanarjuat* or *Whale Rider* (2002, Niki Caro). The course finishes with Jennifer's wrap-up lecture looking back upon the aspects students find most salient and tying them together. Students' final project papers come due in this week.

JENNIFER: TEACHING THE COURSE ONLINE

Because most of the content was prepared and uploaded before the course began, as instructor I could devote the majority of my time to grading weekly assignments with detailed in-text feedback and comments and regularly participating in discussion boards. One goal of online pedagogy is to encourage both independent and collaborative learning. To this end, we assign weekly discussion posts in the course's second half. Students are required to reflect on one assigned film of their choice related to the week's theme, which they watch on their own, in relation to course concepts and arguments, with particular attention to that week's critical readings. This collaborative process works much like in-class discussion, but every student must participate; no one can hide at the back of the classroom! In addition to their primary posts, due by 11:59 p.m. each Friday, students reply to at least two other posts by the Sunday of each week. Staggering the primary and reply post deadlines encourages students to engage with their peers' ideas (at the very least) twice a week and provides time for ideas to simmer between first thoughts and later responses. I also contribute with follow-up questions, asking for clarification and/or asking students to expand upon ideas and take them in new directions.

For example, discussing *Aquamarine* (2006, Elizabeth Allen)—one of the choices for "Little Mermaid" films—the majority of students initially read it as a heteronormative but potentially liberating tale of the power of friendship between girls. Women's and Gender Studies major Alexandria Van Dyck offered a queer reading which highlighted the unstable embodiment of the mermaid, Aqua, who daily transitions between woman and fish. Deftly linking this physical fluctuation to a challenge to binary sexualities and noting the homosocial bonds between the mermaid and two teen girls she befriends, this student began a conversation that more than half of the class members joined and used to expand their understandings of presumed heterosexuality in film. My own brief question, about a scene in which the girls show curiosity about each others' bodies, helped keep the conversation going by offering a specific moment to ponder. Students considered it in relation to that week's lecture and readings, and back to the foundational reading by Alexander Doty (2000) from week 3. Students appeared most confident and loquacious when discussing issues raised in lectures and critical readings that commented directly on a specific film or tale type.

We encourage students to pick a film of their choice for the final assignment, structured on a twenty-minute conference paper (eight to ten pages) rather than an extended essay—another technique from Pauline's live courses.[17] These essays could develop from the weekly discussions or address a film the student had not written on before. The majority chose to expand upon discussions started on the boards. Pauline's goal of de-Disneyfying the course met with success in this final project. Only two students looked at Disney films, one addressing *Cinderella* (1950, Wilfred Jackson, Clyde Geronimi, and Hamilton Luske) and the other considering *Enchanted*. This significantly differs from an in-class course I gave at Ryerson University, Toronto, in which the vast majority of students chose to write on the sole Disney film I permitted, *Beauty and the Beast* (1991, Gary Trousdale and Kirk Wise).[18]

SOME SUGGESTIONS

Although the inaugural run of GFFCF was a success, comments to Pauline from individual students majoring in WGS indicate that despite the advantages of online delivery, they prefer live courses for the better opportunities for getting to know their faculty and fellow students and for the excitement of learning together. Women's and Gender Studies may have to rethink the idea that some courses can be offered online only, and schedule at least a few live offerings of GFFCF and "Gender and Folklore."

Our film studies colleagues often indicate concerns that being limited to teach online-accessible films would compromise pedagogical goals, including that of introducing students to alternatives to conventional fairy-tale films. Before we actually researched what was available, we were apprehensive that our choices would be limited to Disney films. In fact, *Enchanted* was the only Disney film we found online at the first offering, and a number of independent films—including Kaplan's *Little Red Riding Hood*, Neil Jordan's *Ondine* (2009), and *Atanarjuat*—could be accessed. We trust that just as the live course stimulated student interest in seeking other films on their own, via various media, so did the online course. The recent availability of the *International Fairy-Tale Filmography* online facilitates further searches.[19]

In future we may include more vernacular and documentary cinematic folklore texts via sources such as the National Film Board of Canada website.[20] We may provide short supplemental lectures to enhance student engagement with course readings that do not explicitly refer to course films. Or we may encourage discussion of those texts by earlier instructor intervention on the discussion boards with specific prompts. Sustained collaborative learning throughout the course could also be enhanced by having the reading responses of the first few weeks submitted on the discussion forums. In addition, Jennifer has found in other online courses that making peer review of the final project compulsory increases student community feeling and improves the overall quality of written work.

We base our reflections in this chapter upon our personal experiences with creating GFFCF and delivering it the first time online. Anyone considering volunteering for such an endeavor should be aware that preparing a course from scratch online requires approximately double the preparation time as for a live course; retooling for online delivery, as in the case of GFFCF, takes about the same amount of time as developing a course for live delivery. However, the latter process was facilitated by our working together. Jennifer's experience confirms the findings of Philip L. Doughty, Michael Spector, and Barbara A. Yonai that in comparison to live courses, significantly more time is spent on teaching online classes (Doughty et al. 2003). This is in large part because so much communication is transmitted in writing. Each general announcement to the class must anticipate possible questions or misunderstandings that could be quickly addressed verbally in the classroom and must be composed, revised, and proofread before posting. In addition, there is more email communication between instructor and students because questions and concerns cannot be addressed quickly in person.

We met some success in our desire to emulate the best aspects of classroom-based courses and using online delivery's advantages to maintain student interest and enthusiasm in the subject. The required weekly discussion component is a particular advantage in the online class. Every student must participate each week, and although some students will participate more often or with longer posts, all students contribute to discussion. The online format tends to allow students who are disinclined to speak in a live classroom setting because of nervousness to offer their thoughts with less anxiety and at more length. The quality and depth of engagement also appear to benefit from the amount of time students have to think over and revise their thoughts before posting and to clarify their positions when questioned.

On balance, online and live delivery both have advantages and disadvantages; neither is a priori preferable. A certain amount of personal interaction is sacrificed in any online course because of the lack of face-to-face contact and some of the spontaneity of live discussion is lost as well; however, we believe that the advantages of the online format somewhat mitigate these drawbacks. The compensations of teaching the course online include the ability to incorporate lectures from multiple scholars in addition to Pauline's primary lectures. The guest lectures and Jennifer's introductory lecture and final wrap-up make the course a truly collaborative teaching tool that demonstrates scholars working together. Another advantage comes from the depth and amount of student-generated discussion in weeks 6 to 11; it is likely that we will alter the assignments for weeks 1 through 5 to encourage this level and quality of engagement from the get-go.

As discussed, the constraints on choosing materials to create a user-friendly scaffolding upon which to rest the content we wanted were mitigated greatly by our collaboration. We adapted Pauline's expertise, experience, and vision to the online environment with the assistance of Jennifer's experience and knowledge of the strengths and pitfalls to watch for in digital-learning environments. We hope that our willingness to work collaboratively in a new setting has laid promising groundwork for future activities.

NOTES

Thanks to the editors and to Sidneyeve Matrix for helpful suggestions. Note that the course is officially titled "fairytale" (the British usage), but we have changed it here to "fairy-tale."

1. As an adaptation, GFFCF online offers "repetition without replication . . . [an] acknowledged transposition of a recognizable other work or works . . . A creative and an interpretive act of appropriation/salvaging" the live version (Hutcheon 2006, 7). It is "a derivation that is not derivative—a work that is second without being secondary. It is its own palimpsestic thing" (Hutcheon 2006, 9; see also Sanders 2006). Like the comparison between a told or written fairy tale, or a fairy-tale book and film, the online version of the course is neither significantly better nor worse than the live version; it is simply different. *Version*, in our terminology, replicates the usage for traditional fairy tales; there is no original *urform*. Live and online courses are *both* versions, though in this case the live form was temporally prior.

2. I prepared that course for online delivery in winter 2014 with a first offering in fall 2014. This prerequisite-free course, one of several WGS offers at the second-year level that explores topics of general interest, will be available for five years annually online, during which time it will not be offered live. Thus, a prerequisite to GFFCF will be available online. Women's and Gender Studies is also making our "Introduction to WGS," an alternative prerequisite for GFFCF, available at distance. Parallel live versions of that course will continue.

3. Designations of ATU refer to the tale type index originated by Aarne, edited and updated by Thompson and then again by Hans-Jörg Uther (2004), which numbers traditional international folktales.

4. The latter seemed excessive for this course and was unavailable digitally in any case, so we dropped it.

5. Should I offer the course live again, I will show this film later in the course, and preface it with more extensive discussion of the idea that fairy tales are not necessarily for children, and that they explore serious and controversial topics (see, e.g., Turner and Greenhill 2012).

6. At the beginning of the course, I point out that some films I show include sex and violence, contrary to conventional expectations for fairy tales. As a feminist teacher, I recognize that people may have sensitivities to issues like child abuse, so I warn folks specifically

in the course outline and in class about the topic of *Capturing*. Though I offered it, no one took up my option to view another film instead.

7. In Canada, "First Nations" not only refers to Aboriginal peoples recognized in various treaties, but also to the physical spaces, reserves over which they have governmental control.

8. Jennifer's previous online teaching experience demonstrates that a proportionally larger number of online students are pregnant women, new mothers, and mothers upgrading skills before returning to the workforce. It is therefore particularly apt that WGS courses be available to these students, who may be unable to participate in traditional classroom university courses.

9. For details see http://wcdgs.ca/western-deans-agreement.html, accessed March 26, 2016.

10. A MOOC generally closely resembles the pedagogical context of a large, lecture-based class (see, e.g., Glance, Forsey, and Riley 2013). Attempts to use writing assignments rather than machine-marked work meet with mixed results (see Krause 2013 and Rice 2013).

11. For specifics, see http://copyright.uwinnipeg.ca/, accessed March 26, 2016.

12. We may need to transcribe them for hearing-impaired students.

13. For details, see www.surlalunefairytales.com; http://www.pitt.edu/~dash/folktexts.html; http://www.folkstreams.net/; and IMDb.com, all accessed March 26, 2016.

14. As is proper, we capitalize Indigenous and Aboriginal, since they refer to peoples; we would similarly capitalize English or French when referring to those peoples.

15. Social Sciences and Humanities Research Council of Canada, Standard Research Grant, "Fairy Tale Films: Exploring Ethnographic Perspectives" (2011–2015), co-applicants Steven Kohm, Catherine Tosenberger, and Sidneyeve Matrix; collaborators Cristina Bacchilega and Jack Zipes.

16. Often less well-known tales and versions offer greater scope for including queer, transgender, and transbiological perspectives (see, e.g., Turner and Greenhill 2012). Nevertheless, nonheteronormative and resistant readings are always possible (see, e.g., Doty 2000).

17. Weaker students find it less difficult to sustain an argument in a shorter than in a longer exposition; stronger students rise to the challenge of offering complex points of view in abbreviated forms.

18. In the previous incarnation of the Ryerson class, a separate unit centered on "breaking the Disney spell" (Zipes 2005). Most students' final essays defended Disney from academic criticism. I have altered my approach to Disney in this course as a result of teaching GFFCF and have found that fewer students are interested in Disney-dominated essay topics.

19. Searchable at http://iftf.uwinnipeg.ca/, accessed March 26, 2016.

20. Located at http://www.nfb.ca/, accessed March 26, 2016.

REFERENCES

Doty, Alexander. 2000. *Flaming Classics: Queering the Film Canon*. London: Routledge.

Doughty, Philip L., Michael Spector, and Barbara A. Yonai. 2003. "Time, Efficacy and Cost Considerations of e-Collaboration in Online University Courses." *Brazilian Review of Open and Distance Learning*. http://www.abed.org.br/revistacientifica/Revista_PDF_Doc/2003_Time_Efficacy_Cost_Considerations_Part_2_Philip_Doughty_Michael_Spector_Barbara_Yonai.pdf.

Garrison, D. Randy. 2011. *E-Learning in the 21st Century: A Framework for Research and Practice*. New York: Routledge.

Greenhill, Pauline. 2012. "Folklore and/on Film." In *A Companion to Folklore*, ed. Regina Bendix and Galit Hasan-Rokem, 483–99. London: Wiley-Blackwell. http://dx.doi .org/10.1002/9781118379936.ch25.

Greenhill, Pauline, and Steven Kohm. 2013. "*Hoodwinked!* and *Jin-Roh: The Wolf Brigade*: Animated "Little Red Riding Hood" Films and the Rashômon Effect." *Marvels & Tales: Journal of Fairy-Tale Studies* 27 (1): 89–108.

Greenhill, Pauline, and Sidney Eve Matrix, eds. 2010. *Fairy Tale Films: Visions of Ambiguity*. Logan: Utah State University Press; http://digitalcommons.usu.edu/usupress_pubs /70/.

Glance, G., M. Forsey, and M. Riley. 2013. "The Pedagogical Foundations of Massive Open Online Courses." *First Monday* 18 (5–6).

Grimm, Jacob, and Wilhelm Grimm. 1812–1815. *Kinder- und Hausmärchen*. 2 vols. Berlin: Realschulbuchhandlung.

Hutcheon, Linda. 2006. *A Theory of Adaptation*. New York: Routledge.

Kaplan, E. Ann. 2000. *Feminism and Film*. Oxford: Oxford University Press.

Krause, Steven D. 2013. "MOOC Response about 'Listening to World Music.'" *College Composition and Communication* 64 (4): 689–95.

Orme, Jennifer. 2010. "Narrative Desire and Disobedience in *Pan's Labyrinth*." *Marvels & Tales: Journal of Fairy-Tale Studies* 24 (2): 219–34.

Orme, Jennifer. 2015. "A Wolf's Queer Invitation: David Kaplan's *Little Red Riding Hood* and Queer Possibility." *Marvels & Tales: Journal of Fairy-Tale Studies* 29 (1): 87–109. http://dx.doi.org/10.13110/marvelstales.29.1.0087.

Rice, J. 2013. "What I learned in MOOC." *College Composition and Communication* 64 (4): 695–703.

Sanders, Julie. 2006. *Adaptation and Appropriation*. Abingdon: Routledge.

Simpson, Ormond. 2012. *Supporting Students in Online, Open & Distance Learning*. London: Routledge.

Smith, Kevin Paul. 2007. *The Postmodern Fairytale: Folkloric Intertexts in Contemporary Fiction*. New York: Palgrave Macmillan. http://dx.doi.org/10.1057/9780230591707.

Turner, Kay, and Pauline Greenhill, eds. 2012. *Transgressive Tales: Queering the Grimms*. Detroit: Wayne State University Press.

Uther, Hans-Jörg. 2004. *The Types of International Folktales: A Classification and Bibliography*. 3 vols. Helsinki: Academia Scientiarum Fennica.

Zipes, Jack. 2005. "Breaking the Disney Spell." In *From Mouse to Mermaid: the Politics of Film, Gender, and Culture*, ed. Elizabeth Bell, Lynda Haas, and Laura Sells, 21–42. Bloomington: Indiana University Press.

FILMOGRAPHY

Aquamarine. 2006. Directed by Elizabeth Allen. Australia/United States: Twentieth Century Fox.

Atanarjuat: The Fast Runner. 2001. Directed by Zacharias Kunuk. Canada: Igloolik Isuma Productions.

La barbe bleue (Bluebeard). 2009. Directed by Catherine Breillat. France: Flach Film.

Beauty and the Beast. 1991. Directed by Gary Trousdale and Kirk Wise. Burbank, CA: Walt Disney Studios.

La belle et la bête (Beauty and the Beast). 1946. Directed by Jean Cocteau. France: DisCina.

Capturing the Friedmans. 2003. Directed by Andrew Jarecki. United States: HBO.

Cinderella. 1950. Directed by Wilfred Jackson, Clyde Geronimi, Hamilton Luske. United States: Walt Disney Productions.

Enchanted. 2007. Directed by Kevin Lima. United States: Walt Disney Productions.
The Fall. 2006. Directed by Tarsem Singh. India / United States: Googly Films.
"Gingerbread." 1999. *Buffy the Vampire Slayer* (TV). Season 3, episode 11. Created by Joss
    Whedon. United States: Mutant Enemy.
The Juniper Tree. 1990. Directed by Nietzchka Keene. Iceland / United States.
Little Red Riding Hood. 1997. Directed by David Kaplan. United States: Little Red Movie
    Productions.
Mutzmag. 1993. Directed by Tom Davenport. United States: Davenport Films.
Ondine. 2009. Directed by Neil Jordan. Ireland / United States: Wayfare Entertainment.
Pan's Labyrinth (El laberinto del fauno). 2006. Directed by Guillermo del Toro. Spain / Mex-
    ico / United States: Tequila Gang.
Peau d'âne (Donkey Skin). 1970. Directed by Jacques Demy. France: Marianne Productions.
Le piège d'Issoudun (The Juniper Tree). 2003. Directed by Micheline Lanctôt. Canada: Film
    Tonic.
Snow White: A Tale of Terror. 1997. Directed by Michael Cohn. United States: Polygram
    Filmed Entertainment.
Whale Rider. 2002. Directed by Niki Caro. New Zealand / Germany. South Pacific Pictures.
The Wolves of Kromer. 1998. Directed by Will Gould. United Kingdom: Discodog.

Appendix 13.A
Gender in Fairy-Tale Film and Cinematic Folklore

University of Winnipeg, Women's and Gender Studies WGS 3005 (3 credits)
Created by Dr. Pauline Greenhill, Professor, Women's and Gender Studies with the assistance of Teaching Assistant Marie Raynard and Online Instructor Dr. Jennifer Orme

COURSE DESCRIPTION:

Fairy-tale film (movie or TV versions of international wonder tales) and cinematic folklore (representations of other traditional genres in film) express notions of gender that have multiple implications for their creators and audiences. Using feminist film theory, we explore filmed versions of traditional culture primarily for adults. Topics may include postmodern and psychoanalytic perspectives; metamorphosis, enchantment, monstrosity, and abjection; transgender and transbiology; the rise in popularity of adult fairy-tale film; analyses of particular auteurs; adaptation theory; genre and generational shifts and remixes; historic and contemporary perspectives on innovative cinematography and special effects; and/or contemporary iconography.

TEXT:

Greenhill, Pauline, and Sidney Eve Matrix, eds. 2010. *Fairy Tale Films: Visions of Ambiguity.* Logan: Utah State University Press.

available free of charge from http://digitalcommons.usu.edu/usu press_pubs/70/

Other readings as indicated below.

Please note that you will also be expected to purchase at least six films (available on iTunes and/or Netflix and/or store.cineplex.com/store).

ONE "Little Mermaid" film

ONE "Cinderella" film

ONE "Little Red Riding Hood" film

ONE "Snow White" film

ONE fairy tale intertext/composite/fabulation film

ONE film incorporating traditional culture made by members of an Indigenous group

COURSE OUTLINE:

Class 1: Welcome to Gender in Fairy-Tale Film and Cinematic Folklore

Zipes, Jack. 2010. "Foreword: Grounding the Spell: The Fairy Tale Film and Transformation." In *Fairy Tale Films: Visions of Ambiguity*, ed. Pauline Greenhill and Sidney Eve Matrix, ix–xiii. Logan: Utah State University Press.

Class 2: Concepts of Fairy Tale Film and Cinematic Folklore; Gender

Greenhill, Pauline, and Sidney Eve Matrix. 2010. "Introduction." In *Fairy Tale Films: Visions of Ambiguity*, ed. Pauline Greenhill and Sidney Eve Matrix, 1–22. Logan: Utah State University Press.

Koven, Mikel J. 2003. "Folklore Studies and Popular Film and Television: A Necessary Critical Survey." *Journal of American Folklore* 116 (460): 176–95.

Zipes, Jack. 1996. "Towards a Theory of the Fairy-Tale Film: The Case of Pinocchio." *The Lion and the Unicorn* 20 (1): 1–11.

Class 3: Feminist and Queer Film Theory

Clover, Carol J. 1987. "Her Body, Himself: Gender in the Slasher Film." *Representations* 20 (Fall):187–228.

Doty, Alexander. 2000. "Introduction." In *Flaming Classics: Queering the Film Canon*, 1–21. New York: Routledge.

Mulvey, Laura. 1975. "Visual Pleasure and Narrative Cinema." *Screen* 16 (3): 6–18.

Class 4: Home Movies and Documentary Films

Hale, Grace Elizabeth, and Beth Loffreda. 1996. "Clocks for Seeing: Technologies of Memory, Popular Aesthetics, and the Home Movie." *Radical History Review* 66 (Fall): 163–71.

Hearne, Joanna. 2006. "Telling and Retelling in the 'Ink of Light': Documentary Cinema, Oral Narratives, and Indigenous Identities." *Screen* 47 (3): 307–26.

Zimmerman, Patricia R. 1996. "Geographies of Desire: Cartographies of Gender, Race, Nation and Empire in Amateur Film." *Film History* 8 (1): 85–98.

Class 5: Guest Video Lectures

Class 6: The Little Mermaid, Transbiology, and Memetics

Bendix, Regina. 1993. "Seashell Bra and Happy End: Disney's Transformations of 'The Little Mermaid.'" *Fabula* 34 (3–4): 280–90.

Padva, Gilad. 2005. "Radical Sissies and Stereotyped Fairies in Laurie Lynd's The Fairy Who Didn't Want to Be a Fairy Anymore." *Cinema Journal* 45 (1): 66–78.

Sawers, Naarah. 2010. "Building the Perfect Product: The Commodification of Childhood in Contemporary Fairy Tale Film." In *Fairy Tale Films: Visions of Ambiguity*, ed. Pauline Greenhill and Sidney Eve Matrix, 42–59. Logan: Utah State University Press.

Class 7: Cinderella and Cinderfella: (Trans)Gendering Fairy Tales and Their Characters

Lin, Ming-Hsun. 2010. "Fitting the Glass Slipper: A Comparative Study of the Princess's Role in Harry Potter Novels and Films." In *Fairy Tale Films: Visions of Ambiguity*, ed. Pauline Greenhill and Sidney Eve Matrix, 79–98. Logan: Utah State University Press.

Pershing, Linda, and Lisa Gablehouse. 2010. "Disney's *Enchanted*: Patriarchal Backlash and Nostalgia in a Fairy Tale Film." In *Fairy Tale Films: Visions of Ambiguity*, ed. Pauline Greenhill and Sidney Eve Matrix, 137–56. Logan: Utah State University Press.

Williams, Christy. 2010. "The Shoe Still Fits: *Ever After* and the Pursuit of a Feminist Cinderella." In *Fairy Tale Films: Visions of Ambiguity*, ed. Pauline Greenhill and Sidney Eve Matrix, 99–115. Logan: Utah State University Press.

Class 8: Little Red Riding Hood: Feminism and Crime

Kohm, Steven, and Pauline Greenhill. 2011. "Little Red Riding Hood Crime Films: Critical Variations on Criminal Themes." *Law, Culture and the Humanities* online first, September 12, 1–22.

Miller, April. 2005. "The Hair that Wasn't There Before: Demystifying Monstrosity and Menstruation in Ginger Snaps and Ginger Snaps Unleashed." *Western Folklore* 64 (3/4): 281–303.

Snowden, Kim. 2010. "Fairy Tale Film in the Classroom: Feminist Cultural Pedagogy, Angela Carter, and Neil Jordan's *The Company of Wolves*." In *Fairy Tale Films: Visions of Ambiguity*, ed. Pauline Greenhill and Sidney Eve Matrix, 157–77. Logan: Utah State University Press.

Class 9: Snow White: Fairy Tale Horror and Mothering

Barzilai, Shuli. 1990. "Reading 'Snow White': The Mother's Story." *Signs* 15 (3): 515–34.

Greenhill, Pauline, and Anne Brydon. 2010. "Mourning Mothers and Seeing Siblings: Feminism and Place in *The Juniper Tree*." *Fairy Tale Films: Visions of Ambiguity*, ed. Pauline Greenhill and Sidney Eve Matrix, 116–36. Logan: Utah State University Press.

Matrix, Sidney Eve. 2010. "A Secret Midnight Ball and a Magic Cloak of Invisibility: The Cinematic Folklore of Stanley Kubrick's *Eyes Wide Shut*." *Fairy Tale Films: Visions of Ambiguity*, ed. Pauline Greenhill and Sidney Eve Matrix, 178–97. Logan: Utah State University Press.

Class 10: Fairy Tale Adaptations and Intertexts: Fabulations and Composites

Bacchilega, Cristina, and John Rieder. 2010. "Mixing It Up: Generic Complexity and Gender Ideology in Early Twenty-first Century Fairy Tale Films." In *Fairy Tale Films: Visions of Ambiguity*, ed. Pauline Greenhill and Sidney Eve Matrix, 23–41. Logan: Utah State University Press.

Orme, Jennifer. 2010. "Narrative Desire and Disobedience in *Pan's Labyrinth*." *Marvels & Tales: Journal of Fairy-Tale Studies* 24 (2): 219–34.

Ray, Brian. 2010. "Tim Burton and the Idea of Fairy Tales." In *Fairy Tale Films: Visions of Ambiguity*, ed. Pauline Greenhill and Sidney Eve Matrix, 198–218. Logan: Utah State University Press.

Class 11: Cultures Telling Their Own Stories

Gonick, Marnina. 2010. "Indigenizing Girl Power: The *Whale Rider*, Decolonization, and the Project of Remembering." *Feminist Media Studies* 10 (3): 305–19.

Hearne, Joanna. 2005. "John Wayne's Teeth: Speech, Sound and Representation in 'Smoke Signals' and 'Imagining Indians.'" *Western Folklore* 64 (3/4): 189–208.

Siebert, Monika. 2006. "*Atanarjuat* and the Ideological Work of Contemporary Indigenous Filmmaking." *Public Culture* 18 (3): 531–50.

Class 12: Wrap

14

Intertextuality, Creativity, and Sexuality
Group Exercises in the Fairy-Tale/Gender Studies Classroom

Jeana Jorgensen

Many students enter the fairy-tale classroom familiar primarily with the Disney versions of fairy tales, though they are eager to supplement that awareness with knowledge of "the original" tales that (as everyone knows) are darker, sexier, and more violent. Catherine Tosenberger designates this "recovery story" about fairy tales a "rescue operation" designed to uncover the "real" fairy tale and "rescue it from Disney oppression" (Tosenberger 2010, [5.2]). While Tosenberger acknowledges that this approach to fairy tales is as much a construction as any other authenticity-driven narrative, I want to point out that fairy-tale audiences (including college students) who have grown up with the Disney versions as the "real" versions may have also bought into the related belief that they are consumers of the tales, and have nothing to contribute to the creative production of tales. Jack Zipes has discussed the importance of creative storytelling in the classroom, though more aimed at elementary school children. On bringing fairy tales and fantasy into the classroom as a storyteller, he writes: "I believe that there is something subversive and utopian in these genres that can enable young people to develop their critical faculties" (Zipes 1995, 18). Further, critically analyzing and creatively engaging with a genre such as the fairy tale are not mutually exclusive operations. As Vanessa Joosen points out: "Retellings and criticism participate in a continuous and dynamic dialog about the traditional fairy tale, yet they do so on different terms" (Joosen 2011, 3). How and why to navigate these different types of engagement in the fairy-tale classroom comprise the subject of this essay.

In designing a class titled "Dark Desires in Fairy-Tale Fiction" for a small liberal arts college, I wanted to not only give my students a broad

DOI: 10.7330/9781607324812.c014

227

range of readings of contemporary fairy tales based on feminist and queer theory, but also give them the tools to evaluate their own relationships with fairy tales, and the depictions of sexuality therein. In this chapter, I shall share the group exercises I devised in order to provoke students' thinking about the intersections of gender, sexuality, and intertextuality. One of the most successful types of discussion exercises I employed was putting the students in groups with the directive to retell a fairy tale in a specific style or mode. These exercises built on our discussions of intertextuality, in which I emphasized that intertextuality is not always chronological, but can be viewed in relation to an individual's first exposure to a textual tradition.[1] I will evaluate the unique benefits and challenges of these exercises and in closing discuss the role of intertextuality and sexuality in the fairy-tale classroom.

As I was given the freedom to design this course however I chose, I aimed to include a wide range of texts, both primary sources and critical analyses. Examples of the former included tales by Charles Perrault, Marie-Catherine d'Aulnoy, the Brothers Grimm, Hans Christian Andersen, Angela Carter, Anne Sexton, Francesca Lia Block, Nalo Hopkinson, and Emma Donoghue, while examples of the latter included scholarly work by Jack Zipes, Maria Tatar, Donald Haase, and a host of other contemporary fairy-tale scholars whose works appear in the journal *Marvels & Tales* and in *Transgressive Tales: Queering the Grimms* (Turner and Greenhill 2012). My class was to be offered as an upper-division elective, cross-listed between Butler University's History and Anthropology Department and the Gender, Women's, and Sexuality Studies Program. However, there were no prerequisites, so I faced many challenges when trying to make material from anthropology, folkloristics, fairy-tale studies, gender studies, and sexuality studies accessible to my students.

As do many instructors, I use discussion exercises to supplement and reinforce ideas from class lectures and readings. Typical of my teaching style, I lectured most days of the semester, though I made an effort to make sure that each class period included at least some discussion, whether in directed group exercises or informal conversation when I wanted to gauge students' understanding of the material. With eighteen students in the class (approximately two-thirds of them women), the task of getting students to participate was already more manageable than it would have been if the course had been larger. These exercises would, ideally, help the students process the material, reframe it in terms relevant to them, and get hands-on practice with interpreting fairy tales from a number of modes (primarily feminist and queer). By giving my students the creative reins, and encouraging them to apply course concepts in developing retellings of fairy tales, I found that they were able to reach new insights that more conventional discussion exercises might not have accessed. Before proceeding to a description of three specific group exercises, I will outline a few other ways that my course design was geared toward making students active learners.

Given that I had assigned a fairly heavy reading load by most standards for undergraduates—50–100 or more pages a week—coupled with mandatory blog posts synthesizing the readings for each day, I wanted to emphasize other skills in the course assignments. The class met twice a week, for an hour and fifteen minutes each time, so in addition to students' practicing critical-reading skills as noted above, I wanted them to be able to employ concepts from reading and from lectures in their discussions. Further, I wanted students to be able to apply ideas from the class to texts from outside the class. In creating the three short papers (each three to four pages long, double-spaced) that would be due throughout the semester, I hoped to impart lessons about intertextuality, sexuality, and reflexivity that would resonate throughout the course. The first paper, "Versions and Variations," required students to locate three versions of a tale to compare and contrast. We had already covered the concept of tale type by the time that assignment was due, so in many cases students listed tale types in their papers, while in other cases they referred to tales by their best-known title ("Cinderella" rather than ATU 510A). This assignment helped students understand that tales exist in a multiplicity of versions, such that there is no "original" version of a given tale (though the phrase "the original tale" continued to pop up in their writing throughout the semester, a phenomenon that seems difficult to quash no matter how often we reviewed the diffuse nature of folktales and fairy tales). The second paper, "Revisiting Disney," required students to select a Disney film to watch and write about. The film had to be a fairy-tale retelling, and their paper had to discuss the differences in how gender and sexuality were portrayed in an earlier version of the tale that they chose as opposed to in the film. In the third paper, "Scholarly Sources," students were instructed to pick an article from *Marvels & Tales* and analyze the author's arguments, goals, and methods. While the third paper was assigned mainly to help students prepare for their final paper— which would involve doing research and finding sources to support their research question about a particular facet of sexuality, desire, and/or gender in fairy tales—all of the papers invited some amount of reflexivity from the students. There were myriad ways to approach each paper topic, paralleling the messages they were getting from me in lecture that there are always multiple interpretations of fairy tales.

One other component of the course that encouraged awareness of intertextuality, creativity, and sexuality in fairy tales was the contemporary forms presentation assignment. Students had to prepare a ten- to fifteen-minute lecture on a contemporary form of a fairy tale and, in describing it to fellow students, also touch on concepts related to our lectures and readings (sexual desire, masculinity and femininity, queerness, and so on). The medium was up to the student, though many chose to discuss film adaptations of fairy tales (including *Jack the Giant Slayer, A Cinderella Story, Frozen, Edward Scissorhands, Pan's Labyrinth,* and *Ever After*). A few students took the assignment in a more inventive direction, choosing topics such as fairy-tale motifs in children's toys, Japanese manga genres such as *yaoi* and *yuri* (which foreground same-sex relationships and often borrow fairy-tale intertexts), and the novel *Briar Rose* by Jane Yolen (1992). While well-known movies tended to generate the most discussion in these presentations, the students in the audience seemed open to learning about adaptations that would not have occurred to them to research. Some of the discussion questions that presenters asked their peers were on creative facets of fairy-tale production, such as what choices they would have made differently if they were directing the film in question. These creative interventions—generated by the students—echoed the creative interventions I asked them to make in group discussions.

We began the course with a focus on classical tales (those of the French salon writers, the Grimms, and Andersen) and in the fifth week of class started to incorporate fairy-tale adaptations. We watched "Sapsorrow" (1988) from the TV series *The Storyteller* and read Francesca Lia Block's (2000) *The Rose and the Beast: Fairy Tales Retold.* My students latched onto these adaptations, grasping that "Sapsorrow" combined motifs from "Cinderella" (ATU 510A) and "All Kinds of Fur" (ATU 510B). We had reviewed symbolic and literal approaches to fairy tales, so students were able to have an in-depth discussion of the incest motif in "Sapsorrow" and how it can be read literally, as being about actual incest, or symbolically, as being a psychological tale about growing up and displacing one's desire from the natal family to the marital family. Further, that week I introduced the idea of structuralism and asked students to generate universal fairy-tale plot structures in groups. Most of the groups came up with something similar to Vladimir Propp's (1968) morphology, though condensed into fewer than thirty-one functions, perhaps closer to Bengt Holbek's (1987) five moves in terms of condensation and thematization. There was a tendency to leave the structure open ended, emphasizing that the tales could have a happy or sad ending (which is quite a divergence from Propp's model), though in retrospect, we had just read five tales by Andersen, most of them with unhappy endings. One group, rather than make a list of plot points commonly found in fairy tales, drew a plot trajectory that involved dips to represent low points for the protagonist and swoops upward to represent good events. Between the use of group exercises with creative potential that encouraged student-generated models for understanding fairy tales, and the exploration of multiple dimensions of fairy-tale meaning, these discussions helped set the stage for our first creative exercise.

During the week when we read Block's collection, I gave students a little background on Block's life and a list of themes that emerge in Block's work. These included adolescence/youth; cities (especially Los Angeles, Block's home) versus nature; art, beauty, and stories; and conforming versus standing out. We discussed the gender and sexual dynamics of Block's tales, which included loving relationships between women, competition between women, male predators, and women leaving home. We pointed out instances of same-sex desire (a theme that we would return to again and again in the course), transbiology, and other facets of queerness found in the tales. Then I gave students this prompt to work on in small groups (three to five people):

> Select a fairy tale that we have read in class and come up with a retelling in Block's style (it can be one she has retold, but yours must be different)
> Write out at least a plot outline
> Points for discussion:
> Where does your retelling depart from the pre-text in terms of gender and sexuality?
> How does your retelling reflect (or oppose) social norms about coming of age?

The groups decided on different tales to retell, including "Rapunzel," "Cinderella," and "The Little Mermaid." They updated the tales by setting them in contemporary times (like Block did) and by giving them ambiguous endings. One notable text was a retelling of "Rapunzel" set in a modern high-rise apartment with a female protagonist who connects with the outside world through Instant Messaging on her computer. The young man who woos her eventually comes to see her, but her female guardian, overprotective though not magical, misunderstands his intentions and pushes him out the window. He does not survive the fall, and the guardian is sent to jail. This retelling highlights some of the major themes in Block's work—innocence and its loss, life in the city, youthful flirtation—while staying within the confines of the assignment. Students seemed to enjoy the group work and the creative challenge posed to them; the exercise's goals were clearly stated, and we had done enough work setting the stage for understanding what makes Block's retellings distinctive that students did not seem to have trouble working through the possibilities.

The second creative group exercise I gave my students was motivated by completely different concerns. In contrast to the Block exercise, where my scaffolding seemed to flow smoothly into the group work, I found that precisely because I had not done enough setup for the Angela Carter unit, my students would benefit from a chance to process the implications of Carter-style retellings creatively. Specifically, while they seemed to grasp the context in which Carter (1979a) was writing *The Bloody Chamber* and the political repercussions of those tales, my students had an immense amount of trouble with the film *The Company of Wolves* (Jordan 2002).

When introducing Carter's work, I was careful to give life context (her background as writer, her extensive travels) as well as a theoretical context for understanding her tales in *The Bloody Chamber*. We talked about Carl Jung's idea of archetypes (having earlier discussed Sigmund Freud as giving another lens to fairy-tale psychological interpretive methods), so that when we read an excerpt from Carter's (1979b) *The Sadeian Woman* in class, my students would have the background to understand why archetypes are meaningful and powerful (though I personally feel some distaste for Jungian psychological approaches to fairy tales, which I fear I imparted to my students). The excerpt of *The Sadeian Woman* was, I warned them, intensely sexual. I reminded them of the note on the syllabus that in this class we will encounter graphically sexual and violent materials and that they are welcome to review the "Guidelines for Discussion"—posted on the course software— that offer recommendations on how to deal with emotional responses to difficult topics.

Lecture and discussion on Carter's adaptations thus seemed adequately thought out. My students grasped the erotic, gothic nature of the tales' style, while also picking apart the gender tensions and analyzing the changes Carter had made to the canonical tales. Most of the students latched onto various intertexts with ease, though "The Erl King" and "The Lady of the House of Love" confounded some. I suspect this was because "The Erl King" did not correlate with an intertext that we had read in the class and because "The Lady of the House of Love" was quite a bit removed from the "Sleeping Beauty" intertexts Carter evoked in it. By the time we had spent a week on Carter, discussing each of the individual tales in *The Bloody Chamber*, I felt confident about showing students *The Company of Wolves*. This was the only full-length film I showed within class. I chose this film over other fairy-tale films in order to stick close to Carter, to demonstrate that written fairy-tale adaptations are part of a cycle of adaptation that extends into various media, hybridizing genres and conveying different messages by using different stylistic techniques. I was hoping to use the film as a way of extending our discussion on Carter into contemporary times, in order to emphasize the process whereby fairy tales hop media and are transformed into movies, as well as the gender/sexual politics of Carter and beyond.

At least, that is what I thought would happen. My students hated *The Company of Wolves*. I should have been prepared for that possibility, given that I had read Kim Snowden's essay on using *The Company of Wolves* in the classroom (Snowden 2010). She writes that her students' reactions to the film "vary. They may see it as a horror film, a comedy, and/or an adaptation that simply doesn't make sense" (Snowden 2010, 167). My students focused on many of the same stylistic elements that Snowden's did: "There are many seemingly nonsensical elements to Jordan's film such as giant dollhouses, oversized toys, cars out of place and time, and animals where they don't belong" (Snowden 2010, 167–68). My students remarked on these elements as narrative failures, as distractions that distanced them from being able to enjoy the story or focus on the role of fairy tales in the film. They stumbled over the ambiguous ending, reading it pessimistically as the protagonist, Rosaleen, being killed by the wolves that symbolize her sexual awakening. In contrast, Snowden writes about being able to guide her students to a more nuanced understanding of the ending:

> At the film's conclusion, Rosaleen empathizes with the werewolf, allowing him to accept the Other as part of himself. In the process, she transforms into a wolf, thereby fully embracing the Other within. The passive, sleeping heroine (significantly her bedroom is located in a decaying mansion) perhaps awakens and is possibly devoured and incorporated by her powerful, sexual, desiring Other, allowing a new understanding of femininity, sexuality, and power. (Snowden 2010, 175)

Where Snowden succeeded in conveying this equation of open-endedness with empowerment, I failed. It was my first time teaching the film, and the amount of prep work I did for reading Carter's written tales clearly did not translate into making the film accessible and relevant. Now I believe that priming students with a reading of Snowden's essay before watching the film would have helped them make sense of it, and in the future, I will either assign the essay before the film, or choose a different film altogether to screen in class.

In order to recuperate the film, and to give students a chance to process their experience of it, I came up with a creative exercise. This was in part to justify the two class periods we had spent watching the film, and to give my students a discussion prompt that would hopefully provoke something other than the two responses the film had garnered thus far (stubborn silence or scathing critique). The prompt was as follows:

> You get to remake *The Company of Wolves* for today's audience. What would you change?
>
> Discuss which aspects of Carter's "wolf trilogy" you will keep, and which you will discard.
>
> Will you include other references to Carter's tales, or other fairy tales? What about other genres? (legends, horror films, etc.)
>
> Whom will you cast? Who will do the score?
>
> What messages will your film convey about gender and sexuality?

The students formed groups and after some spirited discussion (ten or fifteen minutes) had rough plans for what their movies would be like. Most groups generally agreed to retain references to Carter's other tales from *The Bloody Chamber*; they seemed to have latched onto the idea that the multiple story texts featured in *The Company of Wolves* contributed to an intertextual understanding of sexuality in the film (though they did not like the messages about sexuality that they perceived the film to convey). In what I take to be a comment on how pop culture shapes perceptions, multiple groups decided to cast Hugh Jackman (known for his role as Wolverine in the *X-Men* movie series) as the werewolf Rosaleen encounters. Kevin Spacey was another pick for the werewolf. Many groups that chose older men to play the werewolves chose very young actresses to play Rosaleen and apparently did not see this as a dissonant choice. One group wanted Guillermo del Toro to direct their remake; another chose Quentin Tarantino.

What the groups decided to do with the frame tale was also interesting, and revealed what my students got out of the film's paratextual framing. One group decided to drop the modern-day frame tale entirely, and have the entire story—both the main Rosaleen narrative based on Carter's "The Company of Wolves" and the other vignettes—set in the same past era. Another group also dropped the dream frame tale, and chose to have the story ending with Rosaleen dying in a graphic and violent manner, followed by the words *Stranger Danger* flashing across the screen. This would, to them, convey the message that they wanted to foreground in their remake of *The Company of Wolves*: that ATU 333 versions are most effective as a warning for girls about men's sexuality. This message is not, obviously, the only way to read ATU 333 or *The Company of Wolves*, but it clearly resonated with my students and was a meaning they chose to emphasize.

The third and final creative group exercise arose from different circumstances. I had designed a weeklong unit called "Addressing Abuse," in which we would read about the (supposed) recuperative effects of fairy tales for survivors of childhood abuse. I scheduled this unit to occur in the eleventh week of a fifteen-week semester. We juxtaposed naively optimistic views of the fairy tale's beneficial powers (as expressed by Bruno Bettelheim [1977] in *The Uses of Enchantment*) with more realistic accounts of how fairy tales convey a message of hope for trauma survivors (as expressed by Terri Windling in *The Armless Maiden*). We read a variety of tales, from the Grimms' "The Maiden Without Hands" and "The Juniper Tree" to a handful of Anne Sexton's (1971) poems from *Transformations* and some of the retold fairy tales in the Windling (1995) anthology. After one day of this material, my students were, understandably, sobered by our discussions of how fairy tales frame and transform childhood abuse.

I decided to end the unit by emphasizing the optative potential of fairy tales to encode the experiences of survivors and thereby offer a message of hope to future audiences. However, we did not approach this topic uncritically; in discussing Bettelheim's take on fairy tales, I mentioned the caveats known to folklorists (his potential plagiarism, accusations of abuse, a narrow literary orientation, and so on). We also examined how the uncritical adaptation of fairy-tale roles can be harmful, as seen in the TV show *Dollhouse* (discussed in Jorgensen and Warman 2014). Thus primed with a discussion of the science fiction elements in *Dollhouse*, I led a brief discussion about various types of fantasy literature and science fiction. I defined the fantastic mode for students, distinguishing it from realistic or mimetic types of storytelling that stick closely to reality. In contrast, science fiction and fantasy are both genres that employ the fantastic mode of storytelling—as do fairy tales—because of how they depart from normative reality, using technology, magic, or both. Then I gave my students the following prompt to address individually:

> Take out a piece of paper (you will turn this in at the end of class) and write for one minute:
>> What is a fairy tale that you think could deliver a message of hope if it were adapted in a fantastic mode (e.g. using science fiction and/or fantasy elements)?
>> Name the plot (perhaps even a specific version).
>> Which changes would you make?

The minute flew by quickly, with students complaining that they did not have enough time to develop their thoughts. The way I conceived this part of the exercise, though, was that I was I priming them with short writing exercise so they could begin to develop their ideas about writing a sci-fi/fantasy adaptation of a fairy tale and that this would lead into the second part of the exercise. I asked a few students to share aloud tales that they had decided to revise. Answers included "The Little Mermaid," "Little Red Riding Hood," "Sleeping Beauty," "Snow White," and "Princess Mouse Skin." Then I had them organize themselves into groups, ideally seeking people who wanted to revise the same tale, and do group work using the following prompt:

> Get in groups based on which tale you would like to adapt (multiple groups dealing with same tale—or working solo—are acceptable).
> Generate a plot using speculative fiction tropes (sci-fi, fantasy, and/or horror) to retell this fairy tale with a message of hope.
> Basic plot outline is okay.
> What are you changing from the pretext you chose?
> What messages about gender/sexuality is your telling conveying?

The tales they came up with were amazingly imaginative. A "Little Mermaid" retelling has the protagonist sucked through an underwater portal to a new land where she ends up with legs and falls in love with an "average Joe" who sacrifices his life on land to follow her back through the portal and become a merman. A "Little Red Riding Hood" retelling features the protagonist flying a spaceship back to her home planet. She encounters a mysterious antagonist (the wolf) and first runs away, then fights back in order to defend her home planet, and is victorious. A second "Little Red Riding Hood" retelling has the protagonist being eaten by the wolf, but then being transported to the world of the wolves from inside the wolf's stomach. She is reborn as a human baby and raised by wolves, and eventually forms a romantic attachment with a human hunter who teaches her about being human but also accepts that she considers the wolves to be her family. A pastiche tale that the students named "All-Kinds-of-Gears" has the cyborg protagonist abused by her caretaker, who installs a sex drive (pun intended) in her so that she can be trafficked for sex. She escapes, removes the hardware, and fights for the cyborgs' rights to determine their own gender and sexual identity. A retelling of "Snow White" has the stepmother abusing Snow White before Snow White manages to escape through a portal into a dream/fantasy land. When the queen pursues her in the form of a dragon, Snow White outwits the queen's attempt to poison her, and the dwarves eat the poison by accident, thus maneuvering Snow White into the role of the savior/rescuer.

My students were largely able to articulate why they made those narrative choices: they wanted to empower their protagonists by giving them physical or metaphysical strength, allow traditionally passive heroines to save themselves, and rewrite sexual scripts so that women would not be the ones making all of the sacrifices for love. Building on the ideas that they expressed, I took the discussion of their group work a step further and pointed out that students addressed sexuality by either embracing its role in the characters' lives or by removing it entirely. For instance, the retelling of "Little Red Riding Hood" set in space and the "All-Kinds-of-Gears" tale both stripped their characters of sexuality. The space retelling was utterly devoid of sexual content; the wolf was more of a mysterious predator than a creature with an interest in seducing or devouring the girl. And in "All-Kinds-of-Gears," the protagonist found empowerment through removing her sex drive, and she chose not to reinstall it. In contrast, the female characters in the second "Little Riding Hood" retelling and in "The Little Mermaid" were able to find male mates who understood them, adored them, and made sacrifices to be with them. These divergent approaches to sexuality—excision versus transformation—reflected feminist struggles with how to manage women's sexuality in a patriarchal society. Indeed, many of the fairy-tale adaptations that we read over the course of the semester grappled with this very issue, so I was not surprised to see it turning up in my students' creative exercises.

There were, however, some challenges in implementing these exercises. Some students seem to prefer the kind of group work where they simply discuss a series of questions and do not have to have anything to "show" for it, a stance implied by the mild grumbling when I have told them that they need to produce a story. I am unsure how much to attribute this to laziness, or a fear of not doing the exercise "right" despite my attempt to convey that it was deliberately open ended. I did not assign a specific grade to these exercises, though, instead counting them toward the students' overall participation grades. Interestingly, I noticed that some students balked at having to do something creative. Others seem timid and unwilling to share their ideas with their classmates. I worried that some students would actually prefer to work alone, and I gave them that option for the final creative exercise. As noted earlier, I had given students a one-minute-long individual brainstorming exercise to prepare for the exercise wherein they had to create and flesh out a sci-fi/fantasy fairy-tale adaptation. In theory, an independent-minded person could have used that exercise as a springboard into writing her own solo adaptation. Everyone chose to work in groups instead. My impression is that many students find safety in numbers, especially when they are asked to do something less conventional. Thus, conducting these exercises in groups with a low-stakes outcome seemed like the best way to mitigate these types of concerns.

While I began doing these creative exercises based on the desire to expand my repertoire of group discussion exercises (as well as a flicker of intuition that they might be useful in ways I had not yet anticipated), I was ultimately pleased with the results. When I administered these exercises, I observed that students were extremely engaged when talking with one another. It seemed more difficult than in other types of exercises for one person to remain silent and not contribute much. Everyone seemed to have ideas that they wanted to share with each other. Since getting the students to engage with the material was one of the main goals of the class—rather than allowing them to passively absorb the information and leave it at that—I consider this engagement to be a teaching victory. On a more con- crete level, according to the grade breakdown on my syllabus, participation and attendance count for 10 percent of one's overall grade, so participating in these exercises represents a real part of the grading process. In addition, I was able to evaluate my students' papers and presentations to assess their learning outcomes, and I believe that the creative exercises added a level of nuance to their discussions of fairy-tale adaptations.

Further, the students reported enjoying these types of exercises. When I administered midsemester evaluations to the students to check in about how my teaching style was working for them, a handful specifically stated that they enjoyed and benefited from the exercises in which they reworked tales. At this point in the semester, we had done both the Francesca Lia Block retelling and *The Company of Wolves* remake. One student specifically told me that she enjoyed the tale-reworking exercises because they gave her the opportunity to examine the tale on a deeper level than just observing it on the surface. Based on this feedback, I decided to give students the option of writing a fairy-tale text to analyze for their final papers, rather than assemble texts from literary or collected sources to analyze. A handful of students chose this option.

My ultimate hope for these exercises—and the class as a whole—was to demonstrate to students that just as they are able to rewrite fairy-tale texts, they are able to rewrite sexual scripts. Just as the Disney versions of tales are not in and of themselves bad, the heteronormative sexual scripts incul- cated by society are not bad, though they can be harmful when presented as the only option for how to live, love, and be. I also believe that these exer- cises helped students better understand the nature of intertextuality, and the importance of creative interventions in the fairy-tale tradition. These goals are less tangible than other goals of my course, such as learning basic folkloristic approaches to fairy tales and learning the key tenets of feminist and queer theory, which I can measure by assessing how my students are doing on their papers and other written work. Imparting the ability to critically and creatively relate to stories and the sexual scripts contained therein may, however, ultimately be more relevant to my students' lives, and make more of a lasting impact on them than learning about tale-type numbers. And as the story of my semester draws to a close, I am satisfied with that ending.

NOTE

1. I primarily lectured to my students about intertextuality rather than assigning criticism for them to read on the topic. In doing so, I implicitly drew on ideas from scholars such as Julia Kristeva, though I relied heavily on summaries of other scholars' approaches to intertextuality found in Cristina Bacchilega's (2013) book *Fairy Tales Transformed?*.

REFERENCES

Bacchilega, Cristina. 2013. *Fairy Tales Transformed? Twenty-First-Century Adaptations and the Politics of Wonder*. Detroit: Wayne State University Press.

Bettelheim, Bruno. 1977. *The Uses of Enchantment: The Meaning and Importance of Fairy Tales*. New York: Vintage.

Block, Francesca Lia. 2000. *The Rose and the Beast: Fairy Tales Retold*. New York: HarperCollins, October.

Carter, Angela. 1979a. *The Bloody Chamber and Other Adult Tales*. New York: Harper and Row.

Carter, Angela. 1979b. *The Sadeian Woman and the Ideology of Pornography*. New York: Penguin Books.

Holbeck, Bengt. 1987. *The Interpretation of Fairy Tales: Danish Folklore in a European Perspective*. Helsinki: Academia Scientiarium Fennica.

Joosen, Vanessa. 2011. *Critical and Creative Perspectives on Fairy Tales: An Intertextual Dialogue between Fairy-Tale Scholarship and Postmodern Retellings*. Detroit: Wayne State University Press.

Jordan, Neil, director. [1984] 2002. *The Company of Wolves*. DVD. ITC Entertainment Group,.

Jorgensen, Jeana, and Brittany Warman. 2014. "Molding Messages: Analyzing the Reworking of 'Sleeping Beauty' in *Grimm's Fairy Tale Classics* and *Dollhouse*." In *Channeling Wonder: Fairy Tales on Television*, ed. Pauline Greenhill and Jill Rudy, 144–62. Detroit: Wayne State University Press.

Propp, Vladimir. [1928] 1968. *Morphology of the Folktale*. 2nd ed. Translated by Lawrence Scott. Austin: University of Texas Press.

"Sapsorrow." 1988. *The Storyteller* (TV). Season 1, episode 7. Directed by Steve Barron. United Kingdom.

Sexton, Anne. 1971. *Transformations*. Boston: Houghton Mifflin.

Snowden, Kim. 2010. "Fairy Tale Film in the Classroom: Feminist Cultural Pedagogy, Angela Carter, and Neil Jordan's *The Company of Wolves*." In *Fairy Tale Films: Visions of Ambiguity*, ed. Pauline Greenhill and Sidney Eve Matrix, 157–77. Logan: Utah State University Press.

Tosenberger, Catherine. 2010. "'Kinda Like the Folklore of Its Day': *Supernatural*, Fairy
     Tales, and Ostension." *Transformative Works and Cultures* 4. http://journal.transform
     ativeworks.org/index.php/twc/article/view/174/156.
Turner, Kay, and Pauline Greenhill, eds. 2012. *Transgressive Tales: Queering the Grimms*.
     Detroit: Wayne State University Press.
Windling, Terri, ed. 1995. *The Armless Maiden and Other Tales for Childhood's Survivors*. New
     York: T. Doherty Associates.
Yolen, Jane. 1992. *Briar Rose*. New York: T. Doherty Associates.
Zipes, Jack. 1995. *Creative Storytelling: Building Community, Changing Lives*. New York, London:
     Routledge.

Aarne-Thompson-Uther Index Cited

Animal Tales 1–299

Tales of Magic 300–749

Uther, Hans-Jörg. 2004. *The Types of International Folktales: A Classification and Bibliography, Based on the System of Antti Aarne and Stith Thompson.* 3 vols. Helsinki: Suomalainen Tiedeakatemia, Academia Scientiarum Fennica.

About the Authors

ANNE E. DUGGAN is professor of French and chair of the Department of Classical and Modern Languages, Literatures, and Cultures at Wayne State University. She is author of *Salonnières, Furies, and Fairies: The Politics of Gender and Cultural Change in Absolutist France* (2005), and *Queer Enchantments: Gender, Sexuality, and Class in the Fairy-Tale Cinema of Jacques Demy* (2013).

CYRILLE FRANÇOIS is senior lecturer at the University of Lausanne, Switzerland. His work focuses on the narrative strategies in the fairy tales of Charles Perrault, the Brothers Grimm and Hans Christian Andersen, as well as in their translations. He is the author of several articles and scientific reviews on fairy tales.

LISA GABBERT is associate professor in the Department of English at Utah State University and director of the Folklore Program, where she teaches courses on landscape, folk art, children's folklore, theory, occupational folklore, and fieldwork; her current research focuses on festivity and play in medical contexts. Her writing has appeared in the *Journal of American Folklore*, *Western Folklore*, *Contemporary Legend*, *CUR Quarterly*, *Glimpse: The Art and Science of Seeing*, and elsewhere. Her book *Winter Carnival in a Western Town: Identity, Change, and the Good of the Community* was published in 2011 by Utah State University Press.

PAULINE GREENHILL is professor of women's and gender studies at the University of Winnipeg, Manitoba, Canada. Her recent books are *Fairy-Tale Films beyond Disney: International Perspectives* (coedited with Jack Zipes and Kendra Magnus-Johnston, 2015); *Channeling Wonder: Fairy Tales on Television* (coedited with Jill Terry Rudy, 2014); *Unsettling Assumptions: Tradition, Gender, Drag* (coedited with Diane Tye, 2014); *Transgressive Tales: Queering the Grimms* (coedited with Kay Turner, 2012); *Fairy Tale Films: Visions of Ambiguity* (coedited with Sidney Eve Matrix, 2010); and *Make the Night Hideous: Four English Canadian Charivaris, 1881–1940* (2010).

DONALD HAASE is professor of German and senior associate dean of the College of Liberal Arts and Sciences at Wayne State University. He is the editor of *The Reception of Grimms' Fairy Tales: Responses, Reactions, Revisions* and *Feminism and Fairy Tales: New Approaches*, and general editor of the Series in Fairy-Tale Studies. With Anne E. Duggan, he is the coeditor of *Folktales and Fairy Tales: Traditions and Texts from around the World*, a revised and expanded edition of *The Greenwood Encyclopedia of Folktales and Fairy Tales*.

CHRISTA C. JONES is associate professor of French and associate department head in the Department of Languages, Philosophy, and Communication Studies at Utah State University, where she teaches a variety of French culture, language, and literature classes, as well as Business French. Her research has appeared in *CELAAN Review, Contemporary French and Francophone Studies, Dalhousie French Studies, Expressions maghrébines, Francofonia, French Review, Jeunesse, Nouvelles Études Francophones, Women's Studies Quarterly*, and elsewhere. She is the author of *Cave Culture in Maghrebi . Literature: Imagining Self and Nation* (Lanham, MD: Lexington Books, 2012) and the coeditor of *Women from the Maghreb*, a special issue of *Dalhousie French Studies* (vol. 103, fall 2014).

CHRISTINE A. JONES is associate professor of French and comparative literary and cultural studies at the University of Utah. She has coedited *Marvelous Transformations: An Anthology of Fairy Tales and Contemporary Critical Perspectives* (Broadview Press, 2012) and *Feathers, Paws, Fins and Claws: Fairy-Tale Beasts* (Wayne State University Press, 2015) with Jennifer Schacker; has authored *Shapely Bodies: The Image of Porcelain in Eighteenth-Century France* (University of Delaware Press, 2013); and is currently translating the fairy tales of Charles Perrault under the title *Mother Goose Revisited.*

JEANA JORGENSEN completed her PhD in folklore at Indiana University and teaches in the Anthropology Department and Gender, Women's, and Sexuality Studies Program at Butler University. She researches gender and sexuality in fairy tales, body art, dance, alternative sexualities, and the history of sex education.

ARMANDO MAGGI is professor of Italian literature and is a member of the Committee on the History of Culture at the University of Chicago. His scholarship focuses on two major areas: early modern culture (Renaissance philosophy and demonology, love treatises, art of memory, women writers, female mysticism, Renaissance emblems, baroque culture) and contemporary culture. He is the author of many books. His latest work is the volume titled *Preserving the Spell* (forthcoming, University of Chicago Press) on the Western interpretation of folktales and fairy tales from Giambattista Basile's *Lo cunto de li cunti* to the French late seventeenth-century tradition, German Romanticism, and American postmodernism.

CHRISTINA PHILLIPS MATTSON recently completed her dissertation entitled *Children's Literature Grows Up* and received her PhD from Harvard University in 2015. She has published various articles on fairy tales and fantasy literature throughout her graduate career and is currently revising her dissertation for publication.

DORIS MCGONAGILL (PhD, Harvard) is associate professor and head of the German Section at Utah State University. Publications include *Crisis and Collection: German Visual Memory Archives of the Twentieth Century* (Königshausen & Neumann, 2015); "A New Science of Beauty," on Albrecht Dürer, in *A New History of German Literature*; and articles on contemporary German literature. Recently, her interest in the intersection of visual and literary culture has led her into the realm of fairy-tale and fantasy literature with an article about trees and sylvan landscapes in Tolkien (in *We Should Look at Green Again: Representations of Nature in Middle-earth*, 2015).

JENNIFER ORME'S PhD is in literary studies. She has taught online classes for the University of Winnipeg's Women's and Gender Studies department and both online and "live" classes for Ryerson University's Chang School of Continuing Education in Ontario. She has published on fairy tales and queer theory in *Transgressive Tales: Queering the Grimms*, Pauline Greenhill and Kay Turner, eds. (2012), and *Marvels & Tales: Journal of Fairy Tale Studies* (2015) and on fairy tales and film in *Marvels & Tales* (2010) and *Beyond Adaptation*, Phyllis Frus and Christy Williams, eds. (2010).

CLAUDIA SCHWABE is assistant professor of German at Utah State University and teaches courses in German language, literature, and culture, including fairy tales. She has published on varied subjects, such as East German fairy-tale films, magic realism, European literary fairy tales of the Romantic period, German Orientalism, televisual adaptations of classical tales, and fairy-tale pedagogy. Her work has appeared in *Channeling Wonder*, *Marvels & Tales*, *Journal of Folklore Research*, *Journal: Contemporary Legends*, the *German Quarterly*, *Cultural Analysis*, *Poetica Magazine*, and elsewhere. She is currently working on her monograph *Craving Supernatural Creatures: German Fairy-Tale Figures in American Pop Culture*, which is under contract with Wayne State University Press's *Series in Fairy-Tale Studies*.

ANISSA TALAHITE-MOODLEY is a lecturer in Women's and Gender Studies at the University of Toronto. Her work and publications deal essentially with issues of gender and identity, particularly in the postcolonial and transnational contexts, as well as with questions relating to the intersection of race, gender and identity; postcolonial theory; and women's writing and literature in the context of migration. Her books include *Problématiques identitaires et discours de l'exil dans les littératures francophones* (Ottawa University Press, 2007) and *Gender and Identity* (Oxford University Press, 2013).

MARIA TATAR is the John L. Loeb Professor of Germanic Languages and Literatures & Folklore and Mythology at Harvard University, where she teaches courses on German Studies, folklore, and children's literature. She is the author of *The Annotated Brothers Grimm*, *The Hard Facts of the Grimms' Fairy Tales*, *The Annotated Hans Christian Andersen*, and *Enchanted Hunters: The Power of Stories in Childhood*. She has written for the *New Republic*, *New the York Times*, and the *New Yorker*, and has contributed frequently to *NPR* programs.

FRANCISCO VAZ DA SILVA is a lecturer in folklore and anthropology at Instituto Universitário de Lisboa (Portugal). He has been a visiting professor at several universities in Europe and the United States. He specializes in the study of traditional symbolism in folklore and popular culture, with a particular emphasis on fairy tales. His publications include *Metamorphosis: The Dynamics of Symbolism in European Fairy Tales* (2002), *Archeology of Intangible Heritage* (2008), and an annotated seven-volume collection of European fairy tales: *Contos Maravilhosos Europeus* (2012–13).

JULIETTE WOOD studied folklore at the University of Pennsylvania and Celtic studies at Oxford University and University College of Wales, Aberystwyth. She has served both as president and secretary of the Folklore Society and is currently teaching at Cardiff University and is an Honorary Research Fellow of the Amgueddfa Cymru-National Museum Wales. Her major interest at the present time is the relation between medieval tradition and popular culture. In addition to extensive television and radio work on folklore topics, she has published articles on folkloristics and medieval narrative. Her books include *Eternal Chalice: The Enduring Myth of the Holy Grail* (London: Tauris 2008).

Index